Holistic Psychology of Alexander Pint

CATERPILLAR TO BUTTERFLY
A WAY TO YOURSELF

Introduction to practical self-investigation

Written by
Alexander Pint
&
Translated by
Emin Kuliev, MD

skyrocket press

Skyrocket Press
28020 Newbird Drive
Santa Clarita, CA 91350

Cover art by Freydoon Rasouli www.Rassouli.com
Cover design by Emma Michaels
Interior design by Laurisa Reyes

ISBN: 978-1-944722-00-5

FORWARD

When we are born we accept a certain condition, which we can express with the word "separation" or the act of forgetting oneself. That is the essence and the gist of the game of our world, the game we enter as material (physical) beings. When we enter this world, we feel separated. That is origin of all these difficult states and the multiple problems we constantly talk about. We forgot the Source. The majority of people forget who they are, where their real Home is, what they came here for. They feel lonely, they pity themselves, and they don't understand what's going on. In reality, those are the rules of the game played here. This is not an accident, but the specifics of the game chosen by your Soul. The rules, mechanisms, and meaning of this game is the topic of this book.

Do you need to read this book or not?

This book is written, not to increase the amount of useless information in the overloaded brains of respected readers, but to tune your perception to understand the essence of the material you read and what is happening around you.

This book by itself is a method, a system, and a possibility of getting to know one's essence and mechanisms of the generation of questions, problems, and desires in a respected reader.

Quite possibly, you may want to understand yourself better, solve some kinds of problems, or achieve Harmony, Love, Beauty, Health, Wellbeing, Wisdom, or Awakening. In reality, everything strives toward one goal—Wholeness and Harmony.

So, how can a man find this wholeness in himself? That is the question deserving our attention as it leads us to the road to our self.

This mastery of movement to develop the unifying consciousness, consciousness not divided by the conditioned mind into a multitude of fragments, we call **Holistic** psychology. Unified consciousness is the consciousness of a human being who has become aware of himself or herself. It is a unity of male and female, external and internal, spiritual and material. It is freedom from this fiction and illusion that by force of habit we consider to be ourselves.

Who takes this road, and how does he or she do it? Everyone is different, but, there is something in common for everyone who really walks this walk. It is based on this commonality, that we view peculiarities of the journey of every single individual to himself.

In this book you will find the most interesting and unexpected—the mirror image of yourself: your thoughts, convictions, beliefs, images, feelings, and actions, and, most importantly you can become aware of them.

What kind of reaction will it produce in you? Meeting with your own self is the most amazing of all the possible events in the life of a human being.

So, who are you, respected reader, in reality?

If I give a book with blank sheets of paper the title, "At this time, you cannot receive any help from my book," one could possibly decide to take offense. If I offer a comprehensive and superficially understandable book, some may get excited. "How wonderful! How deep!" People would follow this external expression, making it a source of exaltation and argument, digging into the book for advice, poetry, exercises, and stories. If I publish no books or a tiny book, scientists would laugh at it and disable the minds of prospective students through a literature of opposition worse than they do now. Mixed–up students would add to the confusion, thinking up more conclusions and trying to peg them on others.

If I write a big book, some would call it pretentious.

If I code my book, people would imagine it full of mysteries and start to uselessly ponder it trying to understand.

All these assumptions, as you can see, are justified because it would be very convenient for people to follow them, and not because those assumptions are correct. Far from it, the more you talk about it, the more people will say with irritation: "You do not understand us. We don't behave this way. It is you who are devoid of understanding."

But, if I say all this and you, even for a brief moment, are able to sense the gist of my message, paying attention to every item, I would be satisfied.

(Bahaudin)

How this book was written and how to read it

This and our other books are created as one of the forms of distant education by the School of Holistic Psychology. Work in the school is conducted in different forms, including group work of practical self-investigation. This book brings forward materials accumulated in the work process of one of these groups.

Participating in this work were the leader of the School of Holistic Psychology, Alexander Pint (his speech is typed in a normal font) and members of a group of self-investigators (their speech is italicized).

The best way to use this book is not to use the usual style of reading, where one is only interested in finding an interesting piece of information. In this case one is using primarily the conditioned mind which possesses limited possibilities of perception and understanding.

While investigating the reader's perception of religious, philosophical, psychological, and esoteric literature, we found some interesting consistent patterns. In particular, the majority of readers do not look for something really new, something which could potentially change their worldview, even though they usually insist they do. Primarily, they are interested in confirming their convictions and beliefs. In this case, the reader cannot receive anything substantially new from this book but can further reinforce his or her old, habitual opinions.

The desire to read a particular book frequently comes from one part of the human being, while quite different part participate in the process of reading, rendering its opinion. This shows the fragmented and confrontational inner world of a human being. This happens to one not only when one reads a book, but in many other situations brought up by life.

That's why we recommend you to use this book for self-exploration, and to get to know multiple processes that work simultaneously within your consciousness at any given time in an attempt to bring them together.

True awareness, i.e. the understanding of the essence of what is locked in the book or events that happen to you, comes only with harmonious perception, which encompasses not only the intellectual sphere, but also emotional and physical centers. In such a case, not only you analyze reading material on an intellectual level but live through it physically and emotionally.

This book is written to create the possibility of direct participation in the work of self-exploration of your own internal world, of those problems and questions you find important at the present moment. So, do not be surprised if you find yourself in certain unusual states while reading this book.

This is not a literary entertainment. What is important here is the realization and awareness of your thoughts, feelings, and sensations emerging as you approach these hidden zones to which painful experiences are attached. As a result of this process, one can free oneself from the weight of past problems and illnesses.

In reading this book, be aware of thoughts, feelings, sensations, and desires which surface in response to what you are reading. Observe not only the development of the dialogues between participants, but most importantly your reaction to them. You will see that they will bring up in you certain thoughts, feelings, and sensations. Observe them. That will allow you to make maximum use of this book.

Many first time readers have a desire to reread it again in full or to review certain chapters. Every revisit provides one with an impulse to become aware and to achieve a deeper understanding of surfaced questions and problems.

Look at this book as an interlocutor with whom you are entering into a deep conversation to get an insight into yourself.

Furthermore, any spoken or written word somehow becomes separated from the speaker, from the events that happened during its pronouncement. The word is an intermediary between a speaker and a listener, writer and reader. It equally belongs to both of them. Each one of them brings in his own understanding, perception, and life energy. That is why talking and listening, writing and reading is one encompassing process of communication, and the fewer the barriers, created by hard convictions, opinions and notion, the clearer, and the freer the communication.

This book is an introduction to this kind of communication with you.

TABLE OF CONTENTS

•◆•

INTRODUCTION

•◆•

Peculiarities of the current condition
of human beings and society

Society is currently in a state of fundamental change. All the main paradigms acting in different spheres of life are in a process of change: economic, political, cultural, family, etc. What's happening now represents the most radical revolution on the face of the planet. Nobody can escape participating in this process. What are the main tendencies of this process and what does it mean for each one of us?

First of all, what is happening now is an expression of laws having impersonal characteristics and reflects what is happening in the Universe, i.e. dimensions of this process are not circumscribed by the borders of the Earth. The perception of these laws acting on Earth is being transformed. People are about to open up new perceptions. They will understand the world through unconditional love. That love is the opposite of conditional love, which has a dual character and can easily transform into hate. Unconditional love is a love of a different dimension, which lacks duality, separation, or a fragmented way of perception. This love has at its core unity and interconnectedness.

Secondly, every single one of us is, in essence, a representation of this love but does not understand this due to our habitual perception of the world as comprised of physical bodies separated from each other and existing in a state of contradiction. This kind of perception is being conditioned by the human mind which is dominated by self-reflection, i.e. constant analysis and judgment of everything pertaining and happening to ourselves and those around us. Self-reflection can be seen as a collection of images that are formed, fixed, and maintained by the conditioned mind. The mind creates an illusion of its separation from and opposition to other people and the world at large. The laws on which the personality operates limit the possibilities of a human being and prevent him from seeing himself as he really is.

Every single human being present on Earth now has enormous possibilities which can be actualized in the near future. However, the process of opening those possibilities is not mechanical. It requires certain efforts for one to become all one can potentially be. Only those who sense what is happening and understand this great chance we are being offered can achieve this transformation.

So, what is this work of self-realization and transformation all about? First of all, this work requires an understanding and awareness of its necessity. If this understanding is absent, one would not want to change anything in oneself and would remain in a state one is used to, while constantly expressing dissatisfaction with the conditions of the life that is being lived. It is impossible to be aware of the situation and of oneself if one does not understand why one needs it. Nobody can force one to become one's real self. This can only occur on one's own free will and active choice. Quite a few people are faced with this choice, but not many acknowledge it. This necessity of making a choice appears and is being reinforced now. That is a fact. On the other hand, this fact is not being seen by everyone. That is also a fact. And why do some people fail to see it? They fail to see it because they do not want to see it. Why? They don't want to see it because to see and to become aware of the necessity of making this choice means to understand the inevitable necessity of moving away from the old, habitual perception of oneself, others, and the world in general. But the inertia of habitual perception is very strong. Try to stop a train moving at sixty miles an hour. It is hard, though possible. For one who becomes aware of the necessity of changing one's own perception, laws of different reality come into play—the reality of the unified world. Understanding those laws allows one to change what was previously seen as unshakable and habitual instantly.

This understanding requires desire, desire which can only come from the depths of one's heart—the desire to connect with oneself and to enter the world of Reality, Wholeness, Wisdom, and Love. Laws of Love are easily understood by the heart, but not by the conditional mind which has taken the place of the ruler within the human being and makes one unable to live a natural life.

The nature of conditioned mind is separation, fragmented and narrow perception. One has to learn to see it from the side, to observe the mechanisms of its work. This is **awareness**. By becoming aware of the false in oneself as being false, one moves toward the truth, toward understanding of oneself.

This kind of work requires a special education, since for the majority of people it's neither habitual nor known. To accomplish this kind of work, the School of Holistic Psychology was created. Holistic Psychology is a science that studies the whole human being and the laws of life creation through love. Only creativity in love can lead the human being and humanity out of the dead end of fear, hatred, weakness, and pain. So let us open ourselves to infinity, to the unknown, and finally allow ourselves to become what we really are.

Awakening of being as a way

Everything around us is Unified Consciousness that taking different forms plays with itself. Everything we perceive as a physical reality is just a projection of our conceptions, a reflection of our mind. Those conceptions are being projected onto the screen of Unified Consciousness, the way a movie is projected on a screen in a theater.

In perceiving the physical world, we only see projections of our minds. That is why everything that happens to us is not the only possible option; it's just a movie dreamt by our mind. This world is a result of our worldview and by changing our worldview we change our perception of the world, change what we consider to be the only reality.

Unified Consciousness expresses itself in different forms. A human being is one of the manifestations of Unified Consciousness. The Soul of the human being is consciousness or energy. Just as with any energy, consciousness has the potential to be aware of itself.

This capability manifests itself as attention. Attention characterizes the direction of energy of Consciousness.

The Not Yet Awakened Soul (Consciousness) directs its attention only outward, away from itself, i.e. toward the "body-mind" it embodies. It totally identifies and equates itself with the given psychophysical form.

The sleeping soul is not aware of itself until it has developed and embodies the "body-mind" capable of accepting the energy of awareness, i.e. to become an instrument of the real "I"(Spirit).

iv

The awakening of the Soul begins when at least part of this energy of awareness starts to return back to itself. In the beginning it may be experienced as an instantaneous, flash-like experience. Considering that this state is unusual for the sleeping Soul, it may be qualified by Personality (false "i") as accidental or abnormal. False personality adamantly resists those states because the return of energy to the Soul, i.e. awareness, represents a threat to false personality as it feeds precisely on this energy of consciousness (Soul).

The Soul that starts to wake up, during a short wakeful state (awareness of itself), starts to see the world as it really is, i.e. its real "I" (Spirit). But, falling asleep again it sees only the illusory world, created by the distorted perception of false "i" (false personality). If those states of awakening of the Soul continue to recur, the Soul starts to jump around, unable to understand what's going on. The Soul tries to combine the illusory world of false personality, previously accepted as real, with the opening of the true reality, real essence, and the house it came from.

The human being whose Soul starts to awake, experiences a state of alarm, and starts to seek something he cannot yet understand. Those "kicks of awareness" are associated with very unusual states that force one to search. One doesn't understand what's going on, but feels it.

This is that call from the world of Reality which points toward the only true direction, toward oneself. This direction is opposite of the direction one previously held. One's attention, i.e. energy of awareness, starts to move. The beginning of the Way toward the real "I," toward the House of reality, begins with a 180 degree turn, a turn toward oneself.

This is the beginning of the Great and the most difficult period in the life of a human being. False personality, sensing the threat to its own survival, starts to resist this out flux of energy (energy of awareness of Soul). It uses very sophisticated and sneaky methods to prevent the process of awakening of the Soul. The fight of true "I" and false "i" for the Soul begins. Becoming aware of itself, the Soul sees its real "I" and reality, and falling asleep again perceives only false "i" and illusion.

During this period of time, the human being (body-mind) at one time is under the rule of its real Owner, and is suddenly under the influence of the false "i." It is important to not underestimate the slyness and sophistication of games and tricks used by the false "i" to maintain its power.

The voice of the false "i" at this time is more common and recognizable for the human being (body-mind). It is understandable, since prior to this time it has ruled undividedly. It knows him very well, all his weaknesses and disharmonic aspects. It evolved because of them and tries to reinforce disharmony and imbalance of the main functions of the human being (body-mind).

During this time, one needs a correct education directed toward the strengthening, broadening, and reinforcing of one's ability to become aware of all the functions of body-mind. Special schools should play a role in this education. At the cornerstone of this education should lay a real understanding of one's self, practical experience of self-understanding (self-investigation), a clear vision of the processes occurring on the global scale and their effect on humanity, different groups of people, and each individual in particular.

Holistic Psychology is a science of the whole human being. It studies facts and the laws of evolution of human consciousness, i.e. the process of awakening of the Consciousness (Soul) of the human being and humanity at large. It studies reality and the movement to the next dimension.

The only real evolution of the human being is evolution of one's consciousness (Soul), i.e. vertical evolution.

The evolution of a human being, described as scientific-technical progress is an illusion, a false evolution. It is horizontal, a mechanical process.

Vertical evolution cannot progress mechanically without the understanding of the human being, which in itself is impossible without self-investigation or self-awareness.

The human being who is not yet aware of himself or herself is just a complicated mechanism, blindly carrying out the laws on which it operates. The mechanical existence of a human being cannot lead to vertical evolution or to the state of being whole.

Vertical evolution is possible only when conditions providing appropriate flow of the awakening of consciousness (Soul) of a given human being exist. Two required factors for the vertical evolution to start are the readiness of a human being to begin the practical work of self-investigation, and the help offered by people who have already gone through this work. These people have an understanding of the meaning, aims, and methods of this work, and are able to use them in working with other people. Therefore, the success of this work depends on at least two conditions: the readiness of individual to start work and the presence of people capable of providing the necessary help.

This Way cannot be chosen by the human being himself. The Way chooses one. One entering the Way will have to part with the habitual mode of living. This way is for people who are ready, and who at least have started to understand that they cannot escape it. Dissatisfaction with oneself and one's life is not enough as this work asks for much more—understanding of the impossibility of continuing the previous way of life, i.e. the way of life that

is mechanical and devoid of awareness. The desire to obtain different occult and magical abilities is a hindrance on this Way. The only force propelling one on this Way is the strength of the desire to know one's real "I," and to become free, whole, and aware.

Work is only possible for the human being who understands that at the present time he is completely unknown to himself. Everything he or she previously considered to be his or herself is an illusion and a lie. The deep understanding of this fact is the beginning of vertical evolution.

The real is only what one has become aware of: thought, feeling, or action. Any functionality one is not aware of is mechanical—it maintains the old stereotypical perception of the world and by default recreates the false world of false personality.

The human being who is not aware of himself is not capable of changing himself, others, or circumstances. At the same time he lives in an illusion of the possibility of such changes. He thinks he chooses and determines his thoughts, actions, i.e. his destiny.

Only by coming to awareness of one's own total mechanical nature and inability to influence anything, as well as by acceptance of this situation as the only real fact, may one become aware of the direction of the true Way. Only a robot, aware of itself as being a mechanism, can stop being a robot and start on the road toward his liberation from a mechanical existence.

Main Concepts
of Holistic Psychology

• ◆•◆ • ◆•◆ • ◆•◆ • ◆•◆ • ◆•◆ • ◆•◆ • ◆•◆ • ◆•◆ • ◆•◆ • ◆•◆ • ◆•◆ • ◆•◆ •

Real "I" (Spirit, Owner) – Unified Consciousness. The Source of all and everything. Energy at rest. It expresses itself in the movement and multiplicity of forms.

Soul (Consciousness, Energy) – a seed of Unified Consciousness, possessing the potential of self-awareness.

human being (body-mind) – a tool for the expression of the plan and purpose of Unified Consciousness. The bioenergetic mechanism composed of five functions: mental, emotional, moving, instinctive, and sexual.

Human Being – The human being, possessing awareness of oneself as a whole, represents part of Unified Consciousness.

False personality (False "i") A mental-emotional construct appearing on the basis of functional mechanism of the conditioned mind. False personality should dissolve, transferring control of the body-mind to real "I." False "i" exists in a form of images, perceptions, beliefs, convictions, stereotypical reactions, and body blocks, all having dual nature. False "i" represents many separated and disagreeing with each other parts and pieces. False "i" shows itself in the physical world with the help of actions conducted by the body-mind, in which it has formed and remains.

Distorted perception – An illusionary perception the conditional mind has of itself, others, and its surroundings.

Clear perception – A vision of Reality by consciousness, possessing full awareness.

Reality – The perception of life coming from full awareness.

Illusion – The perception of life coming from sleeping, unawakened consciousness.

Attention – The characteristic of direction and the peculiarity of movement of energy of consciousness.

Identified attention – Consciousness perceiving and reflecting only the external portion of itself. While this process occurs, consciousness (Soul) identifies itself with what it perceives (what it looks at). Identified attention has a tendency toward fixation, fragmentation, and inflexibility.

Free attention (awareness) – Consciousness simultaneously aware of external and internal sides of itself, of what is happening; consciousness seeing itself as a whole. Consciousness, aware of itself, doesn't identify completely with what is it looking at, with an external form. Free attention moves easily and flexibly, able to perceive multiple external forms.

Mechanical reaction – Mechanical, stereotypical actions of the human being representing an effect of perception and management performed by one's conditioned mind and false personality. It is a result of contemplation and choice, and as such, is done with delay and distortion in regards to what happens at the present moment.

Spontaneous action – Free action that comes from a clear vision of reality. Spontaneous actions occur without any intervention of the conditioned mind or false personality, and therefore are not determined by reflection (pondering and choice). Spontaneous actions are natural and instantaneous and respond to the necessities of the current moment.

Mental function of the body-mind – The function working with the energy of thought.

Emotional function of the body-mind – The function working with energy of emotion.

Moving function of the body-mind – The function working with physical energy.

Sexual function of the body-mind – The function working with sexual energy.

Mental function of the body-mind – The function working with the energy of thought.

Instinctive function of the body-mind – The function providing the proper work of physiologic functions and systems within the organism of the human being.

Five expressions of single energy – Every single one of the functions working with a type of energy of Soul (Consciousness) and corresponding to it. All five types of energy in reality are one energy of Soul (consciousness) manifesting itself through the body-mind (human being).

Self-awareness – A way of returning to oneself through a self-investigation of the functions of one's body-mind and the types of energy with which they work.

Self-investigation of the body-mind – An investigation by the way of self-observation of characteristic functions of one's body-mind and types of energy which they work with.

Self-investigation of false personality – Tracking of the main traits of false personality and their mechanical reactions in different situations of life.

Self-observation – The main method of self-investigation. In order to self-observe it is imperative to redirect the attention of consciousness (soul) toward oneself.

Learning to Self-observe – The act of learning to be self-aware.

Learning of self-observation (awareness) – One of the main objectives (tasks) of the School of Holistic psychology. Learning and training of awareness makes sense and can only be applied to a soul which is ready, i.e. a soul that has gone through a certain way of development, necessary to start the process of awakening.

Awakening of a Soul (consciousness) – The stage of self-awareness of being, leading to the complete awareness by the soul of itself, i.e. creation of a whole being.

Additional energy kick – Necessary in the early phase of the process of awakening of the soul that is ready for awakening. An additional energy kick is necessary for the redirection of identified attention of the soul 180 degrees, i.e. toward itself.

An additional energy kick is necessary for the awakening soul to overcome the inertia of identified attention and to be able to release habitual personal attachments to multiple external aspects, such as mental images (symbols) and corresponding to physical objects, reflecting them.

Attachments – Attachments of a false personality, i.e. what false personality identifies with. There are three main categories of personal attachments: to security, to pleasure, to power.

CHAPTER 1:
HOW THE CONDITIONED MIND RECEIVED POWER OVER HUMAN BEING

•◆•◆ • ◆•◆ • ◆•◆ • ◆•◆ • ◆•◆ • ◆•◆ • ◆•◆ • ◆•◆ • ◆•◆ • ◆•◆ • ◆•◆ • ◆•◆ •

The problems of safety and fear

Let us investigate where these concepts of **danger** and **safety** came from. They were created by the dual mind. If there is a danger zone, there should also be a safe (danger-free) zone.

How did the mind ascend the throne? It did so with a motto of "Safety." Look, one's **personal safety** is one of the basic things constantly troubling human beings. One never feels completely safe. Do you know a single person who feels totally safe? **Do you yourself feel totally safe?**

Do you think a soldier at war throws himself at a tank because he is not afraid of anything anymore or because he **came to** such a **threshold** that he is unable to **withstand fear** any longer?

What is fury? **How is wrath born?** Why do you get **irritated**? Is not fear a common ground of those emotions? Would you get wrathful or furious if you were not afraid? If one is not experiencing fear, one is usually calm. So, where is

1

the root of all this? Logically, it is fear. Personality fears the loss of the known. **Fear is a reaction of the mind** to something that does not belong to its conceptual framework. It appears that the mind, in trying to escape fear, starts to fight with itself. If it were not for the mind, one would not have a concept of "danger—safety." They are two points on one scale, two sides of one coin. You say, "Dangerous," and at the same time think about a safe, danger-free environment. How can someone find out what "safety" is? In order to do that, we need to know what "danger" is. Both concepts are creations of the mind.

Why do they say that the **mafia is eternal**? Let's consider a person who decided to start a business and opened a small shop. Some "tough" guys show up and say, "We are going to protect you, and you are going to pay us for protection." He says, "Actually, we work in a nice neighborhood, and we don't have any gangsters around here. I never had any problems here…"

"You have not had any problems? Hmm, that is strange. Okay, we will see you in a few weeks."

The next day his car is burned down, and store windows are shattered. A week later, they show up again and ask: "So, how are you? Is everything quiet around here?"

"No, I have a problem. The store was broken into…"

"Okay. Didn't we tell you it is not safe around here? We need to protect you."

Isn't this how the mind works?

In reality, the body coming into this world is threatened with danger: it may not be born at all, it may not be delivered properly, it may be given a wrong shot, and it may just perish. All this can happen. The threat to the body really exists. But let us take a look at what happens to the child as it grows up. I think you will agree that **the most important thing for**

parents, especially for the mother, is the physical well-being, security, and health of the baby. Her anxiety related to real and possible, but most of the time far-fetched problems connected to the **safety of the child** is transmitted to the child. The child is constantly being told what to be afraid of. The problem of safety is **reinforced** in one's mind **from early childhood.**

We are saying that the **mind promises to provide** this security to the body. In reality, we all know that something traumatic can happen to our body: we can get hit by a car, we can fall and get hurt, etc.

For the human being who lived during the time of the mammoths, the **threat of bodily injury** was constant. Therefore, for safety he used a stick in the beginning, then the arrow, then the tank, and then the atomic bomb. That is how the mind progresses toward solving the problem of personal safety. It did so under the **motto of protection** from danger. But **it itself** created the deadly weapon, threatening one in return. Can you see how two sides of one coin are being developed simultaneously? Talks about security instantaneously create danger.

I don't want to deny the fact that the body of each and every one of us, at a certain moment, one way or another, will be destroyed. **This is a fact.** But based on this fact one's mind creates a constant threat and gives birth to constant fear. **Around this fact,** people create philosophical and religious systems. The mind promises to provide a safe situation and positions itself as a professional. It says, "I will solve it. I will solve this problem." And then it proceeds to create religious systems, introduces the concept of karma, eternal life, etc.

The mind pretends to be able to solve the problem of life and death. I understand the rationale of this when we talk about the physical protection of the body. For example, a man is working with fire and he needs to protect himself from burns. He creates some kind of burn-proof garment. Another gets under water and creates a waterproof diving suit. Thought working in a technical direction creates the necessary conditions to protect the body.

Technical methods and solutions are necessary and they are not being negated by me. I do not deny scientific-technical progress and gladly use some of its products. But the mind pretends to achieve something else. **The main problems arise** not because someone decided on a different brand of air conditioner in his house. Look how many years we had a cold war between the US and the USSR. And do you think it did not reflect in the psychology of people on both sides? During the cold war, there were people committing suicide, saying that atomic war was imminent and everyone would perish anyhow. The Russian people said, "It's okay if we didn't get a paycheck this month. Pray we won't have a war." What is it but the work of the mind? What is it but a similar problem born in the mind of a certain group of people who, irrespective of how paradoxically it may sound, pretend to take on the role of **saviors of the country**, nation, and humanity? The same principle is being used by politicians. **Divide and rule**. They come, divide, and then say: "I know how to solve it now."

The external world reflects the mechanism of work of the mind, which is working in each and every one of us.

So, what is fear? Where does it come from? In reality, fear may be that basic force which moves a person, which does not know anything but the dual mind.

Psychological and physical time.
The mind is thought, thought is time

What is thought? Is thought time? And what is physical time? Is it different from psychological time? For example,

4

tomorrow I need to wake up at 9 am. What do I do? I set the alarm clock to 9 am. I agreed to meet my friend at Kursk train station at 10 am. He knows where it is, and I know where it is; we are both on Moscow time. If nothing unexpected happens, we will meet as agreed. This is an illustration of the usefulness of knowing physical time and space.

But did you notice that sometimes a minute can be as spread out as a full day, while sometimes a day can fly by like one minute? Is there a difference between psychological and physical time? If there is, then what is the mechanism of this psychological time? Why does it sometimes move so fast and sometimes slows down?

When the mind finds something interesting, time speeds up. And when the mind is interested, what happens to the mind?

Again, what is time? We just figured out that when the mind is interested, many thoughts pass through our head. Many thoughts. What does this mean? Is it feasible for two or more thoughts to simultaneously appear in one's mind?

How is it related to psychological time? What is psychological time? When does it speed up, and when does it slow down? If thought is time, is time without thoughts possible? **If thought were absent, would time be possible at all?**

Because the necessity of time in the physical world is obvious to a human being, he **decides it should also exist** in his internal world. This is obvious to the mind. The mind is thought. **Thought is time**. Why do we always want to postpone solving a problem, to think it over? We constantly stretch things, both pleasure and displeasure. Who is interested in it? The mind. This is its way of controlling a human being.

Thought and time are **products of the mind**. It supports them and views them as something obvious.

And what then of the **immortality** some people are so eager to have? Immortality, as the mind sees it, is a constant continuity of thoughts, albeit the same thoughts. If the mind were immortal, it would infinitely reproduce the same thoughts over and over.

Therefore, what do we see? We see the **transfer of laws of the physical world** into the psychological world, and the appearance of physical time and space there. Moreover, the mind receives **limitless power** over our inner world. A human being does not even question its rule.

He looks at the physical world, the world of solid bodies and says, "Yes, of course, there is time, there is space, and I act as it is given; how can I act otherwise?" He does not question it. He does not understand that the internal world can operate in any other way.

In this reality of chronological time and three-dimensional space, the mind is king, and nothing can replace it.

And so we have what we have, because the conditioned mind and dual thought are sadness and suffering; the mind's essence is separation and conflict.

What happens in your internal world?

The Ideal—constant pursuit of illusions of the mind

The world of forms, the physical world is material. **Space and time** are present there. If I want to meet someone, I would agree on a certain time and arrive at a certain place at that particular time. If I don't know where the place or time of the meeting is, we are not going to meet. That is why one cannot disregard time and space in the physical world.

Now, let us look at **what happens in the psychological world**. We can call the internal world of a human being the psychological world. How is the psychological world of the majority of people made? Does it look like the external, material, physical world? How does one lives in this internal psychological world? What kind of questions and problems develop there?

Let us say that someone is accepted by a university and spends five years studying there. Why did he apply there? What kind of **internal necessity** drove him there? What would he say if asked? Most likely he would say, "I want to be a specialist in such and such field." Now, the question is, "Why does he want to become a specialist?" He may answer, "Lawyers are making a lot of money, and that is why I want to become one." Or, he can say, "Without higher education I will not have a career and will become a street sweeper."

In reality, we see that the **majority of people believe they need to become specialists** in something in order to receive some kinds of goods and pleasures. Therefore, in order to get those goods and pleasures, they need to specialize in something. What is similar in the answers of those people? We can see that their internal world has **two images of themselves**, i.e. **present and desired.** They want to arrive at spot B for one or another reason. Next, there is a process of transferring from spot A to spot B.

Take psychologists, for example. What do they do? They specialize in solving the problems of the internal world. What is a problem in a nutshell? A problem is dissatisfaction. Someone says, "I am like this now, but I want to be different," and a conversation follows on **how to make the situation better**. Nobody questions how the problem is positioned. It appears self-evident that this particular human being is not very "good" at the present time from a religious, psychological, moral or some other point of view. **Everyone agrees on this**, both the client and the professional. More than that, economics, politics, and education are **built upon that** premise. You have to be smarter—go learn. You have to be healthier—go to the gym. Your figure is not the best—go shape yourself. Is not everything around us based on that concept? Economy? Business? I don't have something, therefore I need something. I want to transfer from state A to state B.

All of this tells us that the internal psychological world of a man is based on the laws of the physical, material world. Then **what do we have** in our psychological world? We sense a constant, chronic state of deficiency and consider this state to be self-explanatory. That is why we constantly **try to correspond** to some kind of **ideal image** of our-selves and reach it with the help of one or another method. As soon as, internally, we agree to strive toward some kind of ideal image of ourselves, we immediately have a chronic problem, which requires application of a constant effort. And then psychological time appears. Now, I start thinking and planning something, i.e. the mind is getting involved in this work. Actually, it was never turned off. It is always on. It constantly works and constantly aims to "improve" one. It says, "You are not polite enough. But it is okay; we are going to correct it. Your speech is not perfect; we are going to improve it, too. You have a problem; we are going to solve it." That is how the mind works, and that is what it **collects energy for**.

And what kind of ideal image of yourself do you pursue?

The false owner of the inner world

The world we see using physical vision is a material world. What does this mean? It means one can physically touch it. I can touch a table. I can touch a tree. I can touch a stone on the road. I can touch an automobile. This is material. This is material reality. It changes.

Two thousand years ago, a completely different reality existed in the place where you are currently sitting. There were no big houses. Cars were not driving through the streets. Everything was completely different. Years passed by. Physical reality was changing. A lot was brought into this physical reality by human beings who physically embodied some of their thoughts. You live in houses and drive cars. There were no houses here before, but then skyscrapers were built. Does reality change? It does.

In what way does it change? It is changed by a human being who stores and increases certain knowledge of physical reality. He learned how to do many things. He discovered electricity and built cars. Multiple gadgets appeared that made life more comfortable. We see science developing. New technologies are being created which bring more and more comfort into our life. TVs were small, and now they are huge. All this is a result of the movement of human thought. Thought, which then materialized, created some kind of physical reality, which has more comfort and more physical possibilities. This is called technical-scientific progress. Now let us take a look at it from a different point of view. **Physical technical-scientific progress exists, but can we say that internal, psychological, spiritual progress exists?** You understand that I am talking about a different sphere now. **Can I physically touch and feel the psychological world** of any given human being? Can I touch someone's psychological world as I touch a car or any other physical object?

This is a different world. How was this world created? What kinds of laws govern this world? Who created this world?

Every human being has an **internal world**. Inside this world is where all the **main problems** are, where **life's**

problems are. I am talking not about problems of technical-scientific progress, not about problems of comfort, salary increase, i.e. what is being realized and present in the external world. I am talking about problems that create psychological and physical suffering. I am talking about problems that, **for every human being,** are of the utmost importance, whether one is aware of them or not. I am talking about problems philosophers, religious leaders, and psychologists are trying to solve. They do not occupy themselves with material things nor do they create new technologies. They pursue different things. They study the internal world. They try to tell us they **can solve** these life problems.

It is interesting to see **how they solve them**. And it is interesting to see how they pose these problems. Because, depending on **how the problem is positioned,** it will be solved in the future. Problems can be positioned in such a way that one can only arrive at a certain definitive result.

So, what is happening in our internal world? What kind of questions do we have there? How do we pose them? How do we solve them? As far as I understand it, if you are still reading this, you are interested in these questions. These questions bother every single human being, but not everyone is aware of them, and not everyone is ready to spend the time or make any efforts to solve them.

How can I approach my own internal world? What is happening there? What did I create there? What laws operate there? Why do I suffer? Why am I not satisfied with what is there? Who decides what should and should not be in my internal world? Who is the owner there?

If we were to look at this, we would see that the apparatus used by a human being to solve the problems of the external world, i.e. technical problems, is being used to position and solve the problems of the inner world. This apparatus is the mind. The mind operates not only in the external world, where its work is justified, but also in the internal world, where its work and actions are not justified. This is not the sphere one can enter with this apparatus, but because the majority of people don't know any differently, they try to use it everywhere.

What does the mind do when it turns toward the internal world of a human being and tries to create something there? It does the same thing it did while working in the outside world. It uses the same concepts. It is impossible to create technologies by working with one or another form of matter not using concepts of time and space. Everything is built on that. The mind transfers it all into the internal world. That is why inside the internal world of a human being, in his psychological world, time and space are present. This is very important because as a result, the mind gets complete power inside the internal, psychological world. That is where separation, conflicts, sufferings, and wars are coming from as an effect.

All this is in view of the fact that we have multiple psychological, philosophical, and religious doctrines; all of them have not changed us much. We can see that. **Did the internal world of people change?** When the internal world of people change, the external world should change also. We can see that the external world did not change. Not only have wars and conflicts not been resolved, but their frequency and severity have been exacerbated. Why is there no change with so many doctrines and systems? **Maybe something very important is missing? Maybe something very important—the capability to acquire self-knowledge and understanding of true "I," the understanding of reality— is lost.**

The powerful of this world, or professional occultism

What is your perception of life? Do you want to spend your life defining and **explaining life, or spend life living it**? Many people try to explain life. They write books and create multiple conceptual models and systems explaining it. They try to confine life to their view and call it "the investigation of life."

There are many people who study, investigate, and **define love**. I remember a few years ago there was a famous writer who wrote a lot about love. I think this guy did not have time to love, because he spent all his time writing about it. There are people who write a lot or spend a lot of time contemplating life. Can one think about life and live it simultaneously? **May one enjoy** beauty **and think** about beauty?

I went to a concert once, accompanied by a professional musician. I was sitting listening to a violin concert of Beethoven. Meanwhile she was constantly touching my hand saying: "How can someone play this way? They are not keeping the pause long enough here. Their instrument is not tuned properly." This person is a **professional of the art**. Please, pay attention here. She plays multiple classical pieces. She knows the biographies of Mozart, Beethoven, and many other composers. She can tell us many stories about them. But how does she listen to this beautiful music? **She listens professionally.**

The professional is the one who **knows: "How."** Professionalism is a **question of technique**. "How?" is a method, a technique.

For example, a professional driver knows different ways to handle a car during difficult situations. A professional surgeon knows how to open up someone's belly and remove an appendix using many different techniques. Professionals are usually **proud of** and talk about **different methods.** What is a party of professionals? It is a collection of people who get together to discuss the question of "How?" One says, "This needs to be done this particular way, while another retorts, "No, this should be done that way." The third one introduces some other method, etc. They have certain gradations, stages, and steps of professionalism. They use degrees and awards to distinguish each other.

Professionalism usually appears in a **technical world**. I understand this word in very broad terms, as the technical world is present in the art, science, and religion.

May one be a professional of life? For example, people come to one such specialist and ask him, "How should we live?" He replies, "This is my profession. I will tell you everything." What does it mean to be a professional? It means he or she has a very broad vision, and knows "How." In this concrete case, this concrete human being can be called a **professional of life**, i.e. **one who knows how to live**.

Take a look at how many people **make a living** out of it. And who are they? They are professionals. Suddenly astrologist, mediums, and others pop up. Let's take any system. At the top of the system there is one **big professional** and many **smaller professionals**, who distribute this system. They teach others how to live. A huge army of professionals exists now in religious, esoteric, and psychological worlds.

This is business. However, this is the sort of a sphere where it is extremely difficult to determine or prove something. It is almost impossible because everything is based on faith.

The professional occultist can be spotted miles away, because he is interested in the question, "How?" **He answers questions**. He does not ask questions. He answers them. Moreover, he answers every single question. He always has a number of methods, and his methods are the best.

Actually, it is sufficient to consider one professional hunter in order to understand what professional hunters are all about. You may examine one professional administrator in order to understand what an administrator is. It is possible to examine a **professional wizard** to understand what wizards are. Any professional sphere has a certain pattern that needs to be learned. If a man wants to enter this sphere, there is a certain image he needs to correspond to; there are many variations, but in a nutshell they all boil down to the same thing. That is why **all professionals look alike**.

For example, what is **a true healer**? How is he different from a healer that is not true? When a mother kisses a child who fell and hurt himself, she might have never heard of healers and healing. She just **loves and kisses** him. Is she a true healer? The kid stops crying and the pain is resolved.

Someone comes dressed in an exotic costume and starts to move his hands up and down, finally charging five hundred dollars for his visit. The patient is impressed to the point of forgetting what was hurting. He just forgot. He was impressed and shocked.

In reality, all these professional mysteries and methods are quite simple, but professionals of science, magic, and occultism are not interested in opening them up. **Who would feel reverence** and respect toward science, academicians, and professors if they did not write those smart books which nobody except them can even read? This is all **attributes**. Some kind of an image, a projection they create. One may take a "short-legged idea" and cover it up in expensive cloth sewn from concepts and ideas. **Something has been created** and now many people start to **believe in it.** One professional will not "pluck the eyes" of another professional. They both understand that their professionalism is based on an illusion of the mind. They are both interested in the creation of an image of importance. Whether they understand it or not, they do create this image. **And what is behind it?** Most often we are dealing with **simple and primitive** things. Only nobody will ever disclose this secret. The one who finds it knows, and the one who does not can easily be fooled. All this, in my opinion, is not that serious. **Whoever wants to be fooled** will be fooled. It happens in all different spheres and walks of life.

However, there is an important aspect to consider here. Let's say two conmen are fooling a group of people. Both of them are after easy money. That is why they play these games that always circle around the money. Conmen don't **say that they teach living;** they are interested in money, while professional **occultists say exactly that.** They talk about interesting and very important things. They talk about truth, beauty, harmony, health, and other things. Professionals of life talk about eternal values. The appearance is created that they have **answers to the most important questions**.

If you want to learn the English language you go to an English language teacher. If you want to learn how an automobile works, you go to a mechanic who knows how it is made. If you want to know what truth and life is, similarly, you try to find a corresponding professional. The same a**pproach is applied everywhere.**

A professional knows answers to the questions and knows his methods. He knows "How?" If one who positions himself as a professional is unable to answer the question "How?" or "What happens to me?" or is unable to explain what needs to be done, **he would not be** a professional. Therefore, what do you think the professional is **concerned** with? Beauty and harmony? No. They have different, more earthbound and practical interests. Professionals are interested in professional things. They are interested in a **number of techniques** and answers to the question "Why?" They also like to foresee the future. To do that, one doesn't need to be an astrologer. One just needs to ask a person what he had experienced prior to this moment. The exact same thing **will follow**. So, those professional **secrets,** in reality, are quite simple. However, for many people, they represent something so important that they start "praying" to them and, as a consequence, become dependent and enslaved.

No one can be a professional of life. No one. Life has to be lived. That's why to explain and define life is just to waste time and energy. I would not try it. **I prefer living**. But one can investigate those who try to explain and define life. That is what I do. And it is very interesting to investigate the mind that stands **between life and us**. It is precisely what prevents us from seeing life as a whole. The mind with its distorted vision, with its half closed lens tries to get everywhere we look. It always gets its nose into everything.

Imagine an amazing waterfall that is being blocked by a huge wall. People are very keen on finding out what that waterfall is. They pierce the wall with small holes and now everyone can look through them. And what do they see? One sees a fly sitting on a hole and, not having any idea what a waterfall is, says, **"A waterfall is a fly."** Another looks and sees a tree, and a third person sees something else. All of them talk about it adamantly, "I saw it. I know!"

There is a new and interesting business spreading around—spiritual business. Look what happens. Some big and important teachers show up and say, "We have a magic mantra. It is going to cure you. Just make sure you don't ever tell anyone what it is." The cloud of secrecy is created. One starts to repeat something. It is irrelevant what he was given. I can ask you to repeat any given concoction of words, for example "Coca-Cola," "Herbalife," or "Toyota Camry." What is going to happen to your brain? It will get somewhat dulled, and one imagines that it quieted down. Actually, the main source of agitation and anxiety has not been resolved. Just because I told you "Coca-Cola," and that you were repeating it for two hours does not mean you were freed from your personality. Nothing has changed. But, the illusion of change was created. You start to believe that you are doing some kind of important work—meditation. But this is not meditation at all.

It cannot change anything. Dullness of the mind is not equivalent to calmness of the mind. There are people, let us say, on the dull side. Their mentation process is very slow. Does it mean they have a quiet mind? No, it is just dull. Any mechanical action leads to dullness. And this is what it is all about. What do you do when you mechanically repeat a mantra, prayer, positive statement, or something of this nature? You repeat the same thing over and over again. And how is it different from any other habit? Another habit is formed which leads to dullness of the mind—not to liberation of the mind, but to its dullness.

Many people talk about meditation today, not understanding what it is. It is neither a reflection, nor a concentration. Thinking is one of the activities of the mind. Meditation is another activity of the mind. It is a different activity of the mind.

What and who is a human being?

What is a human being? Who are those creatures populating the Earth and calling themselves humans? A Russian writer Maxim Gorky used to say, "Human being—it sounds proudly." Many think that humans are the highest creatures on Earth. I question this. If that were the case, and the human being is really the highest creature, how many of such people populate the face of the Earth?

There are many human-robots, acting mechanistically. Who are they? Are they human beings or not? If you tell someone that he is not a human being but a robot, it would be considered a grave insult. Not many people would like that.

So, what is a human being? When one is born, people say a new man is born. What happens to him in the process of development or growing up? Personality or ego is formed. What is it? Is it not a certain collection of habits people call character traits? Actually, **a character is a stereotypical way of reacting to the external and internal stimuli. It's a mechanism.**

I would like to figure out if personality can be equated to a human being. We have a body and that part which forms later, i.e. personality. When we talk about someone, we talk about his personality, right? We can say that he is good, kind, truthful, punctual, suspicious, jealous, envious, irritable, etc. There are quite a few definitions of personality, and the majority understands and equates personality to a human being.

But if a human being is a supreme creature, and if it sounds proudly, then why does he live this way? If we impartially look at how people live, it is impossible not to see constant conflicts in relationships which lead to wars and murder. Is it possible for someone to call himself a supreme being and at the same time participate in killing of other similar creatures? And this destruction occurs even without a biological necessity. Animals eat each other in nature, but they only do it when they are hungry. Humans do not eat humans, but at the same time the number of people killed by people is enormous. May such a being call himself a supreme being?

Someone may say, "Yes, some people kill. But those are criminals. I am not one of them. I am not doing it, and I would never be able to." But is this true? Does not every single human being possess everything that is present in the whole of humanity? Does not every human being contribute to what has happened and is happening on the face of the Earth? **A conflict is a consequence of separation, fragmentation of the perception of the human being himself, when one fragment of the brain condemns and criticizes another fragment.** That is the main reason for all conflicts and wars. But does not every single one of us have this separation? Is it not true that every single one of us brings this separation into the world we live in? Can one call himself a human being if one is internally divided?

Perhaps you are just afraid of the law and punishment and that is what precludes you from carrying out your internal and external conflicts to do something legally forbidden. Deep down the essence and the cause of every conflict is the same. It is **internal psychological separation.** Let's say I have certain convictions that I am unwilling to change, and that is assuming I have never been in conflict with the law. Does it mean that I have not contributed to the conflicts and wars around the world? Is it not true that not only are we not ready to part with our convictions and beliefs, but that we constantly force them onto others?

Here is a good example. I am sitting in front of the TV watching another brutal conflict saying, "What is going on? It must stop." But am I not the same? Can I easily give up my convictions? Have I never tried to force them on somebody else? So, what is a human being?

Human beings have quite a strong tendency to reproduce and to survive. Multiple species of animals and plants were unable to survive in the rapidly changing environment of the Earth or could only survive in certain places that had a required milieu. Humans, on the other hand, survive in different circumstances and conditions. This is one of the distinguishing characteristics of the species—the ability to adapt and survive in changing circumstances, not only physical but also psychological.

That is why to a certain individual human being the conditions of other people may seem to be nightmarish and unbearable. He says that it is better not to live at all than to live in those conditions. However, if you talk to those other people, it may become obvious that those people are quite content with the way they live. They do not want to change anything. Humans, having developed extreme survival skills, can adapt to almost anything. But this is life in hell. This is a hellish life if you look at it impartially.

A human being gets used to anything. During war, in jail, in extreme weather conditions a man will find his pleasures and sorrows, saying that this is how it is and it could not be different. However, some questions arise. Is this how the superior being should live his life? Who created this creature and subjected it to such a life? Should a human being carry out some other role? Is this amazing survivability, adaptability, and, on the other hand, unwillingness to change required by nature for some other aims? Nature would not allow the development of this particular specimen without a reason. Therefore, for one reason or another, this particular development is acceptable to nature. But is it acceptable to the human being himself?

If we were to look at the situation impartially, we would see that the majority of people don't want anything else. Many may say they are discontent with the way things are, but not many are ready to change anything in their own life. So, what kind of species are we? What is it to be human? Maybe what we have in us presently is just a potential for becoming human? Maybe this is just a possibility to become a human being? Maybe, as a butterfly is born from a cocoon, a Human being can be born from what we call "human" now. Maybe every single one of us has the opportunity to become Human but is not utilizing it, because we believe that we already are human. But then what are we right now?

What do we have? First, we have a body. A body provides us with an opportunity to be present in the material world: to move, act, see, hear, and feel. And what is present in the body: what directs it?

What would psychologists say about it? They would talk about personality: its formation, peculiarities, characteristics, and factors shaping it. They would suggest multiple definitions and classifications of personality and methods describing it.

But what is personality? They say in Russian that "one has to become a personality." The adolescent is told, "You do not have a personality yet, but you may develop it." There are certain expectations of what a real personality is. For example, there are expectations of what the real male personality is, as well as what the real female personality is, and these are looked at during a child's upbringing. Upbringing itself is a process of the formation of these personality traits, these peculiarities of character. So, what is being formed in the body: the human being or the personality? In my opinion this is a very serious question. As you can see, it is not self-evident to me that the personality and the human being are the same. I think the human being is something completely different. Therefore, I ask, what is that they try to instill in a child? It seems to me that this is precisely personality that they try to instill, i.e. the compilation of certain views, beliefs, habits, traits and peculiarities that allow the formation of something in this particular body, that latter allows one to enter the society.

A country needs workers and soldiers. The process we are discussing allows a child to become another worker or a soldier. So, who is it that brings up the child: parents or society? To whom does the child belong? It appears that the child belongs to his parents, and it is through parents that society brings up a child and inoculates him with the traits it requires. Parents are already members of the society. Now they have a new body which they need to bring up, to create a personality that will become another member of society. So, who owns this personality: the parents or society? Here is another question: to whom do the parents belong? Is there anyone here who can say that he or she belongs to nobody? If one is to look objectively, one can see that everything the majority of people usually call a "human being" is personality, while personality is a compilation of something programmed by society. There is nothing there, but what already exists in society. It is a certain fragment of society, which is called personality.

So, what is a human being? What is a personality? Does personality want to become a human being?

What is personality? It is simply a fragment of society, which incorporates certain beliefs, views, convictions, and opinions already existing in one or another stratum of society. Is personality then something individual? What happens when this personality disappears?

You probably know how an automobile is assembled. Multiple parts are assembled together. This collection of separated parts turns into an automobile. But what if I were to meticulously disassemble this conglomerate of parts one calls an automobile, into separate pieces, and then put them in different places? Would one still be able to call this collection of separate parts an automobile? Just few minutes ago there was an automobile here. Now, there is just a collection of certain parts. Can you call this collection of parts an automobile?

So, what is personality? When different fragments of certain convictions, believes, and thoughts concentrate in the body and the mind, this entire conglomerate is called a personality. What would happen if we were to take this personality and disassemble it down to separate parts, i.e. all those different convictions, beliefs, and opinions of which it consists? What would be left behind? Would there be anything left?

Let's take a concrete personality and assume that it has certain convictions. Every single one of these convictions I am going to pick up separately and put aside. It has certain beliefs. I will take them, separate them and put them aside. It also has certain preferences; let us say of a physical nature. These I will also separate and put aside. What will I have left? I have just divided this personality into the many parts of which it was composed.

Next, I am going to return every single part to the source it originally came from. For example, one is convinced that only communism can save the country. He has this strong conviction because he is a communist. I will take this conviction and return it to where it is belongs, i.e. the communist society. Next, we take some other conviction. For example, the conviction that a man should lead a woman, or the reverse, that a woman should lead a man. Again, I would take this conviction and return it to where it originally came from. Do you think I will be able to find all the sources from which these convictions came? Yes, these are certain fragments of society. Certain convictions are concentrated in certain parts of a given society, i.e. in certain groups of people that carry these convictions. Therefore, every single personality can be sliced into building blocks, and these blocks can be returned to where they originated. What would be left of a personality as a result of this action?

A human being is sometimes called a social animal. We can see that a human being is composed of social parts, i.e. parts that came from society, and also of animal parts. If we were to remove everything that was imposed by society, i.e. personality, we would be left with just an animal walking on two legs.

We have said that the mind is a headquarters of personality formation. Certain convictions, beliefs, and opinions are introduced into the mind, and then it starts to use the heart, the emotional sphere to feed those concepts with energy. And what do we have then? We have a social animal. But usually animals kill other animals only when hungry, when instinct drives them to look for food. A human being, on the other hand, can kill another human being not because he is hungry, but because of certain ideas of his personality. So, what does this socially added structure, i.e. personality, gives us? Does it make an animal called human being more humane compare to other animals?

Now, let's take a look at the evolution of the human animal from the animal state to the state of the social animal. An animal does not have convictions; it cannot kill because of convictions. It can kill only when it is hungry. A personality, on the other hand, will kill because of convictions. For example, out of the conviction that it is the most powerful one or from its desire to possess something: a woman, a man, a town, status, a car, a building, a corporation, etc.

Physiologic hunger can be satisfied by a certain quantity of food. The hunger of Personality is insatiable. Vanity, jealousy, wrath, grudges are all reactions of a personality to unsatisfied desires. To satisfy these desires a personality can kill other people. And what is most important, it will do it deliberately. One can premeditate a murder. What other animal on the face of the Earth can premeditate a murder?

Let's take war. Multiple lives are taken by wars. Generals deliberate how to better destroy the enemy. This is an organized murder, and it takes huge number of lives. Of course, we can say that is not related to us personally. I did not kill anyone, and I am not about to kill anyone. But does not every one of us carry his own separateness and conflict?

CHAPTER 2:
MECHANISMS OF PERCEPTION
AND
REACTIONS OF A CONDITIONAL
MIND

❖—❖ • ❖—❖ • ❖—❖ • ❖—❖ • ❖—❖ • ❖—❖ • ❖—❖ • ❖—❖ • ❖—❖ • ❖—❖ • ❖—❖ • ❖—❖ • ❖—❖ •

How do you perceive your surrounding reality?

You are now reading this text. How does your mind react to it? It is possible that your mind pays specific attention to certain fragments and starts to assert, "I agree with this part, but that part is wrong." If you are capable of simultaneously reading and observing the working process of your mind, you can see how it reacts to what is being written here.

The mind usually reacts in one of two ways: it is either in agreement or in disagreement. The mind is like a computer with memory; it tends toward what is habitual. For example, I say, "Long live the Socialist Party." A socialist would say, "Yes, yes, yes." On the other hand, if he hears something contrary to his convictions, he would say, "No, no, and no." If you start to observe the working of your mind you can see that this is exactly how it happens. Your mind either agrees or disagrees.

Everything around you is an opportunity to see something. While observing the same event, person A sees one thing, while person B sees something else. One sees a conflict, another sees the possibility of enrichment, yet a third one sees it as boring and loses interest.

We are surrounded by what we call: the world, reality, illusion, etc. Irrespective of what you call it, this is something that can be seen. That is why the main question is what our ability to see is? Irrespective of the topic we discuss or the questions we ask, the differences that appear initially are superficial. They can be narrowed down to the mode, character, and **peculiarities of our perception**. For example, a man asks, "Why did Stephanie leaving me hurt so much more than Veronica leaving me?" This is also a question of seeing. He just sees it this way. But this can also be seen from a different point of view, making it less painful or even pleasant.

What do people do all the time? People try to change external circumstances in order to receive what they want. If they are afraid of losing something they value, they create conditions that will prevent the loss. They bring the object closer and try to protect it. But there is another option here. We can observe and **investigate the mechanism of our perception itself**.

We can see that any question, any problem, formulated or not yet formulated is the result of one's **perspective, i.e. his vision of something**. The way one formulates one's problem depends on what one considers to be important. Usually, in defining a problem or considering a question, one formulates a definitive theme. Theme is something usually considered as existing outside of oneself. One talks about it as something separate and external, something defined and circumscribed. Yet what if we were to look at it a little bit differently? What if we were to talk not about a theme, which is something separate from a given human being, but to talk about a **human being who has a certain way of seeing this problem**?

What one defines as a theme and how one sees it may in reality specify the peculiarity of one's perception, one's vision. This vision may be broad or narrow, blurred or clear, but this is a vision of a particular **human being** who, by himself, is **an instrument** that defines **what he can see**. This is very important to understand!

When asked a question, I always try to shift the focus of attention from the theme to the one who brings up the theme. I try to show that what is important is not the investigation of some outside, abstract theme but the investigation of this **human being himself as a receptive mechanism.** In particular, what was it in him that gave birth to the understanding of the importance of this theme?

Try always to return to yourself, i.e. to identify the mechanisms which determine your ability or inability to see something. This is very important. This is precisely where all the answers to your current questions, as well as future questions, lie.

So, what is it that determines one's ability to see? How and why does the **possibility of seeing** something develop? Both humans and other animals have physical sensory organs with which they perceive the material, external world. However, our perception differs from that of other animals. For example, in a dog's perception of the world, the sense of smell is dominant and extremely important. Different creatures use their organs of perception in completely different proportions. When I say, "To see, to perceive," I mean all sensory organs, not only vision.

So, what is it that allows us to see the whole picture, and what prevents us from it? Behind all these physical organs (eyes, ears, skin with its nerve endings) is the brain. It accepts all the incoming signals passing through these sensory organs and processes them. It is quite a sophisticated system, but in a nutshell, that is how it works. Two different human beings may react differently to the same situation. One sees it one way, another sees it differently. Even though the source of external influence was the same, each sees it differently. What conclusion can we make here? We can conclude that this apparatus—the brain, and what is being built on its basis—the mind, in a certain way filters, picks up, and differentiates all information that comes through all those sensory organs. **And why is it that certain things are perceived and others are not?**

For example, you are sitting in a room and there is a wall in front of you, you say, "I am tired of looking at this wall. I want to see something else." I offer you, "Then take a look at the window located behind you." But in order to do so, you have to turn 180 degrees, and then you will not see the wall. You reply, "But I can simultaneously look through the window and keep the image of the wall." And to this my reply would be, "That is exactly what you are trying to do all the time." **This is an attempt to sit on two chairs.** Moreover, those chairs are sprawling. You can try to connect them, but there are things that are not connectable, which cannot coexist together. You can try to see something that is incompatible with what you have, and at the same time, you are not willing to release what you have. You can say to it, "I am not ready yet," but then you will not be able to see anything unknown to you, because the window into the unknown is closed by the wall of what you don't want to release—the habitual. It follows then that all the questions you ask are just rhetorical questions. In reality, the answers to all these questions are not in a faraway land but are in your ability or inability to understand the mechanisms of your own perception, i.e. to learn to understand yourself as a receptive mechanism.

If you really want to understand yourself in this way and are ready for it, study this book attentively and apply it in your daily life.

Your spectrum of perception

Some people go to see old movies, but after seeing the movie, they are left with what they already had. Why is it that people watching the same movie see it completely differently? Why do some people, discussing different films, say exactly the same thing? Have you noticed this?

An acquaintance of mine went abroad. On his return, I asked him, "So? How was it?" He replied, "You know, we would wake up in the morning, buy five bottles of beer and have fun." I said, "Great. And what happened then?" "Well, then we would go to the beach, buy three more bottles of a different brand of beer, and have fun." So, he went to an interesting place. He spent a week there drinking beer. He remembers the beer and its brands very well. Everything else was left **behind the screen**.

What is it one wants to see? A man can travel to exotic places but only see the same thing there. At the same time, in his own words, he is looking for something new, and he pays money for it. He would spend a thousand dollars going to one place and three thousand going to another place. He would come back and proudly declare, "I have been there, and I have been over there." "And what did you see?" If we listened to him attentively we would learn that his vision was set at a very narrow range, such as new cars, different brands of beer, beautiful women, etc. In other words, from a huge variety of things around him, he usually chooses one thing only and fixates it in memory. Always and everywhere he sees only this very thing, missing everything else.

Let's take a camera. Imagine we are standing on the bank of a river. Nature around us is beautiful, and we want to take a picture of it. We pull out a camera and happily press the button. However, coming home we discover that we forgot to remove the lens protector. Great camera, expensive lens, but nothing was captured. The lens was covered. But let's assume we opened it, tried to adjust the camera's settings, but did not do it correctly. Then instead of the beautiful image of nature we would get something fuzzy and ugly. Using the camera to record something interesting and important for us, we are asking a question and trying to figure out, "How to tune it up better?" We are not professionals, but we can find someone who can explain to us how to do it. We understand that if our camera is not focused, the picture is going to be correspondingly fuzzy.

But do we understand this in relationship to our own perception?

The focus and fixation of perception

The only thing the mind is after is to **provide security for itself**. Security is the most important thing for the mind. What does the mind do when it works? It drags its past experiences into the future, i.e. it repeats the same stereotypes all the time. But it also watches out not to exceed the limits of what is "permissible." During the process of manufacturing technical parts, the ranges of "permissible" are defined. If "permission" is not allowed, the part is labeled as defective. So the brain itself creates problems and suffering for us, but simultaneously it watches to make sure it is working properly, in order for this suffering not to take us outside the limits of what is "permissible." Going beyond these limits is called insanity.

"Insanity" is a situation that occurs when the mind becomes incapable of controlling itself inside the borders society considers normal. The degree of permissibility can be different. If something happens to the brain and it becomes inoperable, one exits those "limits of permissible" and becomes insane. The mind creates problems and the mind itself keeps these problems inside the habitual borders. That is what is called a normal life. There is a **normal life**, and there is **an abnormal life.**

Abnormal life starts when the mind exits the limits of the habitual. This exit is not followed by insanity in people who learned to exit habitual notions simultaneously creating new, broader and freer notions, i.e. new worldviews. They can change the focus of their perception and move from one perception of the world to another. The mind of such a human being is very elastic and is capable of easily changing its own conceptions and stabilizing its perceptions. That human being is capable, while being aware, of changing his perception, of seeing the world differently. More importantly, he is capable of controlling this process.

Someone who is capable of being aware and of controlling his or her **focus of perception of the world** will not become insane. The borders between normalcy and insanity are relative. Psychiatrists themselves talk about it. Some people are strongly **fixated,** and certain provocative situations can bring them to the verge of becoming abnormal. Every single human being has certain fixations. In some people they are stronger than in others. These fixations constitute the basis of one's personality. This is something people do not want to question, but nobody can fool Life.

Life is a flowing river, and the current of this river may pick one up and throw him into situations, which will influence these fixations, i.e. convictions, opinions, beliefs. Then he will be unable to hold his mind in any kind of brackets. It will get off the rails, as they say. **Permission will not be sustained by the mind any longer.**

Who can guarantee that this will not happen to him? Many people have a very strong fixation on something. They have very strong convictions and try to force them onto the people surrounding them. They are not pacified until others are convinced. They themselves create situations that expose them to **contrary convictions and opinions,** and those situations can "throw out" their mind causing it to exit the borders of controlled "permission." No one can guarantee himself to be free from it.

To exit the borders of perception of the conditioned mind is possible either through the understanding of its limitations (awareness) or through insanity.

Which direction are you taking?

Attention and its direction

Every single one of us **has attention,** and perhaps this is the most valuable thing we possess. Where do we direct it? Attention can be directed outside as well as inside. How do **you use your attention** in order to see and understand another human being? In order to see another human being one should, for a time, **forget one's personality**. One needs to stop identifying with everything one considers to be himself. **What do we consider to be our self?** It is our interests, convictions, values, sorrows, and thoughts. That preclude us from seeing what is really happening around us.

Every single one of us has attention, but why is it that one sees something important in a certain situation while another does not? For example, two friends are listening to the same person or reading the same book. One **was able to hear** and understand something, while another could not. Why?

What is occupying your attention now? How are you reading this book? What do you understand?

Perhaps, you are paying attention only to words and common logic, but not to the essence of this text. What do you want to understand?

Let's pretend you are anxious right now because of some money you owe to a bank or stressed out by friend's sickness or a paper you writing. **Would you be able to see and hear anything unrelated to your immediate concerns and stresses?** You probably would not.

If your attention is occupied by something you consider important, you simply would not be able to see anything except your internal voice, which constantly reminds you about your problems.

Usually people react to words. Let's say you are concerned with money right now. In your head, your mind constantly plays, "Where am I going to get the money? Where am I going to get the money? Am I going to get the money? How will I pay for this and how will I pay for that?" However, there is no mentioning of money in the book. What are you going to react to? Will you hear anything if between my words your key word "money" is missing?

What do you, immersed in a state of internal **replay of your problem react to**? Can you even react to something unrelated to what you consider to be your problem?

What problems interfere most with your understanding of what you are reading now?

34

On what do we spend the energy of attention?

Inside a man's head there is a **constant internal dialogue that does not stop for a minute**. Multiple internal voices talk and discuss things that a man calls, **"my current problems."** But he has not only one problem, but many. He brings them anywhere he goes, and all those problems are circulating inside his head.

What kind of problems prevents you from understanding what you are reading now? Perhaps, 1% of your attention may be directed toward what is happening right now, while 99% is occupied by very important work of circulating the problems the mind does not want to let go off, problems the mind wants to maintain and reinforce all the time.

Attention is that internal currency a human being possesses. Attention can be transformed into money, for example doing some business or into writing a book if one is a writer or a scientist, or into some art object. A man's attention can be transformed into fighting someone who has insulted him, or into a blessing.

We only have **one thing—attention.** We carefully count the money in our wallet, but where do we allocate our attention? **What do we spend it on? Is this attention directed** toward oneself, toward the problems one has, or devoted to others? Perhaps, I devote my attention to another human being just because he or she solves my problems? But then I devote my **attention** not to another human being, but **to myself** through someone else.

Are there many people around you to whom you pay attention? Have you ever had a **full one second** in your life during which you have paid your **full attention to another human being**? Have you ever paid one second of your full attention, **forgetting all your problems,** personal desires and ambitions, to another human being? Is not this **true happiness?**

How much attention do you devote to the understanding of what is written here?

The mind is the reanimator of the past.
The mind is the reanimator.

Hospitals have Intensive Care Units (ICUs). Admission to an ICU means that patient is on the border of life and death. It is unknown whether he will survive or not. Energy, i.e. life, is leaving him. Without energy the body turns into a cadaver. ICU doctors do everything in their power to revive the life in a body.

What does the mind do? The **mind reanimates the past.** This is its constant and only occupation. It reanimates images, thoughts, convictions and beliefs. As soon as it stops doing so, the past disappears because, in reality, there is no past. The past exists only in the memory of the mind, in those neurological cells of the brain where this information is written. **Reality is like a river.** It flows and changes every minute. The mind, on the other hand, grabs the past and reanimates its images. It reproduces itself. It reproduces what it already has. That is what the mind is, and **that is what it does.**

Now let us look at the question of **energy distribution** in the human being. How much energy do you think is needed for such a reanimation? How much energy is being used to reanimate the cadaver? How many cadavers are there in one's mind, in one's memory? How much energy does one need in order to constantly maintain and reanimate all this, every minute, every day, every month, every year, all life long?

That is **what energy is being used for**. Where does it come from? If you were to conduct an impartial self-observation, you would see that the mind steals the major part of one's energy. During the feudal system this was called, "rent."

In a feudal system, a lord would take almost everything his slaves had, leaving them a bare minimum in order for them not to die and to continue to work for him. **Our mind is this feudal lord.** It uses the energy it collects to reanimate the cadavers it contains: images, ideals, convictions of the past.

You may ask, "Is there anything except the mind?" Yes, there is, but how does it function? How much energy is there for its functioning? **How much energy** is in one's heart? How much energy is in the sexual center of a human being? How and for what purpose is this energy spent? We are surprised when we get an ache here or there, but the mind meddles with everything. It wants to control everything. It interferes with the work of organs it should not be touching. It starts to dictate its terms, its views on how the organism should function, and that leads to diseases.

How does your conditioned mind behave?

The duality of perception

What stands **between you and life**? For me, every single human being is life embodied. He himself is this life. But the majority of people view themselves differently. The personality has a completely different image of itself. Where was this image born? It was born in the mind. The mind is dual. The mind **gives birth to duality**. That is how the mind perceives life. But does duality actually exists in life, or does **duality exist in the mind's perception** of life? When you talk about life, who within you is doing the talking? Talking about duality, do we talk about **life as it is** or do we talk about the mind's perception of life?

The conditioned mind does not have other concepts of life except dual, but is there anything else? Is it possible that behind this duality lies something else, something **not dual?**

What do you think?

Perception through image

When you have a very sharp image of another human being, what do you have? Certainty. This is what personality and the mind appreciate the most. The mind loves certainty. As soon as uncertainty appears, the mind immediately tries to elucidate everything and put everything in its place, call it a name and make it definitive. It always strives toward certainty. In these terms, you "win." This particular human being is clear for you, i.e. he does not carry any uncertainty.

But, what do you lose when you see another human being as a precisely defined image? Quite a lot is lost. Only a small number of human beings can really see other people. They are capable of seeing the essence of things, the essence of the human being. It is possible only in one situation: if you look at this particular human being unconditionally, impartially, without an intermediary, which is our image of him. Between every single one of us and another human being there is always an intermediary, a mediator. Have you ever thought of that? This mediator is an image through which we look at this human being.

How is this image formed? Let's say one has a wife or a husband. One has a definitive image created by his family of how a husband or a wife should be. This is related not only to a husband or wife, but to everything else: how it should be at work, how I should be dressed, how should another person be dressed, how the weather should be, how snow should fall. **In regards to everything in this world, we have our own conceptions, images of how it should be. Those images are formed and are present in the mind, and in using them, the mind appraises everything with which it comes in contact. It constantly appraises, "Yes" or "No." I either agree or disagree with it. Nothing else happens.** Everything written here can be seen from this standpoint. You nod your head and say, "Yes, this is so." It means that your experience, which determines your understanding of what I am talking about, triggers certain associations in your mind, which, it seems to you, are in accord with what I say. And then you say, "Yes." If what I say brings up associations that are not in accord with your experience, you say "No."

Do not hurry to agree or disagree with this. Listen to what is happening in your internal world. What do you think? What do you feel? What do you sense? What do you want to do?

The fragmented nature of perception

Life is something that cannot be defined, something that is impossible to express, but is only possible to see and experience. When we try to look at something, how do we do it? Through what lens do we look at everything that surrounds us?

Look around you. What do you see? Most likely you are going to see some parts, fragments of what is around you now, not the whole picture.

When we look at something, we see only fragments. Our perception is fragmented. We look at someone but only see a fragment of him. If we were capable of seeing something as a whole, if we were to see a human being standing in front of us

39

as a whole, then we would see the whole of Life. But we only see fragments. We only see parts.

Life exists and will continue to exist regardless of our personalities or our conditioned minds. Are we able to see the life that really exists? That is the main question because everything else is a result of it—to see life as a whole, to see even something as a whole... But who prevents us from seeing it as a whole? The question of seeing is a defining question. In reality, awareness is seeing.

How do we see things? When we look at something, we see parts and pieces of it. Then we try to connect and unite them. But the question arises: why don't we see it as a whole, but only as bits and pieces? Why? Who is looking? Is it our fragmented mind? Yes. That is why everything we see is partial and fragmented. The mind uses vision, hearing, touch and other senses as instruments to see something. Eyes, ears, and skin allow you to see a lot, but the mind can see only what it is ready to see now.

Is your mind ready to see the fragmented nature of your perception?

The likable and not likable is a prism of perception

The mind wants to recreate something that used to be useful to it or will bring it pleasure. Its memory contains written information of what used to bring pleasure, i.e. the image of it. What can pleasure be connected to? For example, it can be connected to Beethoven's music or some person or a nice car. The mind has saved a certain number of pleasurable experiences, and it strives to recreate those pleasures again and again. When we look at something, the mind will extract from it exactly those parts that will allow us to re-experience this pleasure.

40

What is it that the mind does not want to see? What does it try to escape? An object may be right in front of your eyes, but if in your mind it is associated with something unpleasant, you will not want to see it. Is that so or not? What does your experience tells you?

You may see that there are things that are pleasant to a certain degree, things that are not pleasant to a certain degree, and neutral things, which at present time are not yet associated in your mind with being either pleasant or unpleasant. Do you think this division of things to pleasant, neutral, and unpleasant may have some relationship to what your mind selects from the surrounding environment? Does it affect your perception?

The mind usually notices something pleasant or unpleasant, i.e. emotionally colored as positive or negative. However, what is pleasant for you may not be pleasant for another man. No two human beings will completely agree in their assessment of what is pleasant and what is unpleasant. Our perception, defined by the mind, by its attachment to pleasure and its desire to resist anything unpleasant, extracts from the environment some fragments, associated in our memory with something pleasant or unpleasant. Anything not associated with something pleasant or unpleasant, you may not notice at all.

May we consider this type of perception to be perception of the whole?

Is this related to our perception of certain things and situations only, or is it related to everything else? Every time we look at something, we demonstrate this fragmentation.

You are reading this book now. Are you aware of this mechanism of your perception now? Become aware of it now!

Internal separation and aggression

When the mind starts to understand that all its attempts, all movements of thought, are limited by a certain border which it can't cross, something unusual happens. The majority of people want to share something they know and, in return, receive an agreement in regards to what they consider to be true. They experience displeasure when they do not hear confirmation of what they know and pleasure when what they know is confirmed.

Look how aggressive a man becomes when he is not allowed to say something he considers to be the truth. He starts to exhibit strong aggression and to force his truth on his opponent. Take a look around you and observe how a communist oppresses a capitalist, and capitalist oppresses a communist, a Jew oppresses an Arab while an Arab oppresses a Jew. What is at the core here? The Jew is not agreeing with the Arab, while the Arab is not agreeing with the Jew. It happens because they have different convictions. Not only do they want to maintain those convictions, they also want confirmation that they are right. When someone new shows up not agreeing with their "holy scriptures," they start bullying him into agreement.

Let's say we had an argument. There is nothing criminal here as long as neither one of us is physically hurt. But where does that border lie? In reality, I may just be afraid of punishment, while my mind may want to destroy everything that disagrees with it. Can we see this in ourselves?

Many people say, "Yes, feuds and hatred are everywhere. Brother is fighting brother. How will we live?" Politicians say, "Everything is going to be okay. We understand what needs to be done. We need to connect this and this. We need to push for a new reform." But we see that none of it is working. We need to turn toward ourselves to investigate not the external environment and social processes, but our internal worlds, because all this is a result of the mind's perception. Everything we observe in the external world, in political, economic, social or any other movements, we can see in our own mind. This is where the main problem is located, where separation and fragmentation exists. One part of our mind strikes against another part of our mind, and this internal conflict and fight, which we can observe inside ourselves, eventually develops outside, in political, economic, social, cultural, and all other spheres. Until we see this in ourselves, until we get to the bottom of it in ourselves, no real changes in external life are possible.

What happens to the mind that collides with itself and sees that it is pounding within the same sphere, unable to jump outside the borders of the prison it build for itself. What is the movement of the thought? People praise the movement of human thought and call it technical-scientific progress. Where does this progress take us? What kind of progress is it? Is there any spiritual progress? Is the human being really developing? Where are his thoughts directed? What is the movement of thought? Where does it move?

Agreement or disagreement instead of understanding

What does "understanding" mean to the mind? What does "he understands" mean? It means: he agrees. When we read something with which we are in agreement, it just confirms something we already agree with. While doing that, we can say that we understood, let's say 25% of it. What do we mean when we say that we understood 25% of it? We just found confirmation of something we already knew, i.e. in reality we did not get anything new out of the book. We just confirmed what we already knew. Meanwhile, we state that it is a very good book, and we learned a lot from it. But was there any understanding at all? Was there any attempt on the part of the mind to understand anything at all?

The mind is not interested in learning anything new; it is only interested in confirming what it already knows. Do you think this peculiarity of the mind shows when you read this book? Does it always show up in your perception of new ideas?

The mind perceives only what it already knows. So, it agrees with new information and says that it is valid. You say that this is very interesting book, you liked it a lot, and your friend should read it too. Your friend calls and tells you last night's movie was amazing and you should see it. But you watch this movie and get "nauseated." Why? You say you are not in agreement with everything in this movie while your friend was on the verge of ecstasy.

Consider a movie where a family quarrel is being depicted. The wife approaches her husband, who has just come from another woman, and slaps his cheek. "Bastard, I ruined my life because of you," she screams. "You ruined my youth!" Some women in the theater say, "This is the truth. This is a real movie," because they had similar experience. Other women say, "It is impossible. What is this?" They have never had such an experience. They say, "I have ruined his life. That is why he goes to see another woman." So, what do you see in movies, books, and other people? What does your mind perceive?

The mind needs only one thing out of two: to agree or to disagree. When it sees something that corresponds to its notions, it agrees and says "it is good." When it sees something that does not correspond, it disagrees and says "it is bad."

Why don't people understand each other? Because a human being only acts in two ways: agrees or disagrees. In either case nothing new happens. Nothing new enters the mind because it superimposes everything onto the image that is already there. If one says he understands, it does not really mean he does. He just agrees with it. Some people agree more frequently, some less. In either case, nothing new happens.

If you just agree with what is written here, what can we say has happened? You did not try to enter the essence of the words, did not allow them to enter you and give them an opportunity to spend some time inside of you. You just said on the entrance:

- White?
- White.
- Come on in.
- Black?
- Black.
- Go away.

Agreement or disagreement.

I am talking about one thing only: true understanding, in particular of what I am saying will appear only when your agreement or disagreement leaves you, allowing you to simply listen. It would only happen when the mind stops appraising. One of you may think, "Yes, it has happened already. I already tuned in, and I already have it." No, this is not so, and that is why I constantly need to point this out to you.

Try to become aware of this right now! What are your thoughts, feelings, sensations? What do you want?

The fight of the fragments of the mind

Let's assume I have an idea that social progress in Russia can be only connected to the development of capitalism. What would hinder the movement of this thought?

45

For example, if socialists were to disagree with this thesis, they would try to destroy the idea. The direction of this thought is in contradiction with the direction of socialist thought. It is similar to two knights coming toward each other with lances in their hands during a tournament, trying to pierce each other. Is it really so? Can you observe it in your mind? Perhaps neither socialism nor capitalism concerns you very much. Your thoughts may move differently. What kind of movements are those? How do they occur?

You can see it in yourself. When you have a thought, there is always another, opposite thought present. Those parts of your mind start to scream and work to convince one another. The one that currently has more energy wins.

What can we see during this observation of ourselves? We understand that all this is happening in some self-contained sphere of our mind. There is fragmentation there. The mind is dual. Every thought, image, and idea inside the mind creates its opposite. How do I know there is light? In order to know what light is, I need to know what darkness is. Light means less of darkness. It means that inside my head, a constant comparison of these two opposite images continues. So, what is this fight about, between what and what? It is the fight between the opposites. Between the contents of those opposites that happens to be inside one's mind.

Let's take a look at physiology. Many of you know that the brain consists of two parts. This is a physiologic appearance of duality of the mind. I say certain words; for example, I say, "A tree." What appears in your head? An image. Why does this image appear? What is the physiologic mechanism of this image? Certain cells of your brain contain information about this concept, they get activated, and an image appears. I activated certain cells of your brain which in return produced an image. If, for example, I say, "what a horror," what happens in your mind? Most likely some kind of an image appears related to an unpleasant feeling. What happened? I activated certain cells of your brain, which contain certain information and certain feelings you previously experienced in relationship to this. You can see it, if you want to, of course. I can say certain words and you will start to experience depressed states because they are connected with painful experiences. For example, I say the word "bankruptcy." Recently your company went through a bankruptcy. You start to react to this word with the state of emotion through which you recently lived.

Our mind contains multiple concepts and images. Moreover, as we just discovered, these concepts are dual. If you have a concept and an image of beauty, then you also have a concept and an image of ugliness. Where and how does this conflict in the mind develop? Conflict between what and what develops in the sphere of the mind? Take any given concept, and you can see that it is dual. In the sphere of the mind, one has two opposite images, two opposite teams of cells, as those images are contained in certain cells. And if I talk about a concept, then immediately a team of cells is activated, which corresponds to this concept. If one team is activated, then obligatory, another team would become activated, opposite to the first one. They start fighting. As soon as something is named, it activates an opposition, duality, and incompatibility in the sphere of the mind. The fight has just begun. Take something which is colored very pleasantly for you: a concept, an image. Do you see it?

Would you allow yourself to see the opposite of it now? Do you want to investigate the opposite of this pleasant image you just saw?

If you really experience strong pleasant feelings in relation to this image, it means, mandatorily, there is an opposite image

47

that will be colored equally strongly but with negative feelings. What kind of an image is it? Do you see it?

Every single one of us has a collection of such strongly saturated emotional images, and each one of these images has its own highly emotionally saturated opposite image.

So, what is it that you want to see and don't want to see in the world that surrounds you? What do you notice fast, and what is it that you most likely would not see, would not allow yourself to see?

Imagine it the month of May outside. You go to the park and experience what you have experienced previously in this context, i.e. big pleasure. How about this other, opposite, negatively colored image? Do you want to see it?

It appears that everything is great. That is where we are and what we have, and we don't need to think about the second part. True? "Summer, summer…don't you ever end," as the song goes. But what in reality is going on inside your mind, which has two opposite, strongly colored emotional images? If you do not see it, does it mean this opposite image does not exist?

No. It exists. Moreover, it insists on being seen. It asks for attention. It wants to develop itself. It wants to be seen by you. What do you do in order to not see it? You suppress it. But what does it mean to suppress an opposite image? How do you do it? It is as if you were pushing it, hiding from it, fighting it, not allowing it to develop. You spend a lot of power and energy doing it.

How many images do you have that you do not want to see and constantly suppress?

There are as many unpleasant images as pleasant images. Now let us look at how much energy you spend to suppress those images that you do not want to see in yourself.

You spend as much energy doing it as you spend in contemplation of pleasant images.

We already discussed that the human mind constantly seeks pleasure; its main principle is to find as many pleasures and to hold on to them for as long as possible.

Accordingly, it spends as much energy to suppress those images that do not bring pleasure.

Now we can see the balance and the energy quotient of a human being.

Knowing that, is it strange that people are getting sick? Is it strange they have difficult time moving their legs? They spend their energy suppressing their own manifestations.

But is it possible to cure oneself of this condition using some kind of medicine?

Many methods were invented by a human being as the means of escaping himself—alcohol, drugs, etc. You may have a drink, imagine you have escaped the situation, but tomorrow you will feel even worse. Your hangover is as bad as yesterday's high was good.

The mind keeps itself in a certain balance, negative and positive images alternate. Some Russian proverbs describe this situation well: "It was great, wait for misfortune" or "Life is like a zebra—one stripe white, another black." These sayings reflect the mechanism of the operation of the mind—this rotation is impossible to escape. You can try to suppress not to see the negative image, but it will always pop up. You will never be able to escape, because it is inside you. Is it worth trying to run away when you know this mechanism?

I encourage you to become aware of this mechanism right now.

Anxiety and conflict

Observe the play of your mind. One part of your mind, for example, may say, "I need to date this guy." Another retorts, "I should not date him." One part says, "He will fool me," while another replies, "No, he will not fool me." These conflicts constantly arise between the fragments of the mind.

What is insanity? Observe an insane person. He screams one thing, then another. What a normal human being tries to hide is obvious in an insane. All his internal "i"'s are trying to outcry each other. One "i" says one thing, while another "i" insists on something else. One part pulls in one direction, while another pulls in a different direction. Take a look inside yourself, and you will see that you, similarly to the rest of us, have an insane mind. Its insanity is in its disquiet state. When I say, "turn your mind off," I do not ask you to destroy it. I ask you to quiet it down. In a quiet state, the mind develops capabilities it does not have in its usual, excited state. **All those false convictions of the mind should die.** The mind of a sentient being transfers into a quantitatively different state.

Are you ready to renounce at least one of your false convictions?

The inability to see anything really new

Can we say we really understand the book we are reading or really see this particular human being? We say, "A new guy came in." But what kind of a new guy is he when we are unable to see anything new? This guy is not really new but an old one, because in every next guy, we see the previous one. Meanwhile, people always say, "I want new acquaintances, new impressions, and new feelings." Many businesses are built based on this desire: tourist attractions, entertainment, etc. Every day new singers, movies, and books appear. But are we capable of really seeing something new?

You think you have a variety of ways of perceiving the world. I, on the other hand, tell you this is not so. I say that everything can be boiled down to two assessments: "I like" or "I don't like." Let's take, for example, your perception of some pop singer. If you like her, you like her because her legs are skinny or well-developed, her voice is deep or soft, the lyrics of her songs rhyme well, etc. Then follows the "spin," and it appears that some kind of variety exists, while in reality everything is being "spun" on the same pivot—I like. Some other people spin on another pivot—I don't like. I do not like her because she is not fashionable, because her name is dumb, because with a face like that she should stay home, etc. But it is spun on the same pivot—I don't like.

We are considering the mechanism of mind's perception. Behind this seemingly big variety hides a very simple working scheme of the mind. This is a perception in the framework of a binary code. Wherein, if the listener is a scientist, he will explain his opinion scientifically; a plumber will explain himself in a simple language. But in reality everything boils down to the same thing: either "I liked" or "I did not like."

The question arise: why is something being liked or disliked? Who is finalizing this assessment? What do you think?

The creation of an illusion from words and images

Why do we create theoretical concepts?

Long ago, ancient man collided with an external side of life, and saw problems he was unable to solve. Those problems shifted his attention to his internal world, where he saw chaos and fear. Then he invented something unknown and called it

God, who he could now refer to indefinitely. He could fantasize and talk about God using beautiful, but completely meaningless words that take him away from what is really happening.

This is a very important fact. This is something that frequently happens to every one of us. Please, pay attention to this. We take some kind of an assumption, i.e. fantasy, concept, and then standing on it as if it were real, start to develop certain conclusions. **Why does every conversation become meaningless as soon as you take as an assumption something you don't really know?** It happens because you put your foot down on the soil that is not real, on the illusion.

You can see that every one of us constantly stands on something that is not real. Using this fictitious and unreal substance, we try to arrive at something real. What is most important for us is to find and to be able to see reality. Those who know reality talk only about one thing—reality. They talk about the present moment. They talk about what is here and now. This is the only vision that is meaningful; everything else is meaningless, because whatever happened in the past is gone, and what will happen in the future is not here yet. What does the human mind do? The mind projects the past into the future. This is a good statement. I think you have already heard it, but does knowledge of these words signify your understanding of their meaning? Open psychology books and you will see these words. Many repeat and rewrite those words. If they understood them, they would already be enlightened. They would become those who see reality. But there are not many of those. Words are spoken. So, what is the value of words? This is very important because we usually use words to explain concepts and notions, and every single one of us, with certain pleasure, pronounces some words and thinks to himself, "How smart I am! How rightfully and smartly do I talk! Now I know this and that and soon I will learn something else." The mind is very happy with this. But does our knowledge signify our understanding? This is a very important question. How often do we ask ourselves this question?

Stereotypical reasoning

Let us assume you brought to the surface some stereotypes reflecting the mechanical nature of your mind. What do you do next? Would you be able to **observe them in different situations** of your life?

Let's assume you know your stereotype, and a situation develops during which you start to exhibit it again and **suddenly become aware** of it. In such a case, it starts to change just because you observe its manifestations. Do not fight it. Just observe it very attentively. You want to see all its subtleties and nuances. If the stereotype has not been exposed, and you have not become aware of it at least once, you would not be able to observe it and to be aware of its manifestations. But as soon as you are aware of it—something changes. We are going to observe it in ourselves and others.

This is very interesting. If someone were talking, and talking, and talking and then suddenly stopped and started to listen to another person—this is awareness. **He suddenly became aware of his stereotype**. This would be visible. This would be obvious. This book is written in order for this to happen, for our consciousness to broaden a bit.

Give yourself a present by becoming aware of one more of your stereotypes.

Certainty and uncertainty

What is comfort? What is economy directed toward? Why are so many things being sold? Why do new offers constantly appear and some people get excited about them and run after some new product or service? What do they want?

They want comfort. I can sit in a car and talk to someone a thousand miles away. I can be eating a sandwich sitting in a chair in front of the TV getting the latest news and information. This is comfort. There is **physical comfort and psychological comfort.** What does the mind want? The mind wants to have psychological comfort.

When is the mind in a comfortable state, and when is it in discomfort? Perhaps something unusual happens to a human being. He wants to find an answer, a **definitive explanation** for what is happening to him. What happened is incomprehensible and **does not fit** into his usual frame of reference, requiring his **mind to look for** explanations elsewhere. Until he figures out the answer, his mind is in a state of discomfort. When he finds the answer, his mind gets comfortable. The mind gets comfortable only when it has **found the reason**, determined the situation and chosen the solution. Then and only then does it quiet down. Then it considers it knows and has resolved the issue.

There is an interesting story about Hodja Nasreddin. Once, while walking late at night, Nasreddin suddenly saw three horsemen. He got frightened and started to run. In the process, he stumbled down a hill and wound up in a cemetery. Pushed by fear, he hid in an empty casket. The horsemen, having seen a man running so fast, decided to approach him in order to help. They opened the casket and inquired, "May we somehow help you?" Answered Nasreddin, "If you ask a question, it doesn't mean you can get a straight answer." They asked him a second question, "Why are you here?" to which he replied, "In reality, I am here because of you; and you are here because of me."

Are there questions that cannot be answered immediately? Would you allow yourself to ask such questions?

What would happen to you if a question appeared to which you did not have an answer? If you have a question to which there is no answer, **what happens to your state of mind?**

The conflicts of the mind are transmitted to the body

Where do you think the emotional and informational memory of the mind is? Do you think they are located in the neurons of the brain only? Are they present in some other parts of the body? Why do you think you have a recurrent pain in your back or some other part of your body? Why, for example, when one person shows up, does pain in your back become more pronounced, while in other situations some other pain gets exacerbated? Why do you think you suffer from a certain disease and not from another? Why is a specific organ affected? Why does a certain thought take you "outside of yourself," and makes your body unbalanced? Why does this happen? In my opinion, this is influenced by the mind, by what has been written there.

Emotionally charged information of the mind's memory is located in different organs of a human body. If one is to use a broader view of the human body, one can see that the body carries all the weight of memory. Recollection of old conflicts leads to the drop of this energy charge from the emotional level to the level of the body. At certain point, it is impossible not to feel it. In many people the conflicts between polar convictions of the mind escalate to such a degree that serious diseases appear in their bodies. Then they become interested in health improvement and start going to the doctors. And they can continue doing it until the day they die, because the essence of their problem cannot be understood or solved by contemporary medicine. The source of the problem is in the mind; all their problems were created by the mind. The body itself knows **perfectly well what it needs** and what it does not need, but when it is ruled by the mind in conflict, it becomes unbalanced. This imbalance leads to accidents and diseases.

What has happened to your body lately?

Reaction instead of action

Are we aware of what is happening to us?

Why do we act this way? Why, at certain times, do we not act at all? Where do our actions, deeds, movements originate?

Our life consists of actions. One action, for example, causes us to feel proud, while another action can generate a different feeling. For example, why do you feel guilty when you miss your mother-in-law's birthday? Why do you feel pleasure attending a party to which you were not even invited?

One is constantly doing something. Where are these actions coming from? How do they arise? Is it really necessary for one to perform these actions?

Do you act yourself or is someone acting through you? One grabs a rifle, screams "Hurray!" and, with insane eyes, runs toward the enemy line. He kills one soldier, a second, a third, and then he is killed himself. Later on people call him a hero and say he died a brave death. This is a deed. People get together and say good things about him: he was a good soldier and every one of them would be honored to die as he did. Posthumously, he is given a medal of honor, a book is written about him, and a movie about him is made. What he did becomes very important. But who did it? **What propelled his body to move forward with an insane, fearful look in his eyes?** What did he think about? Was he thinking about the great heroic deed he was committing?

Inside each one of us there are multiple human beings. Inside each one of us live Joan of Arc, Judah, the Knights of the Round Table, Cinderella, and many, many others. So, you can find the answer to these questions **inside yourself.**

The man in the previous example will not think any longer; **other people will think and talk** about him. They will bring their own thoughts and motives to explain his actions.

What moves you when you consider something to be good or bad? What makes you regret doing something? What excites you when you are doing something else? Who is doing it? **Are you doing it yourself,** or **someone** or **something** is doing it through you?

Every single act of ours is done by us in the eyes of others and by other's will. It would be interesting to find out whose will is behind all our actions.

For example, during World War II Russian soldiers were running into a battle in the name of Stalin. This name had a value equal to human life. The word "Stalin" was on one side of the scale and human life on the other side. Moreover, this word frequently was given more weight than the life of a human being. **Choice did not even exist.** The soldier was offered one thing only—to give up one's life in the name of Stalin.

What would you give up your life for? Don't forget that your lifetime is **limited.** When I repeat certain actions, perform the same actions over and over for ten years, don't I pay for them with my life? Is not ten years a significant part of my life? But if for ten years I did one thing, it means that for the **next**

ten years I will do exactly the same thing. That is why I ask, "What would you give your life for?"

Lifestyle replacing life

How does the **"progress of humanity" evolve**: horizontally or vertically?

What does the mind want? It wants more, further, wider. It recreates what it already has. It just increases its size, volume, space. It quantity increases.

For example, the idea of communism popped inside the head of one person and started to propagate. The old Soviet Union was a propagation of ideas and thoughts of Karl Marx.

What do we strive for in our life? I was making $30 a week, and now I make $300. Tomorrow I would want to make $ 9,000. It **appears** that this is progress.

What can the mind do? The **mind can** do only one useful thing: it can **surrender**, put the weapons down. But as simple as it is, not all of us can see it.

Human beings, just as society itself, go through **periods** of excitement and **enthusiasm.** What are these? These are states of the mind during which **it seems to the mind that it will find something.** It seems to the mind that the way toward happiness, freedom, and wellness is right here. **The mind gets excited.** It gives **this something** a new name and organizes mass movement. When many minds are drawn into this movement, it picks up a name: "New Times," or "New Way." In time, this excitement drops and gets transformed into apathy and depression. A new impulse is needed. Someone shows up and starts screaming that he knows what to do. He calls something else a new name, in reality, repeating something old, something that was done before, and people get agitated again and start talking about new way of life.

People **talk not about life, but about a way of life**. There is an actor's way of life, a hunter's way of life, an engineer's a way of life, a movie star's way of life. Sociologists and psychologists constantly investigate this 'way of life.' Books are written and movies are shot addressing this issue.

How do people get into groups? People are grouped based on their life styles. "You are from our circle. He is not from our circle. You have that lifestyle and we have this lifestyle. If you want to become a member of our group, you should master our way of life."

But where is life? **Where is this Human Being?** We are talking about images. We are talking about different images only.

What is your way of life?

Thought and action

What does one need in order to live such a horrible life, not a life, but a way of life? It is necessary to have thoughts in one's head and to believe in them. If you were to observe your mind, you would be able to see multiple thoughts arising there. For example, you may be thinking: should I marry or not, should I go on a date with this guy tomorrow or not, should I apply for this job or not? You think, think, think and then you do something. For example, you get a job, you marry or get a divorce. Why is it that one thought realizes itself in action while another does not? Why are you reading this book instead of watching TV or playing poker now? Let us try to answer this specific question. Does this book really interest you, or do you believe it is of interest to you?

In order for your thought to be realized in action, it is necessary to believe in its reality. This is the mechanism. This is the mechanism using which individuals are brought to action. This is the mechanism using which huge masses of people are similarly brought to action: hundredths of people standing in front of an embassy screaming slogans, thousands of people going to a soccer game or rifles in hands running toward each other. The mechanism is the same. In the beginning, a certain thought arises. People either believe in it or they don't. The most interesting part of this is that neither the thought nor a man's belief in that thought is coming from the man himself.

How does a thought, which appears in one's head, turns into an action? Whose thought is it? Whose belief turns this thought into an action? And, at the end of the day, whose action is it?

The law of equilibration of duality

A dual mind presumes the existence of good and evil, but do these concepts exist where there is no duality, where everything is one? Those who live in the illusion of duality face the question of what to choose? It appears to them that they must choose, but in reality, they just do what they have to do. That is why, if we talk about the mind perception of what is happening in the world, there is always duality and polarity present in it. Someone discovers atomic energy. What happens next? Someone builds a nuclear power plant. Another builds an atomic bomb. That is what happens. Knowledge, entering the minds of different people is used differently. Let's take electricity for example. It is used to light and warm up a building, but it is also used to operate an electric chair.

Professionals from the occult, war industrialists, and politicians are interested in knowledge only. It enables them to achieve their own personal interests. Professionals always consider any situation from the perspective of their own personal interests. That is why increase in knowledge only strengthen personality and the conditioned mind, making real understanding of oneself impossible. All this, including professional occultism, is a part of a world scenario, in which everything happens as it should happen, irrespective of the fact that it is being liked by some and disliked by others. All this happens and follows absolutely precise laws. So, what is the point of judging something that cannot be understood by the mind and is limited by certain convictions? Because, the majority of people perceive the world through the lens of the mind, and the mind is dual, the law of duality and opposition operates in the world that the mind has created. For example, the appearance of a saint will lead to the creation of a monster. In this way, duality is balanced, maintaining the law of harmony which operates on the scale of what can be called the mind of humanity. The operation of this law presupposes the presence of people executing polar, opposite roles. In this way, on a global scale, these oppositions are balanced. In regards to a particular human being, his way is strictly defined, even though he may think that he chooses it himself. If it's meant for you to exit the limits of the mind, it would happen irrespective of the path you have been following. You do not choose a path, a path chooses you. There are pathways that do not lead to liberation. There are ways that lead to even longer imprisonment.

One may question the reconcilability of the predetermination of one's way with the presumption of the possibility of choice.

Choice exists in the conception of the mind. Let's take, for example, construction. In order to build a house, one needs bricks, cement blocks, and mortar's mix. During construction multiple operations are performed, and as a result, waste materials appear. Some bricks brake, concrete solidifies and hardens. Those waste materials are either thrown away or await their opportunity to become useful in construction again. One broken brick may still be found to be useful, while others may turn into waste.

Is it unjust or evil that certain building materials become a waste? From the stand point of a brick it might be so, but from the perspective of the builder, it is a completely natural part of the process.

What is evil? Evil is ignorance, just ignorance. The concept of evil appears as a consequence of one's narrow and fragmented perception of reality. But from the point of view of a personality the question of evil stands. That is why I consider the discussions aimed to discern the difference between good and evil to be useful. Concepts of good and evil depend on the scale they are being considered on. The death of a dictator, from the perspective of his followers, may be considered to be evil. However, from the standpoint of the people he oppressed, the same event may be seen as goodness.

CHAPTER 3:
FALSE PERSONALITY

• ◆ • ◆ • ◆ • ◆ • ◆ • ◆ • ◆ • ◆ • ◆ • ◆ • ◆ • ◆ • ◆ • ◆ •

How is personality formed and reinforced?

What is false personality or false "i"? What is essential for it? Why and how was it formed? What does it want and how does it reinforce itself? How can it be transformed? What would happen if personality were to die?

In order for us to understand what would happen when personality transforms, we need to understand what the human being represents now. If, during our investigation, we discover that the human being represents personality and nothing else, then destruction of the personality would lead to full destruction of the human being, i.e. nothing would be left behind, nothing at all. On the other hand, if something is left behind, we would be able to understand what is that remains. In order to understand this, we need to carry out an unbiased investigation.

We need to understand how each one of us is made. So, let's figure out how personality develops and how it functions.

What does it mean, "The baby is born"? A physical body appears, and it contains life. A newborn is delivered and starts his life in certain conditions. These conditions start to apply their influence. The baby begins to develop. He acquires certain knowledge and habits. He learns language. We can look at children on the playground and observe that they are different. For example, one is active and another is passive. Why do you think they are different?

An animal does not have a personality, but a human being does. What does an animal want? An animal wants to eat and drink. It needs air. A human being also needs to eat, drink, and have access to air.

Let's see if the personality of a human being has some kind of requirements. What is it that personality requires? We started with a question, "What would happen if personality were to die?" But I have another question, "In what way can personality die?" The body can die, and we know how and why it can happen. If we deprive the body of food, water, or air it will die. What is correspondingly necessary for the survival of a personality?

Personality can be seen as an image. Every single one of us has a certain image of himself, and as a rule, this is the image of our personality. How does the image of your personality change when people consider it, listen to it, or say something about it that it likes? And how does this image change when something contrary happens?

We can see that this entity we call personality, reacts to external and internal stimuli somewhat differently. Why does it happen? Why the personality of one man does not swell when he, for example, plays piano well, while the personality of another man swells up tremendously because of it? One man wrote a novel, which became very popular, and his personality swelled enormously because of it. Another wrote a bestseller, but his personality did not react to fame at all. Why does this happen?

What is most important in your personality? What makes it bigger and what makes it smaller?

Who creates personality in us? If a human being did not have a mind, would he be able to create personality? An animal cannot create personality. A plant cannot create personality. A stone cannot create personality. In order to do that one needs to have the mind, because the mind creates images. By creating those images, it gets attached to them and starts to maintain them emotionally.

So, inside the mind of a human being a definitive image of oneself is created, i.e. his personality. This image is being created with the help of other people. The mind holds on to this image and reinforces it. As we know, the mind is dual. Therefore, for each image of oneself, for example, as a polite gentleman, the mind immediately creates another, opposite image of oneself as a brute. Let's say you identified yourself with an image of a polite human being. You experience pleasure when this polite image receives an external reinforcement, and displeasure in opposite scenarios. Can you see this pattern? Can you observe it in yourself?

You can ask me, "But if the main trait of personality is positive, why would we need to weed it out? For example, politeness is a positive trait, and it can be the main trait. Why would you want to get rid of this positive trait?"

Let's take a look. That is precisely how the mind sees it. It wants to experience pleasure and to avoid displeasure. If you formed an image of yourself as a positive human being, you would constantly try to reinforce this image. If this image is not reinforced, what are you going to experience? What would you feel?

Most likely you would experience **fear**. You need to constantly appear good and pleasant. If you feel you were not polite enough to someone, fear appears. In reality, this is not who you are, you just try to appear this way. You identify with a certain image of yourself and then you want to present this image to other people.

In reality nobody knows what politeness and impoliteness are. Nobody knows what beauty and ugliness are. All definitions are blurred. Morals are also relative. What is considered to be moral in one society is immoral in another. There are no universal morals. If you examine different cultures, you will find that they all have different moral codes. Therefore, those notions only exist in the minds of the people and have nothing to do with what we call reality. That is why they require constant proof and reinforcement.

Let's say I have a certain notion. Let's investigate politeness, for example. It seems to me I behave politely now. But among my acquaintances there may be at least one person who does not think of my behavior as polite, because his notion of politeness is completely different from mine. Is it possible? During our lifetime we meet different people. Every single one of them has his own views and notions, which may not coincide with ours. What seems to be of utmost importance to you, is irrelevant to another man.

Would you be able to be polite to someone whose notion of politeness is completely different from yours?

You may say, "There is a reason in your logic, but using it, you may cross any line" Correct. That is because this line is completely illusory. That is why people are unable to agree on this line and will never be able to do so.

Something you consider to be self-explanatory is not so obvious to others. You consider yourself to be very kind, but there are people who say that you are not kind at all. Meanwhile you are jumping out of your skin trying to prove yourself to be kind. Have it ever happened to you?

You may say, "And why jump out of one's skin? I mean not to appear, but to be. Someone may only want to appear kind, to do something to show off, but another may in reality be kind."

– OK. Are you able to be kind to everyone?

– *Well, one cannot be kind to everyone.*

– So, you reluctantly agree, it is impossible to be kind to everyone.

– *Of course.*

– I understand you consider kindness to be your important quality.

– *Yes.*

– When you meet someone, show your kindness and he confirms that you are kind, do you experience pleasure?

– *You can say so.*

– When you meet someone, show your kindness, and he does not consider you to be kind, saying, "What you are doing, in reality, is not kind." What do you feel then?

– *You cannot satisfy everyone.*

– Do you experience pleasure in such a case?

– *Pleasure? No. But there is no big disappointment either.*

– Have you ever experienced a situation in your life when you showed kindness and were hit back in return?

– *I did.*

– But we just don't want to remember these situations, right?

– *Yes. We do not want to remember them.*

– If one is sincere with himself, one can see that what brings pleasure also brings strong displeasure and pain. If we were sincere, if we were to allow ourselves to be sincere, we would see that pleasure and pain go hand in hand. Pleasure, we receive from the realization of one or another habit or character trait is followed by equal displeasure and pain. There is only one reason for this. The reason is our character trait. It is the reason for pleasure and it is the reason for suffering and pain. To see this is to see a very important trait of your personality.

– *Yes, but should one deny it?*

– I don't want to give any ready solutions. Nobody would deny anything without a reason. We are just investigating. If we lead this investigation sincerely and without preconceptions, we will see that a personality trait brings us no more pleasure than pain, suffering, and disappointments. This is what a holistic vision is, but the majority of people do not see themselves whole. The mind of a human being, attaching itself to a personality trait, wants to see one side of it only—the positive side. And he sees it. He does not want to see the opposite side. At the same time, he cannot avoid feeling the negative consequences of this blindness. He cannot connect one side with the other. He insists that every single act of kindness is connected to the fact that he is kind and shows kindness, but he thinks that instances when he feels bad are related to something completely different. He does not see the real source of his suffering. He has multiple explanations for his suffering, but not a single one is related to the true reason— a given personality trait.

That is why it is so difficult to see it. If you were to see it, you would understand what in reality one or another personality trait gives you. In order to do so, you need to see. You show your main traits and insists on them, because you receive pleasure from them. But you don't see the negative aspects connected to them. You don't want to see it. I am trying to show it to you. Look how difficult it is to see it. One does not want to see oneself as a whole.

The mind is that place where personality forms and develops.

The structure of personality

False personality is a compilation of habitual thoughts, feelings, and actions that link together into one chain. They create a very strong skeleton—a personality structure. In some people, it is very hard, in others it is softer. In some, it has only a roof and a couple of pillars. In others it has a compilation of different exotic structures. False personality pursues one goal only—survival. In order to survive, it needs to reinforce itself. To do that, it can use one method only—constant repetition of the same thing. How, for example, is such a trait as kindness reinforced? How does it manifest itself? In one's personality you can always find such a trait as kindness. It can be small or big depending on how it strengthens itself. For example, if you give alms to every beggar you meet, and then say, "I am a very kind and generous man." People say that about you and you say it yourself. Any given personality trait can be accentuated in order to see how it reinforces itself. **What is the main trait of your personality?**

Let us take, for example, such a trait as **touchiness**. The personality of a human being is a conglomerate consisting of many parts and fragments. In one personality, touchiness can constitute quite a big part. Personality consists of many such parts. Personality may be compared with a house or a tent. The body of a tent is assembled from metal tubes. Personality has a similar structure. For example, **in the personality of one man, touchiness may be one of those big props upon which its whole structure is built.** Naturally, personality tries to strengthen and reinforce its props. In what way can this trait be reinforced? A man can provoke others to brush against exactly this part of him, constantly recreating and reliving this feeling of touchiness. In order to do so, he needs other people

69

who will upset him and make him touchy. In order to be offended, he needs other people who will offend him. In order for one to be offended, one needs partners—actors with the opposite role, i.e. those who will offend.

All these personal traits are illusions, fictions created by the conditioned mind.

Usually a man cannot see the main trait of his false personality. For example, asked, "What are you so touchy about?" he may reply, "No, I am reacting normally. I am not touchy at all." He has this trait, and it is very strong, but the stronger it is, the harder it is to see it.

He does not see his trait the way others see it from the outside. He thinks he is acting normally and naturally. He does not give another thought to this notion: am I touchy or am I not touchy?

We can observe two interesting moments here. First, does he have this trait in reality? And second, does he see it? Is it possible for a certain trait to be strongly pronounced in a man, and for him not to see it? For example, vanity can be strongly pronounced, but many people do not see it in themselves.

The most difficult thing is to determine the chief feature of your false personality. This feature is extremely difficult to see in yourself. It is a cornerstone. Everything is built on it. If we were to remove this feature everything would scatter to pieces. If one were to approach the tent and to remove the main prop, the tent would immediately collapse. The chief feature of false personality (and one may have a few of them) is that prop that holds everything. It can be better seen from the outside. Sometimes it is easily seen from a first glance, and sometimes time and opportunity to be with person in different situations are needed. But in any case, it is much better seen from the side. One does not want to see the chief feature of his false personality. To see it is a revolution. What does it mean to see it? It means, factually, to refuse it, because this trait complicates one's life tremendously. It is precisely this trait that creates the hell in which the human being lives. When one sees this feature (and this means to see what one does in reality and what it leads to), one would never want to continue with it.

If you were able to see the chief feature of your false personality, it would be a revolution. Something miraculous would happen to you as the disappearance of the chief feature of false personality leads to a total transformation of human being.

How does personality maintain itself?

Have you ever seen how a car navigates through a deep snow trail? It is not easy to get out of it. It is necessary to step on the gas pedal hard and abruptly turn the wheel in order to do so. And even if everything is done just right, one may not be able to get out because one does not have enough power. When one travels the trail, one does not even need to hold the wheel. So it is with those main false personality features—they are exactly those hard pressed trails by which the same thoughts, feelings, and actions constantly travel.

How can one exit this trail?

To exit the trail is to get into the realm of the unknown. The trail is a repetition of something known to the mind. Your personal trail is a continuous repetition of the same thoughts, feelings, and actions. It is an infinite repetition of what your mind has experienced before. If, while experiencing it, the mind felt pleasure, it wants to repeat this pleasure indefinitely. If, while experiencing it, it felt pain, it wants to prevent it from happening again. Those are two trails the mind is zapping between. On one hand it wants to attract pleasure and to repeat it, on the other hand it doesn't want some unpleasant thing that happened before to happen again.

You may have seen those huge machines that put down railroad tracks. They move and install rails behind themselves. Then they drag the rails ahead and install them in front. Then they move forward onto these rails, pick up the rails from the back, and drag them forward again. Similarly, one creates his future by taking something from the past. Have you seen this? It is very illustrating. In essence this is the illustration of how reproduction and reinforcement of personality occur. All these emotional, mental, and behavioral trails man constantly moves through represent certain traits of his personality.

Let's take kindness. How is it reproduced? Certain thoughts, feelings, and actions are involved here. For example, a man crosses the street and sees a beggar. What happens? Perhaps, his usual desire is to give alms. First, the thought appears, "He is so unhappy. I need to help him." Then he starts to feel pity. Later, he removes money from his wallet and gives it to the beggar. If that situation repeats frequently, it becomes a habit. I talk only about one of the features, one of the ways kindness exhibits itself. In your case, it may exhibit itself differently.

How does it exhibit itself in your particular case?

Personality as a compilation of habits

False personality has its own laws by which it maintains and reinforces itself. It is a law of pleasant and unpleasant. Personality tries to receive pleasure and to avoid displeasure.

For example, take a rude man. He screams and yells at everyone. What kind of pleasure can be found there? The man has neither friends nor happiness, but he repeats this behavior anyway. If you ask him why he is doing it, his reply may be, "I am just this way," or "I want to achieve fairness and justice," or something of such a nature. Why does he continue to do it? He does it because this brings him a certain pleasure.

Have you noticed that any **habit** has a certain quality—it provides pleasure immediately at its realization? You can also feel uncomfortable if you have not done something habitual. In other words, it may not be pleasure it gives you but displeasure and discomfort of not doing it. Do you see it in yourself?

A man wants to eat. He is hungry, and if he were to suppress his hunger he would feel displeasure. For example, you have a habit of eating at seven o'clock. If you have not had your dinner at seven, you experience unpleasant sensations. Notice how a newborn screams only when he really wants to eat. However, parents are smart, they know that everything should be in order; one should eat not when hungry, but when scheduled. They start feeding the baby at certain times only. Later the baby forms a habit and eats not when hungry, but because of having a habit of eating at a particular time. The baby's organism may not ask for food, but he has a habit. If this habit is violated, some uncomfortable state arises in relation to it. Do you agree? Try to tie your shoelaces differently, not the way you are used to. You would see the power of habit. If you say that the important thing for you is to tie a shoelace and everything else is irrelevant, I would ask you to tie it up with your left hand. At the end of the day you would do it, but it would be extremely uncomfortable and unusual. Perhaps, you would say, "Stop with this nonsense. Why do I need to do it?" You tied them up, but experienced quite a bit of displeasure and frustration because you did not use your habitual method.

Habit is an execution of a succession of certain actions: intellectual, emotional, behavioral. Repeated actions entrenched in a human being are very powerful. If one breaks this habitual consequence, a very unpleasant state appears. We can easily demonstrate this. Try to do something in a way to which you are unaccustomed, not in your habitual way. Or do something you don't usually do. You will have to do those things you have not habitually done before, otherwise nothing new can be created. Try to get in some kind of pose which is completely new to you. Sit down in a completely unusual, not habitual pose. **Do it right now**. Please, become aware of your sensations and feelings in regards to the fact that you have been asked to do something not habitual.

Did you assume a pose which is not habitual? You should be very uncomfortable in this pose. Are you aware of how your feelings, thoughts, sensations change?

First, write down what you felt, thought, and sensed when I asked you to move into this unusual pose. Next, write down what you felt, thought, and sensed while moving into that pose. And thirdly, write down what you felt, thought, and sensed while being in that pose. Please, do this small self-investigation and see what will come out of it.

So, we have at least three psychological spheres: intellectual, emotional, and physical. Thoughts are connected with an intellectual sphere, feelings with an emotional sphere, and senses with a body. You just wrote down your experience of observation from which we can deduce what reacts to changes more, and how it happens in your particular case. **What is awareness? Awareness is the simultaneous vision and observation of your thoughts, feelings, and sensations.** We can simultaneously observe our thoughts, feelings, and sensations. If you observed them, you will be able to write them down. What did you see? What were you able to see and what couldn't you see? How aware are you? Now you can elucidate it.

We were talking about the fact that every single human being has something he does not want to change. These are habits. In order to start changing a habit, one needs to see it. How can one see it? One needs to start doing something differently, not in the habitual way. That is what we just did, if you did it. I asked you to become aware of everything that was happening to you at the time it was happening, and that was your experience of awareness.

Convictions and beliefs

Perhaps, much of what is written here is not in agreement with your convictions. How does your mind and personality react to it?

There are no aimless conversations here. Everything we discuss is very important. If I were to invite you home for tea, then we could lead pleasant conversations. You would say something pleasant, I would agree, and you would go home very happy. But this book is written for a different reason. **We want to investigate ourselves. But how can one investigate oneself already having certain presumptions of how things should be? How can you lead the experiment if you already know the result?** That is how many PhD theses are written. A scientist writes conclusions and then tries to fit data to confirm the results. So, what kind of investigation are we talking about? An impartial investigation can only be performed if the observer is free from preconceived notions. Imagine a situation where a communist investigates capitalism. What do you think his conclusion would be? He would come to the same conclusion Marx arrived at. We all are very well familiar with this in practical matters. If you are in conflict with someone and you want to resolve this conflict, would you invite your opponent's friend to the meeting? No, because you are well aware that his convictions would coincide with convictions of your adversary. He would support his position.

Where is one to find a neutral position inside himself? As soon as we direct our gaze inward, we see a multitude of beliefs and convictions there. We are constantly judging, "This is right. This is wrong." Are we capable of understanding something new while doing that? Is the mind capable of understanding anything new at all, when it is already filled to the top by certain habitual thoughts and convictions it inherited?

We say a baby is born with a mind similar to a clean sheet of paper. Then education starts, i.e. different writings begin to appear on this sheet. With help of words, everything the child is confronted with in this world is being written and defined in his mind.

He is told what is good and what is bad, what can be done and what cannot be done. If he does something that is considered to be bad, he is punished. As a result of this, he develops certain convictions based on his own experience. Those convictions are in his mind. **A human being is a carrier of opinions, convictions, and beliefs received from tens, thousands, millions of hands; transmitted through heredity, upbringing, and culture, while he says, "It is I. It is I who thought. It is I who decided. I want this. I don't want that. This is right. This is wrong."**

Based on what does he consider all this garbage to be his own I? Does he want to figure out what is inside his head and where it came from? It looks like the majority of people don't even want to discuss this. They have their convictions and they defend them.

There are important convictions and convictions that are not so important. For example, I tell you that a camera of a certain brand "X" is not very good. If you are not a manufacturer or distributor of this product, my opinion of it will not concern you much. But if I tell you that you are not a real man or not a beautiful woman, this would be quite important to you. You may become upset and start arguing with me. Look at the relationship between men and women— a constant struggle to prove a certain conviction to each other. For example, she constantly tells him, "What kind of man are you? You can't even make enough money." He gets irritated and tries to prove the opposite or tries to justify himself. What happens here? They try to prove to each other some of their convictions. But let us assume one would get up and say, "Yes. I am not a man." He honestly says that. In reality, he does not give a damn about it. Do you think it would be possible to continue the game of this particular conviction?

Every single one of us has certain convictions which, when touched, make us go nuts. May we suppose that the mind, having these strong convictions, can see anything impartially?

Can you name some of your convictions, which you are constantly defending? What happens to you when someone touches a strong conviction of yours?

One may recite beautiful poetry but only be capable of seeing in it what corresponds to his convictions, not wanting to see what is not fitting. We said that between a man and what he is looking at there is always some kind of an image. A husband does not see his wife, a wife does not see her husband; they only see images of what, in their opinion, those should be: husband, wife, child, friend, girlfriend, etc. We see everything around us through the prism of images at the base of which lays our convictions and presumptions. Convictions are created with the help of words. And what are words? They are thoughts which are the essence of the mind.

So, that where the prison is. It is very difficult to understand that you are in prison. You may have read Gurdjieff and agreed with him that man is in prison. But in reality we do not know our prison. We think that prison is made out of those ropes that hold us: our bosses, who constantly bother us, our neighbors, family members, or small apartments. No, this is not it. The real prison is our mind with its convictions.

What do you think?

How false personality protects itself

It is quite possible that while reading this book, you experience irritation or other negative feelings and thoughts. You are showing your defense system. The chief personality feature uses certain methods to defend itself. You may, perhaps, acknowledge the presence of these features but you will not want to change them. Why? Because if you were really to allow yourself to feel what you can possibly feel, while being aware of what is written here, it could be unpleasant to your personality. I am now talking about your main feature and about the fact that it interferes and hurts you. But you may reply to this, "I do not feel anything unpleasant." Pay attention to this. This is one of the methods of defense your chief personality feature has developed. It has quite a few of those methods. You do not allow yourself to feel. As soon as the chief feature of your personality comes under attack, the defense system immediately turns on, and you insist, "Nobody can hurt my feelings." You turn off your emotional sphere.

We started this chapter with a question, "What would happen if personality were to disappear?" But does your false personality want to offer its place to your true "I"? Have you heard of Koschei the Deathless?

In Slavic folklore, **Koschei** is an archetypal male antagonist who commonly abducts a hero's wife. None of the existing tales describe Koschei's appearance, although book illustrations and movies portray him as an old and ugly-looking man. Koschei is also known as **Koschei the Immortal** or **Koschei the Deathless.** The root of the word Koschei in the Russian language suggests that his name may be derived from the word "kost" meaning "bone." Koschei cannot be killed by conventional means that target his body. His soul is hidden separately from his body inside a needle, which is in an egg, which is in a duck, which is in a hare, which is in an iron chest, which is buried under an oak tree, which is on the island in the ocean. As long as his soul is safe, he cannot die. If the chest is dug up and opened, the hare will bolt away; if it is killed, the duck will emerge and try to fly off. Anyone possessing the egg has Koschei in their power. He begins to weaken, becomes sick, and immediately loses the use of his magic abilities. If the egg is tossed about, he likewise is flung around against his will. The minute the needle is broken Koschei dies.

In order to kill Koschei, one needs to find the needle inside the egg. The egg is inside a duck, etc. As I said, everything is sophisticatedly hidden. A hero needs to complete a difficult and dangerous journey in order to find the needle and break it. The same can be said about the personality ant its traits. Try to pierce your chief personality feature directly. What would happen to it? Nothing. You would find out nothing is there. It is quite difficult to approach the chief feature. It defends itself well. Every habit defends itself. And the habit that happens to be your chief personality feature defends itself in a very sophisticated and subtle way. Your personality builds multiple defense units around it. The chief feature will disappear the minute you see it. It is extremely difficult to see it. To see it, you need to complete a long voyage, i.e. to see all these defense mechanisms which it surrounds itself with.

How does your chief personality feature defend itself?

It is not easy to see one's chief personality feature, but it constantly shows up, because it is a very strongly inbuilt habit. Behind this habit there is a certain thought pathway. Behind this thought pathway there is a certain emotional reaction, which is followed by a certain action. It is a complex structure of interconnected habits that constantly support, maintain, and recreate each other. Let's say you declare one of your convictions. It immediately triggers certain emotional and behavioral reactions of your personality connected to it.

In what thoughts, feelings, and actions does your chief personality feature usually appear?

Problems of personality

The newborn child is thrown into a certain culture and, in a way, is bewitched by images and convictions that already operate in this culture. The way to get out of this bewitched circle is to be aware. In observing your mind, you will see how it creates your suffering, and seeing it, you will not want to continue it. De-bewitching will occur. When you see the mechanism of your own suffering, you will gain power over it. The more you contemplate or analyze a certain problem, the more you reinforce it. The mind thrives on problems. When one comes to a doctor who practices psychoanalysis and says that he has a problem, the doctor gets very excited because for him, it is a method of making money, and the mind of a client gets very happy because its problem was acknowledged. They discuss the problem for a long period of time, reinforcing the problem even more.

A human being, for the most part, is the mind, and the mind is a problem. The more important the problem is, the more important the human being is. People praise their problems. One says, "I feel bad." Another one replies, "You think you feel bad; you think you are in a tough situation? It is nothing compare to my situation. My problem is a real problem; your problem is just a pittance." People are running around with their problems trying to appear as if they were trying to get rid of them. In reality not only do they not want to get rid of them, they want to hold on to and reinforce them. And who wants to do that? It is the mind who is behind it.

I vividly remember a scene from the circus. Two small, stocky wrestlers appeared and started wrestling each other. They proceeded to wrestle and wrestle. Neither of them could win. After a while the blanket they were covered with was dropped and everyone could see that this was one man who was imitating the appearance of two wrestlers. This, in my opinion, is a very good analogy of the mind. It appears to you that you have a problem. You try to figure it out. People can do this all lifelong. They constantly try to solve problems. They think that those are real problems, but those problems were created by the mind. The mind, in turn, tries to solve them. Do you think after solving a problem it gets to rest, appeases itself, and retires? No, it constantly creates other problems, because it does not want to be idle. It thrives when it thinks. It thrives creating problems. Meanwhile, if the problem is serious enough and cannot be solved instantly, a man starts to suffer. He goes to see a psychologist saying, "Can you help me solve this problem?" In reality he does not want to solve it. He wants to be occupied by this problem.

What do you think it is that one does not want to part with more than anything? One does not want to part with one's problems. One does not want to part with one's sufferings. It is paradoxical, but it is so because the function of the mind is precisely in finding solutions to these problems. Like the gut is created to digest food, the mind is created to digest thoughts.

Until we understand how the mind operates we will not be able to move forward. The mind creates problems and solves them. **That is why it is useless to talk about any change. There are no changes. It is impossible to change. Where does the mind get the problem and how does it solve it? Have you ever investigated this? Every single one of us has problems. If we were to look at those problems in their continuity, we would see that it is one recurrent problem. If we were to look deeper, we would see that the methods we use to create these problems are the same.**

Which of your problems do you love the best? Write them down. Look at them from different sides.

There is a big difference between a puzzle and a problem. The creative mind solves puzzles, while the conditioned mind solves problems. The creative mind defines and solves a puzzle, while the conditioned mind creates a problem out of every puzzle.

How is the feeling of pity created?

Why do you feel pity? Why does your mind and personality cling to this feeling? What do you feel when someone pities you? What do you feel when you pity yourself? What do you feel when you pity someone else?

You felt pity toward someone, and now he thinks that you love him. Is that so? You have been pitied; therefore, you are significant to someone. The personality feels pleasure because it has been accepted. Someone acknowledged the problem invented by the personality and all those feelings that appeared in association with it.

82

Pity is one of the main sources of energetic nourishment of false personality. Here is a typical story brought up by one of the students of our school.

"This situation happened between me and my mother. She has been ill for the last few months, suffering from different illnesses. When I came to visit her last time, she was ill again. This time she had a bad electrocardiogram. The reason I tell you this is that suddenly I realized that I behave exactly the way she does. Her illnesses represent a defense reaction. She constantly repeats, "You do not pity me. Look how tired I am. I carry the weight of the whole household on my shoulders." She constantly tries to have us, family members, pity her. Now, I am able to see how one operates in order to be pitied."

Try to see how pleasure and suffering walk hand in hand. One says, "Take pity on me. I feel unhappy." But he needs to become unhappy in order for you to pity him. It's a vicious circle. Some people make themselves sick in order to be pitied. What kind of thoughts do people entertain before suicide? "They will pity me when I die."

That is the thoughts people have, "Yes, you will all see me die, and then all of you will pity me. You do not appreciate me, do not acknowledge me, do not pity me; you just wait and see what I am capable of doing."

That is how far the chief personality feature can take one. It can lead to the self-liquidation of a human being. After that, can you say that this chief personality feature is helpful? You can say that in case you continue to see only the things that bring you pleasure.

An old parable talks about a passerby who, while walking through a dark street, encounters a man kneeling down under the streetlight looking for something.

— What are you looking for?

— I am looking for my key.

The passerby decides to help. He spends two hours helping and kneeling under the streetlight. Eventually he asks:

— Listen; is it possible you have lost it somewhere else?

— Of course, I lost it by my house.

— So, why are we looking here?

— Well, it is dark over there, while here it is quite bright.

That is what constantly happens. We look only where it is warm and full of light. We don't want to search where it is dark. That is why we only see one part of our personality and do not want to see another. But until we do see it, we will not be able to understand anything about ourselves or other people.

Here is another story told by a student.

— *My neighbor called and asked if she could come in to borrow money. When I opened the door I saw three young men beating her up. I felt pity for her and went outside to help her. I tried to break the fight. But, neither the young men nor the girl paid any attention to me.*

— Do you think you pity the girl? Is it possible that you pity yourself?

One is swimming, bounced by the waves, submerging under water and struggling to the surface again. He persists. Suddenly, a boat full of people appears. They get him out of the water. He screams and yells, "What did you do? Damn you! I had only 100 yards left to beat the world record!"

Everyone sees a situation from his own angle. Feelings experienced by someone involved in a certain situation **may be completely different** from the feelings of someone who is observing the same situation.

Where are you coming from when you try to interfere in certain situation? Where are you coming from when you try to save someone? Are we coming from our assumptions about the situation? I would like to figure out **what happens in reality** when you **try to save someone,** when you try to **interfere**, when you say, "This is not right."

Are you trying to **help another human being or yourself**? Do you differentiate the nuances of your real motive?

If you pity yourself, you start to see yourself in another human being and pity him. That leads you to perform different actions. For example, for many parents the process of upbringing a child is in pitying him, i.e. in pitying themselves. But who sees this? Who really wants to see it? How much of what we do is brought on by the feeling of pity?

We do something and then we say that it was right. We always say that it was right. In truth, we may have serious doubts whether it was right or not. But in certain moments we say, "This was the only way it could have been done." What is this fight for truth, and what do we really want when we try to save, help, and put another human being on the right path? What do we really want?

Feeling of pity is similar to hydrochloric acid. It eats up the soul. It eats up the heart. It kills one's aspirations. Feeling of pity implies that something is not right. Try to understand: empathy and pity are two completely different things. If I feel pity, I look at someone and I think, "You could have been different, but you are this and that, and I feel pity for you." There is denial of reality in pity. In reality, we do not see another human being but only see ourselves in him or her.

Do you want to see the mechanisms of pity development? This feeling arises as a result of your perception of how the world should be, of how surrounding circumstances and a given human being should be. When you see a discrepancy between how, in your opinion, things should be and how they are, you feel pity. Make a note of the fact that feeling of pity is experienced by you. A beggar you pity may experience completely different feelings. He could be completely satisfied with his life and not want to change anything—your expectations of how he should live may not interest him at all. Therefore, the feeling of pity is not experienced by him, but by you.

What's going on here? The fact is that one personality tries to prove to other personalities that it is better. This is characteristic of any given personality. This is just a fact. So, why do you experience pity in regards to this fact?

This feeling of pity arising in you, as you assert in relation to him, pertains not to him, but to you. Whom do you pity in reality—him or yourself? You pity yourself but somehow you project this feeling onto him. Why does this feeling appear in you precisely in relationship to him?

Is this so? Perhaps, you see something in him that you do not want to see in yourself? Is it possible that your feeling of pity is your reaction to certain unfulfilled desires you don't even want to see in yourself? If you don't see it, you will always experience this feeling of pity toward yourself. Moreover, the man you think you pity holds you based precisely on this feeling. If you do not want to see the motives and the mechanisms of pity in yourself, you will depend on the man you pity completely—will he change as you want him to change or not?

You condemn yourself to a long-lasting feeling of pity. I don't know how long it will last, and you don't know either. Do you like this feeling?

If you think you experience this feeling because of another man, then to get rid of pity you need to do something with him, to change his life and his convictions. If, by your logic, this feeling is connected to him, you need to do something with him in order to change something in yourself.

What does it mean to eliminate something? For example, what does it mean to eliminate the feeling of pity? It means it will stop coming back. You can try to quiet it down for some time. You can push it inside and suppress it. But in such a case, it will not disappear. It will be reinforced. If you want to continue to suppress this feeling, it means you don't want to see certain things in yourself. But everything will come back. To eliminate means to eliminate. It means it will not happen again. In your case, does it recur? If yes, it means you are constantly on the hook. In order to change something, you constantly try to change something in another person. You cannot do that. You can only change yourself. Only when you acknowledge that everything is connected to you, that you experience pity toward yourself, and not toward someone else, will you have a real opportunity to figure out the mechanisms of the appearance of this feeling in you and the possibility of changing it. You need to see it. You need to understand that everything is related to you, that you pity yourself, not somebody else.

The only thing and the most important thing one can do is to understand that this feeling is coming from inside, that you experience this pity not toward someone else, but toward yourself. You don't need anything else. You don't need to understand what it is and where it is coming from. You need to see it as a fact. Seeing is action, seeing is resolution. One does not need a help of a psychologist. This is quite simple. Yet, it is quite difficult, because one does not want to do it, does not want to see it inside oneself, because it is connected to a painful experience. One needs to touch this painful experience and to illuminate and declassify it with the light of awareness. All this happens instantly as a flash of light while all this psychoanalysis, theories, concepts, looking for the causes, etc. are just a prolongation, just an unwillingness to see facts as they are. It is just another fallacy. Many people entertain the illusion that there is a professional out there who can help them. No, you can only help yourself.

Pity and empathy are completely different things. Empathy is an ability to see facts as they really are—clearly. Pity is your own reaction to your inability to see those facts. It's a fact, for example, that this particular human being does not want to follow what you consider to be a right course of actions. He says, "I know what is right, and you don't know." Those are just facts. However, because you want to believe that what you are doing is right and it contradicts with what he says, he behaves inappropriately. Also, because you have a close relationship with him, the relationship you are not willing to jeopardize, you say, "Look at him. He is a pitiable human being. He does not understand. I know, but he does not understand, and I pity him." But in reality, one feels, thinks, and acts one way, while another human being feels, thinks, and acts differently. These are facts. When you experience a desire to change something in another human being, but he does not want to change, and at the same time you have quite strong ties with him, you start to experience pity. This pity is seemingly directed toward him, but in reality it is directed toward yourself, because you are connected with him by those knots. You may say that he is walking in circles, but you are also walking in the same circles, because you are tightly bound together. That's how things are.

Personality and suicide

Why do people commit suicide? As a rule, someone who commits suicide wants to **prove something.** As we have discussed, the mind represents a collection of convictions. In between these multiple convictions there are certain convictions that constitute **the base of the personality** of a given human being. These **particular convictions require** constant reinforcement of their righteousness. The mind wants to be in agreement with these convictions and to reinforce them. **There is no life** for the mind outside of the realms of what it considers to be most important, i.e. its convictions. One man may kill another man or commit suicide because of his convictions. Look how the mind resists something that does not correspond to its convictions.

Russian writer Mikhail Bulgakov in his famous novel "The White Guard" described white officers committing suicide on seeing the destruction of what they considered to be **holy**. Life goes on, but **they** don't want this life. An old white guard says, **"If life does not correspond to my conviction**, then better no life than this new life." The body could have lived for many more years, but the mind destroyed it.

So, who initiated the suicide? It was initiated by the false personality who said: my way or the highway. **Behind every action** there is a certain conviction. You have to see it. This is very important to see.

And what kind of convictions of your false personality can lead you to commit suicide?

Morals: Who needs them? Personality and morals

Are you bothered by society's morals? Do morals belong to the personality or lie outside of personality?

Personality is a product of society. Personality reflects what happens in a given society, given culture, and given subculture. In fact, personality is a reflection of a certain slice of societal morals, convictions, standards (positions on multiple things). Therefore it belongs to society. That is why morality is something personality holds on to. It belongs to it. But **what kind of morals did personality absorb**? The morals of personality are defined by everything it absorbed from its surroundings.

Can a human being who is considered to be immoral in a given society have holistic vision?

Let's try to figure it out. Is the criterion **moral or amoral** important in order for one to see holistically? Morals have nothing to do with one's ability to see. Moreover, one can say that moral vision is quite a distorted vision.

We can look at different cultures, different nationalities, and different time periods and see that morals are relative. At one particular time, two different places have different morals. That is why this type of morality has nothing to do with what can be called holistic vision. It is a very strong fragmentation that **starts to have a very strong influence** on how people think and behave. That is why a man who really wants to see something clearly, without distortion most likely will be considered to be amoral—he is outside of accepted morals. When people say that someone is amoral, they mean **he does not share their moral norms,** norms that happen to be accepted where they live. A man may have his own moral norms, but they may not correspond to the norms that surround him now.

Usually, personality is quite disturbed by a question of whose morals are better and whose are worst. It is a talk of moralists. Are you capable of exiting these limits and going higher, lower, rightward, or leftward? A human being that follows harsh moral convictions will not be able to do so. He will be constantly restricted by the strict borders of these moral norms. It is precisely these hard brackets that preclude him from seeing more. He will see all and everything through the lens of these moral norms. If he takes these moral norms, which are accepted by him, very seriously, he will be frightened to see something not corresponding to them in himself.

There is a small number of people for whom these widely accepted moral norms are not important. Also, there are people who negate everything—these are their moral norms. **That is why people cannot come to an understanding**.

And you, do you understand the relativity and falseness of morals created by conditioned minds and by false personalities?

Duty, responsibility, and guilt

Human consciousness contains **global ideas** and concepts that exert strong influence on humanity. Let's investigate this question, which I consider to be of extreme importance. For example, the ideas of duty and responsibility. Do you think the **notion of responsibility** is common? Quite a lot is built on this notion. Here is a list of opinions on this topic.

"Not a single state or civilization would be able to exist without it, because everything is built on duty and responsibility."

"The release of attachments of the mind is strongly interconnected with duty and responsibility. In order to step away from something, one needs to accomplish his duty. Frequently, one lifetime is not enough for its completion. Therefore, to be free from everything is impossible and may not even be necessary."

So, what is the sense of duty?

You can talk to different people about the existence of the sense of duty and about responsibilities, and they will agree with you. Some other topics may cause disagreement, but the majority will come to agreement here. One will say, "I owe it to my family." Another, "I owe it to my country." A third one, "I owe it to my god." The fourth one owes it to someone or to something else. All of them talk about owing something to someone. This is a very deep conviction characteristic of many people. That is why I think we need to investigate this. If one has an idea of duty, he will materialize it in a certain way; he will accept his duty toward his family, organization, country, a particular human being, etc. If one does something that does not correspond to his conviction of the accomplishment of his duty, he will experience a feeling of guilt.

Multiple mechanical societal laws are built on sense of duty. The sense of duty is indoctrinated into a child from day one. It is being installed through parents, who already have it. It was installed by their parents.

Duty is an assumption that someone owes someone: a child to his parents, parents to their parents, etc. The family is a unit of society. It is through the family that government transmits the idea, without which it cannot live—the idea of duty.

If the idea of conscious duty is introduced into a human being he can be operated remotely, because when one does not fulfill one's duty, one experiences a feeling of guilt. And this is a scary feeling—the feeling of guilt. It is similar to a hook one uses to catch a fish. As soon as it is in, you can move one wherever you want.

Imagine **you swallowed a hook.** It pierced your tongue and someone is pulling the line. He barely needs to pull it and you develop tremendous pain in your tongue. You will run after him. Later, he will not even need to pull on it because as soon as he says, "I am going to pull now," you will start running. And this is what everyone has: duty to this, duty to that, duty to Motherland, duty to parents, duty to family, duty to people, duty to work.

A human being is covered with duties. These are the hooks that can be pulled. May one even talk about freedom? May one talk about free vision? What can one see having a hook in his tongue that is being constantly pulled by someone? Can one see anything except this hook? What is he going to pay attention too? All his attention would be directed toward the danger related to the hook, the line, and the one holding it. Will he be able to pay attention to anything else? Is he capable of paying attention to anything else? Can you imagine what he would feel if someone were to pull the hook?

Can one, having a couple of those hooks in his tongue, have any kind of free opinion? Will he be in control of himself? He can't even lift his head up, because as soon as he lifts his head up, the line pulls up and the hook pierces his tongue. He cannot even turn his head.

How about you?

How to free oneself from feeling of guilt?

A feeling of guilt appears when we have not done something we believe we should have done. If you did not have an assumption that you owe something, a feeling of guilt does not appear. That is the mechanism of this feeling. How can you **get rid of a feeling of guilt? How can you do it?** You need to go deep and to see how your conviction of owing something to someone is born, and how this conviction leads to the feeling of guilt.

"I owe. I must." **Why do you think you owe something?** Until you stop feeling that way, a feeling of guilt will be present. What does one usually do when confronted by this feeling? It is a heavy feeling. One tries to fulfill his duty the best way he can in order to not feel guilty. But that is not the way to get rid of a feeling of guilt. The one toward whom you experience it will want more, because the more you are doing the more pretensions will another have. The more you do, the more expectations there will be. This debt will grow indefinitely. So, what is one to do?

"To allow yourself not to do it," – you may say. But in such a case, you would fully experience this feeling of guilt, at least at the moment when you allow yourself not to do it.

"Quite oppositely, when I feel I can allow myself not to do something, I do not experience any sense of guilt at all. I feel they overdid it with their demands, and I simply do not do what they want. The feeling of guilt does not arise, I am calm, even though I did not do what I was supposed to do," perhaps you would say.

But, you did not get rid of this feeling of guilt at all. You have certain assumptions in regards to what you should have done and what others should have done. If you did it, and they did not, you may allow yourself not to feel guilty. You say, "Yes, it's my duty to do this, but you also should do it. You did not do it. I will not do it either."

This method is sufficient to avoid the feeling of guilt temporarily, but it will not definitively solve the problem. You may be able to use it with one human being, but it will not work with another, who would convince you that you ought to do it, while he does not. The problem of guilt follows you as long as you continue to have the conviction that you owe something to somebody else. In such a case a feeling of guilt always show up. It oozes down one way or another.

Do you want to lower the feeling of guilt or to remove it completely? You can lower it for a certain period of time by inventing different defense systems, but they will be counteracted by new accusations, and eventually you will feel it in full. This is a manifestation of the mind's duality: one part says, "I have to," another says, "I don't have to." These are two opposite poles. When the first is activated, reinforcement of the feeling of guilt occurs; when the second is activated, "I don't owe anything to anyone," the feeling of guilt temporarily disappears, but then it gets stronger again when you return to the first part. "How come?! I still owe something?! What did I do?! How can I repair it?!"

It's horrible that one has to do something based on the fact that he owes something. This is precisely what makes interpersonal human relationships hell. When a man allows himself to see his relationships with his relatives, he can see that those he "loves" the most, he actually "hates" more than anybody else. Why does this happen? **It is the closest people who have the most difficult interrelationships,** because they throw everything at each other. But at the same time they should, so to speak, "love" each other. One needs to see it. Then, and only then, the transfer to something which is not coming from a sense of necessity is possible. **What kind of love is possible because of necessity?** How is it possible? That is precisely how people live.

And how do you live?

Communication: Lies instead of sincerity

— I experienced it yesterday. My parents came home from the country house. We have not seen each other for a long time. We missed each other. I was talking to Mom, and she was constantly asking, "So, tell me, what happens during your studies?" I am telling her, but she does not even understand what I am talking about. She continuously reproaches me, "You have these high thoughts because you don't have to think about putting bread on the table. When I was young, I lived through such hard times; we had neither food nor clothes on our backs. If you were to get in such a situation" And that is our daily conversation.

— This is a theater of close interpersonal relationships.

— She says, "They are playing with your mind over there." I ask her, "Why do you have such an opinion? I invite you to come with me, sit down and listen with me." She replies, "I would not go."

— **There are brothers by blood, and brothers by spirit. These are completely different things.** It is extremely rare for the two to coincide. I think an opportunity to be completely honest, without limitations is a major necessity of a human being. **One has to be honest.** Without it nothing is possible.

It is the greatest happiness, but not everyone wants it. For many it is the biggest danger and fear, because then they would have to encounter themselves.

— *I have this sad experience. A man, very close to me in spirit, suddenly left. I still cannot understand why it happened.*

— Was he close to you spiritually or in some other way? If he is close spiritually, conflicts are impossible. His leaving is impossible.

— *Perhaps, it was not a spiritual but some other closeness. Perhaps, we were close in our opinions, in experiencing certain events we shared. Even at such a level it may be very important. Not knowing any other experiences, this may appear to be very important. That is why separation leads to such trauma.*

— When you have no luck fishing, even a crayfish is a fish. And one gets used to it. But this is not it. When there is a real spiritual connection, there is no possibility of a break, no possibility of misunderstanding or leaving. Even when the physical body dies, there is no leaving.

I don't know with whom or how we are supposed to experience a spiritual connection, but the path to it lies through pain of rupture of common, habitual relationships with people one considered to be his closest. The break shows it was an illusion. **The spiritual relationship is impossible to break.** It is infinite. We all are parts of a big whole. A human body consists of cells, and similarly Earth consists of cells of humanity. All the cells in the body interact with each other. The same interaction occurs between people, especially when people are tuned to the same wavelength. Did you notice that people belonging to one organization and pursuing the same goals are somehow similar? They express something uniform. And if people come to a vision of their predestination, and if at that time, they are also together, it is impossible for them not to develop this interaction. They start to form an organ, which belongs to the wholeness of a different, higher level? Their interactions and interchange starts to happen independently of their being physically together or not. Perhaps you have felt this already.

The deepest communication occurs not when words are spoken, but when a pause is born, in silence. One needs to be silent. **It is during silence that the most important thing happens,** as when the words are spoken, the mind is under a certain strain. It attempts to hear and to understand what is being said. At this moment something totally different may occur and expresses itself.

Why is it so difficult for so many people to be silent? It is especially difficult when new people that do not know each other get together. Have you notice that? People get together and try to talk constantly, non-stop. If a pause develops, it is a heavy pause. How many definitions of silence are there: dead silence, horrible silence, deep silence, cold silence?

Usually one says what people expect him to say, not what he wants to say. One thinks what one can and cannot say. Out of everything we have inside, only a tiny portion is being said and expressed. The rest we don't even allow to our awareness. The ability of one being to say everything to another being is not something totally impossible. Maybe that in itself is heaven on earth, **when you can say everything to another human being,** and when this other human being can say everything to you.

For example, let's take a man and a woman. May a man say everything to a woman, especially if she is his wife? How many men allow themselves to do so? How many women allow themselves to do so? There are certain things, God forbid you would think about let alone say it, or even think that you can think about. That is how we live. Do you understand the horror of it? A human being has something he cannot say. **And**

how do you relate to something you cannot say? Perhaps you consider it to be bad. Otherwise, why can't you say it aloud? What kind of self-expression can we talk about here?

You cannot talk about something precisely because you consider it to be bad or to lead to something bad. For example, can you say to a girl you are planning to marry, "I saw Irene yesterday. She looks great!"? You really felt it. You met your old classmate or first love, and she really looked great. You were very happy to see her. Would you be able to share this with your fiancé? If you were to share it with her, would it make her happy? No. In a best case scenario, she would silently nod her head. It is quite difficult to expect her to share your feelings toward Irene's great looks. This is just an example, and there are many similar examples.

So, what can we say to each other without turning on limitations of the mind's perception: considering, judging, presumptions?

In reality, the human being has lost the ability to be sincere. That's a tragedy of a human being. One cannot be sincere. One forgot what it is. One only says what is acceptable to say, filtering one's words through thousands of filters. That's why **usually only banal things are being said**.

When was a man allowed to say something that really reflected his individuality? A man weights everything he says: is it smart or not smart? How would they relate to my statement? How would I look? Is what I say grammatically correct? That's why usually only commonly accepted banalities are being said. That is what people exchange. A man cannot say what he wants to say. Then he forgets what he wanted to say, he forgets himself.

An opportunity of one human being to say something to at least one other human being is already God's kingdom on Earth. But in order for this to happen, what kind of human being should this other one be? First of all, what kind of human being should I be in order to say what I have to say? Is it easy? Even if you had an opportunity, and another human being who can understand and accept everything you were to say to him as you would say to yourself were near, what would you say? Maybe, exactly at that precise moment, the deepest pause in your life would appear.

What does it mean to open up to another human being? It means, first of all, to open up to yourself. If a man cannot admit and accept something in himself, he simply will not be able to say it.

There are people who create an appearance of being very sincere.

Let's imagine one such guy. He gets himself tipsy and starts talking about everything and everyone. It appears that he says everything he thinks, but this is not so. He does not know everything about himself. He talks only about what he knows well, while he does not know and does not want to know the rest; he does not even allow the rest to his awareness. That is why it seems to him and to everyone around him that he expresses everything he has, while in reality he is not even aware of what he has.

Prior to saying everything you have, you have to become aware of what you have. In order for that to happen, you have to become the one who would be able to do so. Only then, possibly, in connection to it, another human being would appear who would be able to hear you, to whom you would be able to say it. **But as long as the one who is speaking is not ready to say everything, the one who can hear it all will not come.** Those who see things as a whole, understand each other, but in order to understand them one has to become whole himself.

Do you want to switch from lie to sincerity? Are you ready for this?

Agreement without understanding

Complete understanding between people is only possible when they have holistic vision. Because the majority of people do not have holistic vision, they cannot understand each other, but people interact anyway. If they were not to have some kind of **substitution of true understanding**, which is currently inaccessible to them due to the fragmentation of their vision, communication would be impossible. That is why people invented such thing as an **agreement**. In essence, it is that maximum which people with fragmented vision can reach.

Look **how conflicts are regulated**: familial, state, national, etc. Regulation is negotiation. Let's assume people want to come to some kind of compromise. What is a compromise? It's an agreement in regards to a certain case, an opportunity to get to agree with each other somehow. But when people are unable to come to a compromise, to reach an agreement, war either starts or continues: cold, hot, emotional, or intellectual. Everyone here has his own, unique point of view. Those points of view do not connect and everyone tries to impose his point of view on another. But if, for certain reasons, people decide to stop the feud, they try to renegotiate again. What does it mean? It means, they try to reach a new agreement. This is the maximum they can possibly accomplish.

There are many people who have very different religious, cultural, political views, moral and ethical norms, but not all of them are in state of open war. They are somehow capable of reaching an agreement. **What do heads of states do? They try to negotiate**. They try to come to some kind of an agreement. This is the maximum they can possibly accomplish.

100

Based on what they would reach this agreement is a different question. But if people come to an agreement on two, three, ten, hundreds of points, it does not yet mean they have an understanding, because on another thousand points that they did not even touch during the negotiation process they would not reach an agreement. They reach only a partial agreement, and it helps them to have a temporary truce.

Holistic vision has a different scale. We already discussed that a human being constantly pounds in the sphere of the mind, unable to get outside its limits. But if one were to exit the limits of the mind, one would encounter different spheres, which one would try to exit again later on.

So what is the **scope of understanding** that is present outside of the sphere of the mind? Let's say we took people who achieved the level of understanding that is outside of the sphere of the mind. They would really see what happens inside the limits of what is being called the Earth. I presume they would see it the same way, i.e. they would understand each other. They would understand each other well, because their vision is equally holistic in the limits of a given scale of a given wholeness.

If you really understand another human being, you are in complete agreement with him. If you do not agree even on one topic, it means you don't understand him, even if you think you do.

Are you capable of full understanding of one human being?

If your answer is yes, it means you understand everything.

Is this so for you?

To whom does personality belong?

Parents claim to own a child. They think their child belongs to them. It's quite usual to hear, "You are so ungrateful. We fed and took care of you. We invested so much in you. And what do we see now? You don't talk to us the way you should!" Do parents have rights on a child?

Society controls a child through parents? Using parents, another society member is prepared. It is to society that every personality belongs. Using millions of hooks, thousands of "have to" and "ought to," feelings of guilt and patriotism, society holds personality in its net. Parents play a huge role in this.

While a baby is small, parents' influence is tremendous. It is not coincidental that the family is considered to be a unit of society, as it is precisely through parents, through them as personalities and products of society, that this influence is transmitted to a child. Familial connections are very strong. If you say something that does not fit into the brackets of accepted familial relationships, you experience a very strong feeling of guilt. That is how society throws its hooks and keeps personality inside its brackets.

It is impossible to hold a human being, while personality is easily detained because it is a product of society. So, what is a human being? What kind of an opportunity does a human being have? How can this opportunity be realized? What does a man, who starts to see and to release his attachments, starts to hear? What kind of call is it? Where does it come from? And if you start to follow this call, what happens to you? If your personality disappears, what's left behind? Why are we so afraid to let something personal go?

There are talented musicians, talented painters, and talented singers. How are these talents being used? Someone can use piano to strengthen his personality, another can use paints and brushes for the same reason. When talent becomes leverage for personality to strengthen itself, is it really a talent? What is a real talent?

Personality aspires to success and recognition, it wants to be famous, and it does not care what it uses to accomplish this. But there is a musician who plays, because he plays; there is a painter who paints, because he paints. Personality, on the other hand, uses this talent for its own purposes. Maybe this is what people call "God sent." Maybe this is that really important note or melody that one performs with his life, with his whole being. But that talent does not belong to anybody, in particular, to a human being through whom it develops. It is just expressed through him.

A human being like that can be compared to a violin. A violin can be lying on the table and we would not even know what it is capable of. But when a great musician takes the violin and starts to play, they become one, and a beautiful melody is conducted through them. Maybe this is a real talent. Nothing personal is needed when such a union occurs: no admiration, no money, no fame. Everything is already present in what happens. No additional payment is needed. Maybe that is what the real answer to a call is, a call that comes from There, which one can hear and listen to.

But personality wants to usurp and use this. If something would come from There, from those other spheres, personality would want to take it and use it to strengthen itself. But this call cannot be used this way. It just stops its movement. It requires complete cleansing from everything personal. Then it comes. Maybe it is precisely then, a human being becomes a Human Being. A human being from an opportunity of becoming one becomes the one. And then beautiful music is heard through him or her.

What is considered to be a talent in this world? It is something that gives certain fame, right? For example, a writer's talent may make you famous. See, the whole idea of talent is seriously distorted. When I talk about talent, I have a completely different vision. True talent may be subtle—a talent to hear birds, a talent to hear wind, a talent to see a play of clouds.

This is not something which requires any kind of appraisal. **Appraisal** always indicates the interference of personality. It is precisely the personality that wants to be famous, wants to be appraised. Here we are talking about something completely different. We are talking about something invisible and irrelevant for the majority of people, who look for importance. This is something very simple, something completely irrelevant for them. What is in the first place here may be in the last place There. What is being praised and happens to be desirable here has no value There.

You can say, "Well, we live in a society and are brought up to be attached to its judgment. It is very difficult to move away from society's appraisal." But it is impossible to sit between two chairs. It's impossible to develop just a touch of spiritually, while blowing up and inflating your personality. It is possible to delude oneself on the subject. It is precisely for personality, its inflation, that a human being sacrifices the opportunity to become a Human Being. On the other hand if one really wants to become a Human Being he needs to sacrifice whatever prevents him from becoming one—sacrifice personality. But the majority of people don't want to do it and say, "I am already a Human Being. What are you talking about?" They mistake personality for a Human Being.

From personality to a Human being

A Human Being is something that can develop when personality is transformed. But who really wants it? Personality wants to use everything it encounters for its own profit. It would never miss its chance. You want to develop spiritually? Please do so, achieve, become. What is being strengthened then? It is personality that is being strengthened. You want new knowledge? Excellent. Spiritual achievements? Great. Personality attempts to save and hold on to everything. It always wants to win something for itself. But if you stop aspiring toward the ideal, if you let go of everything you saved, then you will feel personality, its resistance and pain.

Pain is a reaction of personality to letting go of something it believes belongs to it and only to it. That is a mechanism of this pain. It's quite simple, but around it, one can create serious dramas and tragedies. In reality, everything is quite simple. Personality does not want to let go of anything it thinks belongs to it. The bigger the "piece" that is "leaving," the more upset personality will be. Personality wants to have, not to be. For personality to have means to be and not to have means not to be. Just being—the state of life without any kinds of attachments—is something completely foreign for personality. The essence of personality is fictitious and illusory, and like every other illusory thing, it requires support and reinforcement; otherwise nobody would believe it existence.

There is an old parable about an Emperor without clothes, you've probably heard before. Only a boy, who could see impartially, being totally independent of the king, could scream out that the king was naked. Hundreds of people who were dependent on the king, could not say it. They, most likely, did not even see it, because it is very difficult to call someone beautifully dressed, knowing that he is naked. Therefore, it is better not to see it and only see an illusion. But this illusion requires constant support and nourishment. To see what exists in reality requires no effort. It is there, and you see it, but in order to see what is, in reality, absent, constant efforts are necessary.

Why is life so hard? Why does it require constant efforts and stress? Is it because the aims and ideals the majority of people try to reach are illusory, fictitious, and unreal? But a man constantly needs to support and to feed those illusions with his energy. That's where those constant efforts and constant stress and tiredness come from. If he stops applying those efforts, stop stressing out, these illusions will collapse like a house of cards. He tries to achieve something, anxiously runs around doing something and only before the end of his life possibly realizes it was a house of cards, and he was using his life energy to maintain it day after day after day, all his life. All societal relationships are a big house of cards, held together only by the efforts of many people aspiring toward societal ideals, running away from reality. Until people share this vision, this illusion will continue to exist. But if these efforts were to be stopped, the illusion would clear away and disappear as smoke during powerful wind. It is impossible to destroy reality, life, and true love, because they exist.

Why do we see so many aggressive people? Why do they try to convince each other of something, to compel others to do things their way? If what they want was real, why would they need to be so anxious, so insistent? **Anxiety develops** precisely in the sphere of the unreal, illusory, and ideal. Take a look at how many people try to support what they call love, good relationships, moral norms, and ethics. Only the things that cannot stand on their own have to be supported. If people stop supporting these things, they would simply disappear. We try to maintain good relationships. We are interested not in communication, but specifically in the maintaining of good relationships. We don't communicate, we maintain relationships. So, what kind of relationships are those that you need to constantly maintain? What kind of efforts do those relationships require? What would happen to these relationships if you stop supporting them? Would you like to try it one day?

What are the assumptions about so called "good relationships" are based on? They are based on "ought to," "must," "advantageous," "easier," etc. Behind them is fear: fear to not perform, fear to not get, fear of guilt, and fear of losing. That is what everything is held on. Meanwhile, we are surprised why we live this way. Why do we perform the melody of sadness, pain, depression, jealousy, anger, and irritation? Why do we maintain this melody within ourselves and others? Do we want to see it? And what does it mean to see it? It means to see the fictitiousness, falsity of relationships we are in. It means to see the lie in ourselves and others. Who is ready for this, will see it. How many are willing to?

How is it possible? I maintained these relationships all my life. How can I change them? It is sad. Look how difficult it is to throw away old clothes. One looks around a house and sees old clothes, old books, useless things and thinks, "Should I throw them out? Perhaps kids will be able to use them?" If it is so difficult to throw away old things, what can we say about the difficulty of letting go of our convictions and beliefs? I was following it my whole life, how can I let it go now? The more time we spend contemplating it, the harder it is to let it go. How is it possible, I spent so much time and energy on all this? And what really is "this"? What was there? It is nothing real, but a lot of thought up stuff. The one who is alive can stand on one's own, the dead one need to be supported. So, what is it that we support and hold on to all our lives? What kind of relationships do we maintain? Who with? Why? Why won't we drop them?

Is there a difference between pity and compassion?

Can one feel both, or does compassion exclude pity?

Do you feel pity toward someone, or do you pity yourself?

To take and to give

Many people find it difficult to ask someone for something. The majority try to solve their needs through action. Maybe you did something similar. In principal, you can stand on the street and beg for alms, but you will quickly get used to it. It becomes daily and habitual work. Your inner state would possibly change, but it does not mean that you understand it and feel it to the end. You just exchanged one habit for another. You were in a habit of not asking, and now you have developed a habit of asking. But as soon as some actions become habitual, you cease to be aware of them.

For example, for those who earn their leaving begging on the streets, begging becomes a habitual, mechanical act. Perhaps you have noticed that some of them beg as if passersby owe them. They don't beg, they demand. People performing what appears to be the same act, i.e. begging for alms, may be in very different states. That is why it is quite difficult to consider that by asking others more frequently, you would be able to get deeper into the state we are talking about.

In reality, you can get in touch with and experience this state right now, right here. In order to see something, you don't need to do anything special. It does not require any kind of preparation or time. No efforts are necessary. You can do it now.

So, what kind of state develops when you need to ask someone for something? To give or to take is similar to inspiration and expiration. It is something that is constantly present in your life. One lives in his body until one stops breathing. To give and to take is the breath of life, coming through the body of each and every one of us. It is the interaction of our internal and external worlds. When I give something to someone, I exhale something into the outside world: my thoughts, feelings, actions, plans. When I take something from someone, I inhale. It enters me. Again, these are thoughts, feelings, etc. What if this exchange is interrupted? What if one tries only to inhale or exhale? Try for five minutes only to inhale or only to exhale. How long will you last? So, what really happens when you want to ask someone for something? What kind of state is it?

Do you suppose one never does anything for another human being for free? Don't you think that the exchange, during which one does something for another, is precious by itself? Should I always be paid for something I do for others? Perhaps when this labor is not paid for by you, you feel a certain unpleasant sensation; you may call it guilt or give it some other name. Then it follows that you see the situation in this light: something was received from one side, while from another side nothing was given. Seeing it this way, the negative state arises. Isn't it based on the concept that every interaction, every exchange with others, happens to represent some sort of labor for you and for another human being that should be reimbursed? The interchange itself cannot be adequate and self-sufficient. Another human being would not do it if you did not ask him to, if you did not pay him one way or another.

Let's take someone very close to you now. In such a case, as we said, there is a credit of trust, in other words "credit card," i.e. you don't pay him back immediately but postpone payment for a certain period of time. He did something for you today. He considers that later, when he turns to you, you would do for him what he would ask you to do. Therefore, between the two of you there is a certain unwritten agreement according to which you can turn to each other, most likely not expecting to be refused.

Between close people scores are harsher, but it may not be obvious as both are in the habit of complying with the agreement. Let's say a husband brings home money while his wife cooks, and there are no frictions between them because both agree and understand it. But, assume he failed to do so, or she failed to cook the way she usually does. Surely some questions would come up.

For example, he may say, "Why is today's soup so tasteless?" or, "Why did you cook this instead of what I like?" It appears that everyone has his own plans, his own expectations in mind, and when those expectations coincide, everything appears to be normal, conflicts do not develop. But when they do not coincide and recur, someone for sure will express a feeling of dissatisfaction because he didn't get what he should have gotten. "Close, too close he was, of course, but somehow he did not give me his fullest."

If we see that the process of interchange happens by itself, and we simply participate in it, should we get anxious on account of who took what and who put down how much? In such a case, **the feeling of guilt** would never appear. But the majority of people have different convictions regarding this. For example, parents do something for a child, and then at a certain moment show a bill. They may also be in a habit of constantly showing it. They say, "Here you go again. I did not sleep nights, I was feeding you and sacrificed my life for you; and now you don't even listen to me!" More often than not, the bill brought up is not for money, but for the child to listen, agree, conform, and follow what is being said. For example, a father may say to his son, "You are going to follow my footsteps. You are going to be a lawyer." But the kid wants to be a musician. Their desires and expectations do not coincide. The father may say, "Boy, did you forget how much I invested in you? Why are you playing the fool?" And here you go; the bill is brought up full price.

These bills are usually not put on the table immediately, but sooner or later it happens. It is the closest people who usually bring up the most substantial "psychological bills." Most people have strong convictions that the payments on "psychological bills" should come precisely from where their efforts, hopes, and desires were directed. If you are doing something for this particular human being or for a certain organization, it is from them you expect reimbursement. And usually you expect it to be no less than the efforts you have made. If this return is not coming or coming with a delay, you start to become anxious first and then get outraged.

Is it true that the efforts you invested in someone or something should be returned precisely from there?

Some religious and spiritual systems talk about the fact than when something comes your way, you should remember who you gave this something to before. If something was stolen from you, it means that you stole something from someone before.

These are some explanations I encounter frequently. Let's say someone was robbed of three thousand dollars. He is outraged and wants this money returned. Why is he outraged? He believes he was not dealt with fairly. He says, "I gave him so much, and look how he paid me back. What is it? I am playing fair and square, and what do I get in return?" And now somebody shows up who says, "You know, you actually did not pay him in full." If he believes this, he has no reason to think that he has not been dealt with appropriately. Yes, money was taken from him, but he did something similar sometime in his past life. Look, this is an explanation; quite a clever explanation. It contains an element of mystery, esotericism, karma, previous lives, etc. Let's say I am such a difficult case that I don't want to believe this explanation. How do I know there is such a thing as a past life? How do I know I met him in the past and took money from him? I am not satisfied with this explanation.

And who needs these explanations? Who is being fed by them? It is personality and the superficial mind, that gave birth to it that are being fed by those explanations. For example, a given personality considers itself to be generous. When it gives money to someone, it reinforces its convictions in regards to its own generosity. Another personality may have, for example, some notions about its entrepreneurship. Then if it makes $2,000 out of $1,000, it reinforces its convictions of itself as a good entrepreneur. But what if personality, instead of receiving back the money invested, would get neither thanks nor profit, or, in other words, nothing of value for what it did? That is what happens when one human being gives something to another.

Who is it that gives? Is it a human being or personality? If a personality gives something to someone, it expects a return, a profit. Profit for personality is a reinforcement of its convictions. If the expected profit is not received, the personality feels fooled. Recently quite a few spiritual entrepreneurs appeared who offer karmic theories and explain what happens in a way to satisfy a personality. For example, they say that profit was not received not because a given personality has poor entrepreneurial skills, but because it should pay its karmic debt. This explanation is well understood by the personality of the entrepreneur, as the idea that dues should be paid fits well into a system of its beliefs. Similar notions may be related to another personality's convictions, such as generosity, fairness, orderliness, etc.

Many people try to mix what they think is useful to them with what gives them pleasure. For example, you like cooking. You are married. If you feed your husband well he may get to be very affectionate. As we can see, one thing does not exclude the other. He is well fed and he starts thinking, "You were good to me, and I am going to reciprocate." Meanwhile, you can experience pleasure from preparing a meal, and then get an additional pleasure from his company. But who is getting pleasure here? Is it personality?

Do we really understand why we experience pleasure, when we receive something or when we give something? Most importantly, who is getting pleasure? Does personality experience pleasure or is it something completely different? What I just called "completely different" is difficult to describe with words, but I think we will touch upon it today. For example, it seems to me that I am doing something unselfishly. For example, I am standing on a crossroad waiting for some old man to show up in order to help him cross the street. I am not going to charge him. Quite the opposite, I will bid him good day and return to my spot, waiting for another old man to appear.

Do we always understand the real source of our pleasures and sufferings? Are we always aware of the motives of our actions? When we do something that does not come from self-interest, don't we create self-interest? Are selfishness and unselfishness two sides of one duality? What we want to receive, acting as we consider unselfishly, may be accompanied by expectations of a certain result, prize, without getting which we would get upset, even though we would never acknowledge this to ourselves or others.

If action comes from personality, it would obligatorily want to receive its prize and one way or another to reinforce itself. I am not discussing whether it is good or bad. This is just so. This is the mechanism of the functioning of personality. To see it means to see something as it is, as it happens in reality. What does personality wants when it gives? What does personality wants when it takes? What are personality's problems connected to this exchange? Personality has multiple problems related to this.

The interchange can be seen as an impersonal process. Usually one breathes without thinking about the profit. It is natural to inhale and exhale. In order to do so, one does not need to be good, smart, stupid, or entrepreneurial. All these concepts of personality are unnecessary for the natural breathing process. Isn't the process of interchange between people equally natural? Don't we distort it ourselves, introducing our notions, opinions, beliefs of how it should be in the opinion of our superficial, limited mind? Perhaps because of this, our relationships with others become so painful, similar to asthma.

To work up the ability to ask is to work on the technical side, on the competence and proficiency in taking something. But even if you learn all this, you would still not exit the limits of your own convictions related to the concept "give—take." Irrespective of our notions and concepts of it, the process occurs constantly and all the time. Moreover, it occurs under natural laws, which are impossible to understand using the superficial, conditional mind, limited by the ideas it already has.

If you decide to start begging in order to work up this ability, it means that your personality wants to acquire the ability to beg. For one who does not know how to beg, the necessity to do so is painful because his personality gets traumatized. If he is refused alms, his personality would feel unimportant and devalued. That would be quite traumatic for the personality.

Now, let's take another one, who knows how to beg. Suppose he has mastered this skill to perfection. He can beg by using different methods. If necessary, he can drop onto his knees, he can crawl, and he can cry buckets of tears. But all of this is just his ability—internally it does not affect him. He is just playing a role of a beggar. If we were to look deep into his personality, we would see that as a result of all these operations—kneeling, crawling, and tearing—his personality got stronger. One may ask: why? It happens because he does it professionally. In reality, he does not give a damn how he does it. The important thing for him is to achieve results.

It is impossible to say that he cannot beg. He can. He begs in a way that it is impossible to refuse him. Perhaps he can use a gun or wet twenty handkerchiefs with his tears. He applies methods that would work on any given human being, and his arsenal is huge.

Let's return for a minute to the concept of karmic debt to someone who robed you. This is not ability. This is a concept that allows one to calm down personality in a situation when it feels strangled, insulted, degraded. Some personalities get calmed by it. This is a very sneaky method, but this method in no way puts in doubt the presence of personality itself, the possibility of its future existence.

But let's ask ourselves again, "Is a human being just a personality or is it something more than personality?"

The question "Give or take?" appears in relationship to profit. You think, "Why would I ask him for something now when I would have to return later?" And now I start to think, what do I gain by it and what do I lose? And when the mind calculates this, I feel dissatisfaction, and I don't want to ask because it seems to me that I will lose more than I will gain.

Do you understand that these are the questions of accounting details? Those are the questions an accountant would ask.

It is not accidental that Judas was an accountant. Did anyone pay attention to this? He was the one who managed financial accounts. I am not judging it to be good or bad. I am just stating a fact. He was dealing with money, and when Magdalena used expensive oil to rub Jesus' feet, Judas got outraged. He said, "What an irrational use of such an expensive product!" We could have sold it and dispersed money among the poor." And what was Jesus' reply? Jesus said, "Don't you worry. The world always had poor and always will have them, while I will not be here for long." This is symbolic. These are two different views on one thing. Someone may say that Judas looks kinder here than Jesus. If the superficial mind, personality approach this question, it would definitely say that Judas is kinder than Jesus. It is impossible to understand Jesus' words with a limited mind, because from the standpoint of this mind, Judas is right!

CHAPTER 4:
LIBERATION
FROM THE PRISON OF THE MIND

•◆•◆•◆•◆•◆•◆•◆•◆•◆•◆•◆•◆•◆•◆•◆•◆•◆•◆•

A typical reaction of the mind to the unknown

The mind gets nervous when it encounters something incomprehensible and unknown, something that it cannot name, define, and classify. Have you ever been in a situation where you encountered something incomprehensible and unknown? What happened in these situations?

When the mind encounters something unknown, it experiences certain states. If you observe yourself, you may notice that most frequently it is a state of fear. The more unknown the thing or the situation, the stronger the fear. One of the most incomprehensible things for the mind is death. **People don't want to see it. In fact, the life of the majority of people is a flight from death because it is the only reality with which no one can argue. Even the mind cannot argue with death, because it is a fact.** One knows that people die, knows he is a human being and understands he will die also. This leads to mindless fear, and one starts to create theories, concepts, and notions of immortality. I don't want to talk about these theories being right or wrong. That is a different question. I want to say that these concepts are created, and they are created in order to calm the mind.

The main quality of the mind is fear of the unknown. Take a look at what one does encountering something unknown. When you start to observe your mind, you will see how it reacts to unknown. **How does your mind react when it encounters something unknown?**

When the mind sees something unknown, it tries to characterize it and put it on a certain shelf by comparing it with something it already knows. Then it quiets down and says, "I already know it." Have you noticed it? Personal experience is very important here. If we don't learn the qualities of our mind, we will not be able to understand anything, because the mind is both the jail and the jailer. Unless we see how it works, we will never be able to escape it.

Observe yourself and you will see how pleasant it is to hold on to this image of yourself as "me knowledgeable, me experienced, etc." The mind is unable to accept something new, but it can give it a name and say that it already possesses it. The mind cannot have new experiences; it cannot have something which is outside of itself. It can only possess what is inside its brackets: words, notions, and convictions. That is why when it encounters something unknown to it, it names it and says, "I already possess it." Certain people appeared who started talking about awakening and the awakened state at the same time, insisting that this is impossible to describe using words. Immediately the minds of other people started to say that they experienced the same state, repeating, "It is impossible to describe those states using words." Try to see what happens. The mind already thinks it possesses it. If it deems it has it, it does not need to go any further. **Only the mind which sincerely says, "I don't know anything,"— may really start an investigation.** It is funny. You can say it now, and it will become a good tradition for you, but it is gibberish. The mind is the greatest illusionist. It can always, not having something, create an image of it, as it is the only way to possess it. The mind will always resist the unknown. Can you observe this in yourself?

When one encounters something unusual, one's first habitual reaction is, "Let's see what will happen." How many times have you reacted this way? Notice that the way I talk is unusual. How do you react to it? Will you be able to understand something new by reacting to it in an old, habitual way?

What do you think, feel, sense right now? Is your current reaction to what you have just read—your usual, habitual reaction? Describe it. Try to see it from another side. Allow something new to enter you.

Exiting the borders of the usual

It is precisely the habitual reaction of the mind that does not allow us to enter the unknown. It is possible to approach the borders of the mind, but no one can tell you what happens afterward. In observing the work of your mind, you can see its mechanical nature, the limits and the barriers it has built based on its own opinions, convictions, and beliefs. To see these barriers is to see the things as they are. It is pointless to talk about the unknown as it cannot be described in words.

Why do I even say this, if the main idea cannot even be verbalized? Did you ask this question? How did you answer it?

Perhaps, you think, "Okay. Let's assume he understands something. But he talks about something that cannot be expressed in words. So, I just have one option—to believe his words. But I want to understand it. How can I do that?" Let's say there is something behind the borders of the mind. How can we get there? If one continues one's search, one will probably be anxious to know how to get to the destination. Then the second question will arise: how to get there faster? One may also experience anxiety in regards to doing something inappropriately or missing another, shorter way to the destination. One may question whether the path is his or whether he needs to be on another, different path. Do you have similar questions?

Many people have these questions. They may not be clearly formulated, some may not be even aware of them, but they do exist. You may not have answers to these questions, but based on what you continue, start, or stop doing, a lot of what is happening inside of you can be seen. Let's accept that you continue to do something. For example, you continue to read this book. Doing this, do you still hope for something or not? If you don't, then why do you continue reading this book? If you do hope, what do you hope for? Are these important questions or not?

What do you think?

What prevents one's meeting with the unknown?

If you open a newspaper, you can frequently see this sort of advertisement, "Opening of the "third eye" with 100% guarantee." Can you imagine what it means to **open** a holistic **vision** to someone who is **not ready for it**? Why do so many people get hooked on these offers? They are interested. What is behind this interest? Behind this interest lays a **conviction that one may find something unknown**, not leaving anything known, habitual.

Quite a few people think they can do it. They think the unknown can be opened up as a curtain in a theater. Here I am in the first row. My wife is sitting next to me with my mistress, brothers, and sisters nearby. I have a wallet full of money in my pocket, and life smiles at me. And now I want something new. Please, entertain and make me interested. And right away the curtain lifts and one can see different worlds: fourth dimension, fifth dimension, etc. That is how many people imagine the opening of something unknown. One already has everything, and now one wants something new.

To be honest with you, **sometime ago I had similar thoughts,** but one day everything changed. One should pay for everything, and for big things one should pay a lot. Some people say, "I am tired of this life. I don't want to live like this. I want to see different worlds." But when the question arises of what one needs to do for this, to deny oneself something, to get up at five am, one says, "No, this is very difficult. I get up at nine." And at the same time one argues with gusto that one can't live the way one lives. It is funny, but you can see it everywhere.

So, how can one release one's attachments that do not allow one to meet the unknown?

There is no universal recipe. Moreover, every single human being is unique. It is impossible to say, "First we are going to release this, and then we are going to release that." I can say only one thing: it is a very painful, hard process.

At certain times it may appear that the most important thing is to **find real knowledge**, a book, or a teacher. I will read and learn, and I will be immediately transformed. That is not how it happens. It does not happen in relation to reading a new book, or visiting a certain holy place, even though the transformation may coincide with it. This process is connected with one thing only—**your readiness to see what interferes with it**—to see the attachments of the mind.

The mind is very subtle and sophisticated, and that is why it is not easy to see all these obstacles. Frequently, one returns to things which appears one has already passed. Why? Why do these things return again and again? Did I not pass them before? No, not yet. And then you can stop seeing your attachments again, stop wanting to see them. One has to have a very strong aim in order to not stop **to fall asleep again**. This is a very difficult process. It cannot be done between things. It is a work that should constantly be with you. Everything should be subordinated to this work. Everything should be aimed toward it. Many people take psychological, spiritual, esoteric, or religious study courses believing they can spiritually develop and evolve between work and personal liaisons. This is quite unlikely, as spiritually development requires all of you. If you leave something in reserve, nothing will happen. Usually one wants to leave something for himself—a conviction that one is smart, kind, spiritual, etc. I am talking about notions, convictions, and beliefs, and not about material things now. Something material, physically visible is easier to leave. It is very difficult to leave ideas, notions, convictions, beliefs, which became self-obvious to one.

There are convictions which many people believe in. For example, one says, "I believe in God." What does it mean to believe in God? Why does the necessity to believe develop at all? This is something not so self-evident. "I doubt that, and in order to overcome my doubts, I believe. I believe more and more. I want to believe." Why? In reality, it happens because I doubt. Otherwise, why would I try to believe so hard?

There are theists and atheists. They support each other in their notions of God. Theists say, "God exists," while atheists say, "God does not exist." But both talk about God and thus support this idea, this notion. They are on a certain horizontal plane, which has two polarities. **These are two sides of the same idea.**

But God is not an idea. God is a unified reality, which no one is able to understand, but can only live through.

Death and the attachments

Does your mind want to know **what death is**? Can you understand what life is if you **don't know what death is**? Does death come at the end of life, or do **life and death go hand in hand**? And if life and death go hand in hand, it means we **die every minute, every day.**

Your mind is so afraid of death because it cannot define it. Even if the mind were to define it, it would still continue to experience an unaccountable fear of it. That is why different theories arose in regards to life after death and the possibility of reincarnation. Are these questions of concern to you? If yes, why?

Are you ready to die now? Do you think life will continue without you? Will you disappear completely? Can you accept your death right now? How about sometime later? Do you want to think about it? And if you start to contemplate this question, where will you arrive? **Is it possible to learn something new** about this **if you were to think about it only from a logical standpoint**? Is this question important to you? What do you do when this question arises?

Would you be calm if I were to tell you that you will die in ten minutes? When you die, **what is it that will die in you?** What do you have the **most difficult** time letting go of now? What are the strongest attachments of your mind and personality? Is it possible to weaken these attachments gradually, or can one release them right now, instantly?

Imagine that you are carrying something. For example, a big and heavy bookcase tied to you by ropes. **How** can you **gradually release** it? It is tied to you. As soon as you move, this bookcase moves with you. Can you tell me how you can gradually release this bookcase? In my opinion, it can only be done at once by **cutting the ropes** connecting you to it. Perhaps, you can reply, "*It is possible to neither sense nor feel these ropes and this bookcase. One can see something completely different in it. In such case it is not heavy at all. I may not even notice it*" That is precisely how the majority of people relate to their attachments. They are tied up by multiple ropes and carry huge weights, **repeating**, "This is not heavy at all. It is not tied up to me at all."

In order to let go of something, you need to see it first. But to see it means to **learn that you have carried and continue to carry a huge load,** which, in reality, is **not related to you** and is not you. But you don't want to do it. People create different theories trying to prove that they are not afraid of death. They **define it,** name it, and **say** that they **are not afraid** of it. How long can you be in such a state? One day you will **definitely find out** what is **really holding you**, to what you are **tied**, not even noticing it. This will happen at the moment of the death of your physical body.

When you **see** what's **holding** you, will you be able to **let go of it**? You did not want to **do it** before. If you do not **become aware of death while living**, you will definitely **become aware** of it when you die, but then you will become aware of death, in a way, **forcibly,** not by your own choice.

All the blocks are in man's mind. If one likes one's religion, one goes to church. If one likes one's car, one drives it. **When a man dies** and loses his body, his consciousness transfers to a different state. If everything external disappears, what is left? Let's assume that what's left is what was in his mind. Then, when he loses his body, he also loses the possibility to fulfill the requirements he had in his mind. Therefore, he has the requirements but not the ability to satisfy them.

So, what is the mind attached to? It wants to constantly repeat what is inside it, what it's attached to. You can call it anything you want: car, vacation, dissertation, God symbol. But all these, in the end, are just thoughts and images. **The mind consists of thoughts and images, and it is attached to itself**, to its own productions. **The image** we are attached to **requires** realization outside itself. Then, **through this image,** you attach to something external, something that has a certain **form.**

So, **what is it that we let go of** when we let go? Do we let go of **an object or the image** of an object? When we separate with someone, do we let go of this human being or do we let go of the image of this human being? When we live with someone, do we see a human being or the image of this human being?

When we feel pity for ourselves or when we feel humiliated or jealous,—what exactly is it? **What** is being influenced: we ourselves or our image of what **we consider to be ourselves?**

So, what is it that we are so attached to? What are we so afraid to lose? What will happen if we lose the image of ourselves? If one's image of oneself is to die, what will one be left with? A and B were sitting on the wall. A was dropped. B disappeared. What was left behind?

When one imagines one's death, what exactly is one so upset with?

So, can we understand life without fully understanding death?

Can one see anything at all when one is having multiple problems, multiple images constantly rotating and requiring immediate attention and search for solutions? And does one really live? Where is this human being? What lives there? What images live in this shelter? Are these images really his? No. So why does he feed them? Why is one so afraid of letting them go?

What about you? Are you ready to release at least one of your major attachments right now?

The attachments to the illusion of the mind

How can one see reality if one is captivated by illusion?

There are different illusions. Some people collect certain illusions, while others collect different illusions. I say to you, "Let go of all your illusions." You can say, "I let go of this illusion, but this one I will not let go of." But that will not work. It is enough to have just one illusion in order not to see reality. It is enough to have just one mosquito buzzing around you in order for you to lose your cool. You don't need a hundred mosquitoes. You can kill ninety nine of them, but if one is left, you will not be at peace. The effect is the same.

You have freed yourself from hundredth of illusions, but have left just one—the favorite illusion of your mind. It will not allow you to get to know reality. One illusion is enough. Do you understand that one illusion is enough?

One says, "I let go of everything, but I will have my faith in God. You will not take that away from me. I don't believe in cars, property, career, but don't you touch my God." But what is it if not an illusion? What is God? It is a word, a product of the mind. Where did men come up with the idea of God? How did men find God? The image of God was created in men's mind. It is just an image, just a product of the mind, but now a man is attached to it. What does it mean "a man is attached to it"? It means one is attached to a certain notion of the mind. But is it possible to enter the zone of unknown, to move to the state of no-mind while holding on to some kind of a belief, a conviction, or a notion of the mind?

126

What kind of the illusions is your conditioned mind attached to?

Freedom and conditioning

A human being is afraid of freedom. In reality, a human being does not want freedom. One talks about freedom, but more than anything, one does not want to have it.

A newborn starts with breast milk and slowly progresses to regular food. During this transition, a child may experience abdominal cramps. But this period, going from usual to unusual, should be experienced. The usual mode for a human being is to be on a leash and scream for freedom. Meanwhile, as soon as the leash is loosened, one starts to pull it in order to tighten it. So, what can we talk about, what kind of holistic vision?

One, being tied up by heavy ropes, holds in one's hands a tiny air balloon screaming, "I am going to fly. I am going to see this city from above." One is tied with ropes ten inches in diameter and holds the balloon, which is almost out of gas, and one screams, "I want to take off. I want to fly."

What can you see if you stand knee deep in a dirty puddle? From such a spot, you can barely see what happens ten feet away from you. But you can see much more if you really take off. But in order to take off, you need to remove all the ropes. However, you can feed yourself with an illusion that you do not have to remove all the ropes, or scream that all the ropes are off and you are flying already.

The mind can throw multiple explanations at you in order not to change anything. This is the most difficult moment. One cannot be helped here. If one does not want to change, saying that one does, while not being ready to let go of the ropes, nothing will happen. People can get together and call themselves spiritual. They will all be satisfied playing this game—the game of spirituality.

Some people that enter our school leave fast. Why? It happens because they can see that they will not be allowed to play the game they love to play so much here. They will constantly wander. They have already been to many schools, and they will probably find other schools. They will eternally walk with their ideas, trying to find confirmation for them. That is what many people do. They don't want to let go of anything. Perhaps, some are satisfied with it.

Why is it so difficult to see, even for the one who really wants to see? Every single human being is completely unique—**unique** in his **attachments.** That is exactly where one is unique, not in anything else. In the **essential** that each one of us possesses, we are all **together**. But in this fragmentation, we are very individual, very original.

Life creates the most favorable conditions in order for each one of us to see it. Try to understand, nothing needs to be done here. One says, "I need to think it through. I need to read on it. Perhaps then I will figure out what I need to let go of and how to do it." It is gibberish. It is procrastination. In reality, it is unnecessary. One needs only one thing—**to allow oneself to really see the state one is in**. If you decide to see it, it will be strongly pronounced. These are the gifts life offers to each one of us in order to help us see what impedes us, to see holistically. And these are not something many will find pleasant, "The door will open up, and I will see this, hear that, and find out what the future holds." If one really wants to have a holistic vision, in the beginning one will see one's own ropes.

Life, in performing the Great Miracle of Love, will reveal the obstacles. How can one talk to someone who stands knee deep in mud, looking down, all tied up, about any broader vision? What will he understand? You can talk day and night, but he will not be able to understand anything. In order to see and to see more, one needs to start liberating oneself. It is precisely during this liberation process that the broadening of one's vision occurs.

Life circumstances allow exactly that. But whether we really want to use these circumstances or not is a different question. If we don't want to see, it will get murkier and murkier. Habitual situations will recur again and again, but we will not want to see their recurrent theme. This is similar to an unpleasant sound that is constantly present, but is not heard anymore. We get used to it, and think it is impossible not to have it around.

True understanding may only come as one slowly releases what is obstructing one's vision. If a completely tied up, enslaved man were able to free himself instantly from everything that ties him down, the sudden freedom will be accompanied by very intense suffering.

But Life, being loving and wise, will not let one experience more than one can withstand. If Life gives something, and you see it, you can pass through it, even though, you sometimes think you will not be able to bear it, that it is above your strength. But you will be able to withstand whatever you are given. This is a real path to holistic vision. I am not asking you to believe everything I say. I invite you to test it. Yet, you need energy to do so.

In my opinion, the only thing worth spending energy on is to open one's eyes. But what does one spends one's energy on? It is very important to understand. There is an old fairy tale called "The flower with the seven leaves," in which a young girl gets a hold of a magic flower. As she picks a leaf, her wish is fulfilled. First, she asks for ice-cream, then for toys. She is overwhelmed by ice-cream and toys. She does not know what to do with them. Next, she wishes to get rid of all of them.

129

That is how people spend their lives. It is a good analogy. But the quantity of one's energy is limited, and when one spends it on something known and habitual, nothing is left for the unknown. So, what is really important to you? What do you really want? What is it you are ready to spend your energy and life on?

There are **many people** who **attend spiritual schools only in order** to reinforce what they think is right. They come with premade answers, convictions, beliefs, and opinions. And all they want is to have them strengthened. They don't want anything new. They involve other people in active, emotional conversations, trying to convince them that what they have come with is right. If they are successful, they stay; if not, they go to other places where they repeat the same thing. Where is their energy going to? **Why is it so important for them to have their convictions strengthened?**

One can come and say that the only true way is Christianity. Another claims it is Islam. The third man insists it is something else, and tries to convince everyone that his way is the right way. He does not want to listen to anybody. Why do people insist on their beliefs so hard? What does it give them? Where do the convictions people carry come from?

Which convictions do you try to reinforce? Where did you get them from?

To see and to let go

A human being learned how to separate. He says, "I am here, and he is there. What can I expect from him?" We always create an image of another human being. This is how we separate ourselves from those with whom we communicate. What kind of wholeness is there, what kind of clear perception? It is pure suffering. Suffering comes from separation, and separation comes from the mind. **Until we understand the nature of the mind, until we become disenchanted with it, we will continue to live in duality, and suffer eternally.** We can suffer more or less depending on how closed up our heart has become. If we have closed it completely, it means we are living dead. There is an Eastern tale about a rich merchant who had many expensive carpets and precious stones in his vaults. One day, walking through the marketplace, he saw a beautiful emerald, superseding in its beauty anything he had previously seen. He gave away everything he had for it.

It is an old and wise story, but we should not take it literally. Awareness is that emerald for which one can give everything one has. But are we ready for it? Every one of us has an enormous number of illusory riches—our attachments. We are attached to many different things, and these are the ropes that keep us in captivity of the mind, while, we want to find something unknown. Can you imagine someone whose arms and legs are tied up saying, "Now I am going to go and find something new." Would you believe him? Millions of ropes are holding him down. He cannot even move his finger, but he insists he is going to go somewhere. Where can he go to? Nowhere. Our mind is that someone who is tied up completely by his own attachments.

What kind of attachments does your mind have? That is precisely what you need to see now. Until you understand and see these attachments, no real changes are possible. What does your mind hold on to? It is holding on to its own convictions. As soon as someone's more or less serious conviction is challenged, he starts to get anxious, agitated, and irritable. Have you noticed this in yourself already? When you start talking about your convictions and beliefs a bit more openly, you will see how strongly you are attached to them. The mind does not want to let go of its convictions and beliefs, because it is so identified with them.

Do you want to develop a holistic vision? A holistic vision is impossible to develop with the help of the mind. Holistic vision is a vision which only appears after one exit the limits of the mind. In order to exit the limits of the mind, you need to let go of its attachments. But in order to let something go, you need to see what it is you are letting go of.

If I don't know, for example, that I have a box of matches in my hand, I will not be able to let it go. Imagine, you are holding a box in your hand. It is full of matches, but you don't know about it. You don't know what's inside the box. You may think it is full of paper. Suddenly, a man walks toward you and says, "Drop your box of matches." You sincerely reply, "I cannot do it. I don't have matches." **You are totally sincere, because you don't know you are mistaken**. You think you are holding a box with paper, while it is full of matches. He continues to insist you drop a box of matches, while in reality you cannot do it as you don't know you have it in your hand. Later on, when you unfold your fingers, you may see a box of matches and realize that you could have complied with his request. But in order to do so, you needed to know what was in your hand.

Why do I use this analogy? I think that is precisely what happens. You **cannot let go of something** that you **do not see in yourself**.

If one has a strong desire to see, one can see it in oneself. That is the wisdom of life. One can only see the fragment that bothers him, and seeing it, one is able to let it go. In reality, it happens simultaneously: seeing and letting go. I may see something in another person, my symbol compares with his symbol, but I have difficulties seeing my own symbols directly. When I talk, argue, and try to convince someone, I am in the brackets of the symbol that determines my vision. This is a fragment through which I see everything. What kind of holistic vision can we talk about here?

In order to really understand this, not just agree or disagree with it, one needs to let go of attachments of the mind. It is analogous to ascending in an elevator. I can get to the second floor only by leaving the first. I get to the second floor, the doors open and I can either stay inside or move forward. If I stay on the second floor, I will not be able to get to a higher level.

We are talking now about the sphere of the conditional mind. To get outside its limits is unimaginable for a human being. But this is not something final. Behind this sphere there is another sphere, which is followed by the next sphere. It is an infinite process. Why do they say that the Absolute is unknowable? It cannot be understood completely. It is always bigger than you can imagine. It is infinite. Vision is also infinite. It can be more and more holistic, and this is what we call real development. It is infinite, but you can only know it by freeing yourself from what prevents you from seeing holistically.

What are you ready to free yourself from right now?

Stop feeding the dying egregor

The consciousness of a human being is fragmented. It consists of multiple fragments received during education and enculturation. **From where** are these fragments **taken?** These fragments are taken from the consciousness of humanity. The consciousness of humanity includes all the experience worked up by humanity. It is from this experience that the consciousness of a discrete human being receives its fragments. But, if the consciousness of a human being is fragmented, then the consciousness of humanity is also fragmented.

Let us take a look at **what is going on in the world now**. Can we say that the consciousness of humanity is getting less fragmented? Can we say that it becomes holistic? Horrible and devastating wars occurred during twentieth century and continue to take place today. Can we say that people's suffering diminishes? No. So, where does humanity go? What happens to the consciousness of humanity and to the consciousness of a given human being? What is human being trying to reach? What is his mind tries to grab?

Multiple books have been written about egregors. An egregor is a structure that a human being, not aware of anything except conditioned mind and false personality, feeds. The energy of men supports egregors. What constitutes an egregor?

An egregor is a huge image with many details. For example, Christianity developed a big and powerful egregor with multiple details. Egregors exist in many spheres: politics, culture, economics, religion, etc.

Every single human being, depending on what has been **downloaded into his mind, is connected** to one of many egregors. An energy link develops between them. But all these egregors are fragments of the mind of humanity, and therefore, exist inside the limits of the closed system of notions and beliefs.

We can see that neither a human being nor humanity at large can exit the limits of their own fragmented mind. They are pounding inside of it as bird in a cage.

Can we say that the mind of a human being and humanity is mindful, i.e. aware of itself?

What is collective consciousness? We already discussed that the mind of any human being consists of certain fragments, which were introduced into it by parents and society. It may be a certain fragment of Christian egregor or some other fragment connected to a political or economic system. Every single personality consists of many such fragments. It does not have anything unknown; it only contains different compilations of known fragments.

Where do these fragments come from? They exist in the collective mind of humanity. There is a fragment there called communism as well as a fragment called capitalism. There are many fragments there.

These fragments were invented by people, their minds and thoughts, and represent smaller or larger images, with more or fewer number of details. All these fragments compile into a certain fragment in the mind of humanity. As memory of a human being records everything that happens to him, so the collective memory of humanity records everything that happens to its entire people, to every single individual human being.

If some kind of an idea, some fragment, was forcefully developed by some people and many people were to believe in it, it becomes a more representative, more powerful fragment. There are certain religious systems that last for centuries. They accrue details, become modified and form **egregors**.

A **human being**, whose mind contains fragments of different egregors is **energetically connected to them**. The convictions a human being has are taken from and supported by a certain egregor. A man is a walking representative of one or many egregors. **Exchange of energy** occurs between the personality of a human being and an egregor. A man gives something to another man who returns something in response. It's a tradeoff that a human being may understand or not. Any given **personality is a carrier** of certain definitive convictions that are picked out **of certain egregorial images** present in

135

the collective memory of humanity. For example, people we call fanatics are those that are completely enslaved by one and only one egregor; **they serve it completely and inseparably.**

How does it connect with a possibility of seeing? To see reality is possible only when one refuses something, when one lets go of some of his convictions. We can see how a certain conviction can make one's vision very narrow. **What does it mean—to insist? It means to separate a certain fragment and accentuate it.** As soon as I separate one fragment, I can only see this fragment. I can't see anything but this fragment, and I start to insist on it.

Which egregors does your conditioned mind represent? Try to become aware of it now. Which convictions does your conditioned mind carry? Try to become aware of it now.

Your changes—who is interested in them?

Of what does the process of a child's education consist? One gets acculturated. First, one is taught the language. What is language? Language is a necessary attribute of a culture. It is a system of notions and convictions about the world, culture, and the society one is born into. Language helps to describe it all. Enclosed within a language are certain notions. **How is a language made?** For example, if I say "beauty," how can I understand what beauty is? I need to compare. **The whole language is built on comparison, on dualities: smart—stupid, good—bad, etc. Therefore, language is also dual**. The child is taught and introduced into this world, which in reality is a jail, and this jail exerts its influence on the child. Language is the first influence. Family, school, multiple societal organizations, work—everything we call society—starts to influence him. The experience the child receives is the

136

experience of society. **So, who creates this jail, and who maintains it?**

A human being himself creates this jail, because his notions of the world and other people are who he is. He is his own jail.

Who gave him these notions? Society did. Who is interested in backing up these notions? It is the people surrounding him. Asking these questions, we start digging, and try to get to the root cause of it. Do you think your family is interested in your program being changed? Do you think your coworkers are interested in your program being changed? Do you think society you live in is interested in your program being changed? No. None of them is interested because it would mean that a ring is going to be dropped out of the mechanical chain. The next question arises, **"Who do you want to satisfy?"** If you were born to fulfill the requirements of a certain human being or a certain organization, then there is no reason to change yourself, since in wanting something new or different, you will lose what you have. But if you want to understand something new and get outside the limits of this mechanism, inside of which you represent some kind of screw, you will be interested in it. All your mechanical surroundings are not interested in it, with a possible exception of people who also want to wake up and return to themselves, to the lost House of Reality.

For example, your wife is convinced that you should make a certain sum of money because she wants to maintain a certain lifestyle. Suddenly, your convictions change, and you say, "I don't owe anything to anyone. I may do certain things if I want to do them, but I may decide not to do them." In the beginning, she will listen and smile, but when she gets it and understands that you are serious, she will stop smiling, and can start doing something about it. If you tell your boss, "You know, you constantly reprimand me. You think I should do something, but I think I should not be doing it at all," at first he will be shocked, and then he may fire you. He will say, "What do I need him for? I will find someone who will do it," and he will find this someone. Therefore, it is really quite an important question, **"Who is it that wants these changes?"**

Spiritual growth—who and how to define it

Who is it in you that wants to move somewhere, and who is it in you that determines how to move? Who determines it? Who is it in you who says, "I am not satisfied with the way I am?" It is the same mind we have been talking about. We say, "To observe, to be aware." But don't you observe yourself anyway? For example, if you were to approach someone and suddenly one of your inner parts were to declare, "Why are you so weak? Why can't you do anything?" **Inside each man there are number of parts—multiple fragments of the mind. One fragment observes another. One fragment does not want to change, while another screams, "What are you waiting for? Get up. Let's go. It is time for a change." But all this is happening inside your mind. So, who is observing whom over there? Who is making this decision regarding who and how is to change? Is change possible at all? And if we were to change, who is it that determines the character of these changes? Who controls how this change is to happen?** Suddenly, someone yells, "Let's change!" – "And what needs to be done?" – "It is necessary to go to school and study Holistic Psychology." – "Excellent. Let's go to school." Then someone asks, "So what happened? You are going to school, did something change?" And the answer is, "No. Nothing happened and nothing has changed," or "Yes. It is amazing and many things changed." What is it that changes there? One part of your brain is observing another

138

part of your brain. The one observing becomes the most important and dominant. It starts to critique the other part. But then it leaves and another part shows up and starts its observation and critique. You may ask, "What makes this specific part dominant?" This question cannot be answered theoretically or philosophically. The answer to this question is practical and can be found only by you. My mind has certain fragments. Your fragments are different. You need to figure out which fragments of your mind dominate and which are suppressed. How many are there? What are they?

Your mind says, "Let's change." Then it says, "Let's not change." The mind is a worker and a controller, a thief and a policeman catching a thief. Can you imagine what is going inside your mind?

Now the question arises: "Do real changes occur in you or all of this is just a play of the fragments of your mind?" I have this question. Do you have an answer?

Self-observation and the knowledge of oneself

Awareness is great power. It separates what you need from what you do not need. We don't have to spend a lot of time discussing what you need and what you don't need now, but this is the major topic of your reflections on your life and destiny, when you sit down and think: "Did I do it right or did I do it wrong? Should I do this or should I not do this? Is this so or is this not so?" **Awareness provides you with power that helps you to discern what you really need from what you don't need.** However, you need to learn how to use it. This is the work you need to do in order to direct your attention inward, into your thoughts, feelings, and sensations.

In the beginning you will observe what is known to you. If you are used to observing your body, you will have multiple observations of your bodily sensations. If you are used to following your feelings, you will have multiple observations of your feelings. If you are used to tracing your thoughts, you will have multiple observations of your thoughts. It is possible that you don't see anything inside of you at all. That is even more common. For now, just start to observe your manifestations in different situations. It is only from this experience that the knowledge of yourself may come.

When you talk about something it does not mean you are aware of what you are talking about. When you feel something, it does not mean you are aware of your feelings. When you are doing something, it does not mean you are aware of what you are doing. When you are thinking about something, it does not mean you are aware of what you are thinking about. Many thoughts can flash through your mind. Are you aware of them? They have passed already. Every one of you experiences multiple feelings and sensations passing through you every minute. Are you aware of them? They are there. So, where is the fullness of the awareness?

How aware are you? In the evening, having lived through a full day, you may say, "Yes, I remember one sensation: I had a sharp pain in my side when someone pushed me on the street." Meanwhile, you have had millions of sensations. During one day you became aware of two thoughts: your boss called you an idiot, but later he praised you. I am exaggerating, but in reality, out of the enormous flow of infinite internal changes, one separates only a few fragments.

Try to start this observation. You will see what you observe, how you observe, how long you are able to be in the state of self-observation. What do you observe more frequently, and what don't you observe? If you were able to simultaneously see your feelings and thoughts while being in a certain situation, perhaps you would be able to notice that certain thoughts give birth to certain feelings, other thoughts give birth to certain sensations. You may notice that certain sensations give birth to certain thoughts and feelings. For example, when you assume a certain pose, a certain thought or a certain sensation appears. That is why habitual poses are accompanied by habitual thoughts and habitual feelings.

Every one of us has a certain number of poses. When you are sitting in a certain pose, you have precisely certain thoughts. You may see them if you start to become aware of them. If you change a pose, something else may appear. Perhaps no thoughts appear, since for this pose you do not have any thoughts yet. They have not been developed. It is exactly in this pose that you can understand something new. When you are sitting in a pose that is habitual for you, certain habitual thoughts and feelings pass through you. For example, when what is written here is congruent with your thoughts and feelings, habitual for this pose, agreement will arise in you. What is not congruent will cause a disagreement. Does anything change? No, nothing changes. It is similar to a radio tuned to a certain wavelength. Suddenly, you get into a completely unusual for you pose. Your habitual thoughts and feelings has not been associated with this pose yet. Then what is written here may enter you. Become aware of the positioning of your body. What kind of habitual thoughts and feelings are characteristic for it? How does it influence your perception of the book you are reading now?

I don't want you to accept my words as an axiom. Try it. Just try it. Everything I say is an invitation to an investigation. You will try it and then you will be able to jump up and get to something else. Any method, any technique used multiple times becomes a habit. For many people, a prayer is just a habit, just a mechanical repetition. It leads nowhere. **Everything that is repeatable tends to become mechanical. What is**

141

not repeatable does not become mechanical. Awareness is spontaneity. Actions of a mechanical human being are easy to foresee. He is programmed. I know what to expect from him. He has but a few ways to think, feel, and act. I can easily predict his actions. But the one who is aware is impossible to predict. He is spontaneous. You never know what he will do. He does not have a template. He always acts in an unusual way. That is a real development or enlightenment. That is awareness, not a mechanical behavior. Unfortunately, even work with awareness may become mechanical. Many people get into that trap.

What about you?

The illusion of meditation

What is awareness? The words "meditation" and "awareness" are frequently used together. Many books have been written on the subject. A man reads and starts to follow these recommendations believing he is meditating and becoming aware. It seems to him he is approaching the final destination. In reality, it is complete nonsense, as it is just a repetition of something. What do people do when they meditate? They get a certain pleasure out of the recreation of certain pleasurable images. For example, a man who considers himself religious, associates his pleasant thoughts and feelings with the image of God, "meditates" on this image and gets a certain pleasure in connection with it. Another man "meditates" on a glass of beer or a well-done steak. If you are hungry, you can "meditate" on anything you want.

People usually don't call it meditation, but that is exactly what happens here. A man walks down the street tired, and suddenly an image of a bottle of beer and a plate of French fries appears, accompanied by an image of a friend he can talk to while having this meal. This is his "meditation." He does not call it meditation, but the mechanism is the same. Many people are sitting around some guru, meditating, so to speak. They just reproduce different images, and consider themselves to be "spiritual." Please, don't talk to them about it; they will not like this point of view.

So, what is awareness? A man becomes aware when he starts seeing the falsity of something he considered to be right and important. A man who becomes aware refuses himself this pleasure—pleasure of being right and important. That is a difficult thing to do. It is difficult to refuse the false personality.

Are you ready for awareness?

The awareness of fear

You can hear people say, "I frequently find myself in a state of an alarm. It bothers me significantly. It is something that is sitting inside me searching for an exit. Being in such a state, I want to break something. Sometimes I do break things. Sometimes, while in this state, I scream at people. If I don't do it, I feel very bad." Have you experienced such a state?

And what if you were to allow yourself to experience such a state? The state of, "I want to break... I want to yell at... I want to..." In reality, you want to avoid this state. But what if you were to allow yourself to get into the very depth of this state? This state is hiding a very important secret. You can find it. You can observe all your states, including this. **There is no fear where and when awareness is present.**

Why does one constantly need to apply efforts, to do something, to explain and to plan something? It is because one is afraid! Because one is afraid that something may not go right. It is a constant fear that is manifested differently. One is afraid one is going to be fired from a job. One is afraid of not having enough money to pay for an apartment. One is afraid of a partner leaving. It is a constant unexplainable fear. One projects it outside trying to embody it in certain people and situations, in order to fight it. But what if you were to try to **become aware of it? Don't do anything.** Do not undertake any actions. **Simply observe** what is happening in you.

Don't push your thoughts and feelings away—just observe them. **Let what happens happen.** Certain thoughts are passing through your mind. Become aware of them. Don't try to turn your mind off; you will not be able to do so. Become aware of what is going on there. **Observe it without any judgment. Don't grade it.**

For example, you see someone who is begging for money, and a thought appears, "Here you go, another beggar. They are all beggars here." Then you observe another thought, "Why am I being so rude? Let me give him some money." What happens here? It is just one fragment of your mind critiquing another. This is not awareness. **Awareness is an observation without a choice,** just an observation of what is going on in your internal world. Let these fragments explore their relationships. Observe them. You are outside of it. Just observe what is happening inside of your mind. You observe the expression of the different viewpoints of certain fragments of your mind. The awareness is observation without any involvement in what you are observing. Perhaps, certain frightening thoughts will appear in your mind, and you will not be able to impartially observe them. You will sink deep into the morass of your own mind again. You have many thoughts you are afraid of. It is a repetition of what happened to you before. The mind recorded everything you have experienced in your life, and now it regurgitates it in certain situations. For example, you are afraid you are going to be fired. Perhaps, it happened to you before. But even now, when you come to work, this fear rises up when you see your supervisor. He is not firing you now, but the image of the past is so strong that when you see your supervisor, you get scared. In your mind, he is already firing you. But this is just the image from the library of your mind. If you become aware of this, you will see it not as reality, but simply as the image from the past. This is a very important moment. The mind constantly reproduces images and thoughts that we accept as real. As soon as you start to think that it is real, you get into a mind trap, and the mind sucks you into its sphere.

What are you afraid of more than anything? Become aware of your fear right now.

Are you ready to perceive something new?

Do you think one has any idea what "new" is when one says, "I want something new?" Why are you happy and excited sometimes about what happened during these meetings you were engaged in during your search for something new, and sometimes disappointed and depressed? What do you think are the roots of the fluctuation of these feelings? Is there something that you usually expect and presume to get by saying that you want something new? Do you have any notion of what it is you really want when you say you want something new?

Have you noticed that a man talking about his desire to experience something new, in reality seeks to repeat certain pleasant states he experienced in the past? And what is a pleasant state? A pleasant state is a state that he calls pleasant— a state he defined for himself as pleasant. If he is able to reproduce this state, he says, "Excellent, everything was great, I experienced something new." But did he really experience anything new? I question this. Did one really receive anything new? That's my question. I frequently observe this during my

145

meetings, seminars, and consultations. When a human being feels good, i.e. re-experiences the state previously enjoyed, he says it was great, something new was received, something helpful and useful, and now he is ready to change and to move forward. He recapitulates a number of criteria convincing himself that everything is all right, that this place is worth coming to, it has everything he wanted. On the other hand if he experiences some kind of feelings that he defines as unpleasant, he says exactly the same, but with an opposite sign, with a minus sign. I did not get anything new, did not receive anything useful, etc. Have you noticed this pattern of reaction in other people or in yourself?

But how will you know you have learned something new? What should the state of a human being be, that will allow him to experience the entrance of something new? Notice, I used the word "enters." I did not use the word, "take." I said, "to experience the entrance of something new." Can you feel the difference?

A man comes to a library because he is not familiar with a certain subject, chemistry for example, and wants to learn it. He burrows a corresponding book, reads it, and now he knows this topic.

Did he learn anything new? On one hand, yes. He took this knowledge and memorized it. We can say he possesses it now. But is this knowledge his own, or did he just memorize something someone else offered? Can he consider this knowledge to be his own? This is question number one. A second question: is this knowledge new? One who wrote a book most likely was stepping on and using the knowledge received from others. It is possible that his views were conditioned by beliefs and convictions shared by a community of scientists working in a given field. For someone not familiar with these views, they are new.

On one hand, this is true. He did not know that, but now he knows. He took this knowledge, memorized it, and can repeat it now. Notice that he already knew what he wanted, what he was missing. He knew what it was and where to get it. But is the knowledge he received from the book really new? Who requested this knowledge? It was requested by his mind in order to fill some kind of a gap, which developed in relationship to his desire to get something, to achieve something. Perhaps he was performing a school assignment. It is connected to the desire of his mind to achieve a certain aim. What if this aim developed due to dissatisfaction of the mind, and is therefore in its sphere? Can one have something new in the sphere of the mind or is it always a repetition?

This was discussed already. Why? Because this book was not written with an aim to increase the amount of knowledge related to the sphere of the mind of the reader. If that were the case, its value would be insignificant. Your mind would rejoice again to receive food so much needed, but nothing really new would happen. What is knowledge? How does the usual establishment of learning understand it? Knowledge is some kind of information transferred to a student in order for him to remember it and to be able to repeat it. In fact, it is tuning of the mind to a strict definitive perspective of vision of what the subject of learning happens to be. That kind of learning makes the mind hard and certain in its rightfulness, which at the end leads to its degradation.

This book is for those who want to investigate what exits the scope of the conditioned mind, created by traditional upbringing and education. We attempt to touch something new and unknown, to see the usual from the unusual point of view. This new vision is impossible to obtain in the ways we are used to, but it can enter us if we were to allow ourselves to become open to it. It can happen if we are able to free our mind from habitual notions, convictions, judgments, and beliefs. Holistic vision allows us to see the limitations created by our mind, and this is what clear vision is, the Truth.

But can the Truth enter us the way a shy person enters a big room full of important people who show displeasure seeing the uninvited guest? Will the Truth be satisfied by a small space in the corner of the room which turned out to be free because no one occupied it yet? Is that the way for the Truth to enter— looking shyly for an open spot? Or, should it enter head high, clearing up everything obstructing its way? What do you think? Should the unknown enter a place completely occupied by old and habitual? Or should it enter as a revolution, changing everything that has been there before?

The state of disbelief—the border of known

When and why do revolutions occur? Let us take social processes. Is the probability of having a revolution high when people have a strong faith in some kind of a symbol: church, monarchy, democracy or do revolutions occur when a state of disbelief develops and acquires power?

When does disenchantment develop in people beliefs? For example, in a country ruled by a monarchy, the force of different circumstances shakes and tumbles the belief in the monarch and monarchy in general. However, because this belief was the main binding force of the country, unbelief and chaos develop. Then some people show up bringing another belief. At the time when the monarchy in Russia started to crumble the Bolsheviks showed up. They believed in communism. And even though they called themselves atheists and materialists, what they offered was just another form of an orthodox religion. They believed in their symbols—symbols of communism, and they were ready to sacrifice in their name.

These sacrifices were made. Many people were killed in the name of "a bright future." That's how one belief was changed by another. The state of unbelief, the absence of hope for better life is a state that leads to revolution, chaos, and riots. How long can a state withstand this condition, and can it be called a state if it happens to be in such a condition for a prolonged period of time? A state is a certain structure that tries to reinforce and keep its power and influence. In order for a state to exist, it needs an ideology and economy, i.e. beliefs in certain ideals and symbols. If the majority of people in a state do not have a belief in the symbols offered by state leaders, the society deteriorates.

That is what we see in the external world. What do we see in our internal worlds? The external world is a reflection of our internal world. What happens in the external world also happens in the internal world of a human being.

What happens to a man when he loses his faith? Hope and beliefs are what the mind, the personality cannot live without. The predominant number of people believes in something. You don't necessarily have to be what they call "a religious person." Everyone believes in something of his own: money, power, prestige, one or another god, etc. If such a human being were to stop believing in something, he would find something else to believe in. Dissuaded in a given political movement, he will search for another. Disenchanted in certain spiritual ideas, he will search and change them for others. He may also find methods to forget. What we are discussing here is nothing but socially developed ways of escape, ways to leave oneself. To believe in certain symbols is a reliable method of forgetting oneself. A belief is something that the personality needs to keep and reinforce in itself in order not to allow the entrance of the unknown.

One believes in something. It is impossible to believe just in order to believe, without a subject. That is why as a symbol of belief some kind of an image is taken by the human mind. Moreover, the majority of people who believe in something do not create this image themselves, but get it readymade in a form of political, religious or some other organization.

Why do so many people require these organizations and the symbols of belief offered by them? They do so because they promise some form of a future prize to believers, in "the bright future" of communist society or heaven in the skies for those who believe in God. A believer can never be by himself; inside of him, the image of his belief is always present, preventing him from seeing anything not corresponding to this image. As a result, he sacrifices himself for the dubious comfort that a belief in a certain symbol provides.

Both hope and belief represent a transfer of the past into the future. This is a way the mind constantly recreates itself, repeating the same story over and over again. A personality thinks, "I feel bad now, and I felt bad before, but I hope I will feel good in the future." That allows a believer to live his days dwelling in an illusion of some future transformation and improvement. But the real transformation is possible only in the present moment, not sometime later. If we were to look at the majority of people impartially, we would see that they live constantly repeating the same thing, believing that something good will happen to them, as a result of which their life will get better. Notice how propaganda is built on this: political, religious, etc. Billions of people live having some kind of hope or a belief. But why do you need hope or belief if you happen to be in reality, here and now? Hope and belief turn us toward the future because we are not satisfied by our present. But what we consider to be our present is only our past.

If you were truly present in reality, in the present, there would not be any need to believe in something. Why would you need to believe in something if you already happen to be in what is? It means you are not satisfied with it, and then the necessity to hope and to believe develops. We are describing characteristics of the mind now. We already investigated it from different sides, and now we are looking at it from another side. This is a very interesting aspect of the function of the human mind and personality because it is precisely hope and belief that do not allow you to get something really new, to see the unknown. It is hope and belief which prevent you from an opportunity to exit the limits of the self-contained, closed, and conditioned sphere of the mind. Hope and belief keep you in a sphere of the fragments of your mind as gravitation keeps you on Earth. Disenchanted in one fragment of your mind, you search and find another one. But the mind contains a multitude of different parts and fragments; to sift through all of them takes a long time and strong effort. There are a huge variety of fragments. Hope and belief turn the point of view from one fragment, which you believe you have exhausted, to another fragment. It is similar to jumping in a swamp, from one hummock to another. Trying to escape, you jump from one hummock to another, unable to see that they happen to create a circle. It seems to you, just one more jump and you will escape, but in reality you move in circles, returning to the same hummocks, not recognizing them. But why are you jumping? Why don't you stop to figure out what is happening to you? It happens because you hope and believe.

Take a look at someone who claims to have met a true spiritual system or has gone through a great training, and who now thinks he underwent amazing changes, improved and is moving toward something substantial and very important. If you are observant, you will notice that he simply believes in it.

He excites himself and other people by the power of his belief. The more he hopes and believes, the more excited he gets, even though it does not necessarily show externally. But after a certain period of time this excitement drops, disenchantment steps into the place of this particular belief, and he needs to apply efforts in order to sustain this belief. His internal sufferings intensify. He becomes doubtful. But the fear of losing the ground offered by this belief prompts him to apply even more efforts in order to convince himself of the righteousness of his belief. It is interesting that he starts to convince others (frequently very successfully), while in reality he is trying to convince himself.

To meet reality and the unknown, you should try not to hold tight to the departing belief, or immediately look for a substitute, but prudently and attentively investigate the state of the absence of the belief. It is a state when the mind stops clinging to any images, symbols, systems, etc. This state is a door into the unknown, a door toward yourself. Will you allow yourself to approach this door or will you run away again, searching for the next illusory hope?" – "Father! Why did you forsake me?" – screamed Jesus as he was nailed to the cross. I presume that this is precisely a signpost to such a state. If you are ready to move all the way to yourself, you cannot walk around this state, because you either change one illusion to the next, the thousand and first time regaining what is called hope and belief, or you throw all this away and enter the state of reality where NOTHING and at the same time EVERYTHING is present at once. It is precisely this state, this reality, that personality and the mind are afraid of more than anything else, because it is a state of impersonality, a state of mindlessness. It is that strip, that neutral zone, which is situated at the very border of the conditioned mind. It is an area of the unknown, where words cannot express or define anything. This is not what the conditioned mind wants to enclose in the word "unknown." This word is used quite differently.

Let's say a certain neighborhood is unknown to me. I drove there, inspected it, and now think it is known to me. The meaning of this word in common day language is completely different. For example, in a TV advertisement the voice behind the screen says, "Kathryn discovered 'Always' tampons." A happy Kathryn tells us how she discovered these miraculous tampons, which were previously unknown to her. Unknown is what is outside the borders of the mind, it is the exit behind the boundaries of power and laws of the conditioned mind.

$2 = 1$

One can find two opposite sides in everything. When someone falls on one side and says, "This is horrible," I say: "Are you sure? Let's take a look from another side." Afterwards he says, "Oh! But this was great." I say, "Hold it. Do you remember what you were saying just a minute ago?" Suddenly, he sees this "great" and this "horrible" simultaneously. To see two sides of something simultaneously is to see holistically.

Our superficial, conditioned mind is fragmented and limited. It is capable of seeing only one side at any given moment, one face of what it encounters. If you have observed your own mind, you have probably noticed that at any given moment in time only one thought is present there. Then it is changed to another. At any discrete moment in time, the mind is limited; it is stuck inside the borders of one thought only, and this thought defines its perception of what is happening. Because any thought is limited and circumscribed in itself, the mind's perception is fragmented, partial. But if the mind is in a state of no-thought, its perception becomes holistic. This is clear vision. This is awareness. It does not require the intermediary of the mind. It does not require the presence of any kind of thought. That kind of perception, external to mentation, is the true understanding. Attempts to express this vision, in words distort it, make it partial and incomplete.

It is very important to overcome the duality of the mind's perception and to see what happens to you holistically.

Look at yourself from different sides. When you see yourself from multiple opposite points of view simultaneously, you get into the position of equilibrium. It is only in that state, that one can let go of what one calls "my problem," which gives birth to pain and suffering. As paradoxical as it may sound, suffering is as difficult to let go of as pleasure, because the mind is equally attached to both of them. It is the interchange of suffering and pleasure that supports and reinforces your problem.

Imagine a rope. One side of it is tied to your hand. The other end is tied to the hand of another human being. Each one of you is pulling on this rope in opposite directions, with equal force. Are you capable of releasing this rope that, due to applied tension, tightens more and more around your hand? You will only be able to do so when both of you stop applying these opposing efforts. Then, the tension on both ends of the rope will disappear, and it will drop on its own. That is the only way of doing it. But in order to do so, it is necessary to simultaneously stop applying all efforts.

Non-effort is a state of being where the mind can see holistically. Thinking is always an effort. That is why "thinking through," pondering some kind of a problem, leads to its exacerbation.

When Buddha went through all possible teachers, all possible techniques, and then, completely exhausted from all these useless efforts leaned back on a tree, he experienced the awakening. It is precisely in this state of exhaustion that it happened to him. He did not hope for anything anymore. He did not hope for anything because he had been through everything: all the teachers, all the techniques, everything there was. Nothing to hope for, exhausted, he leaned on a tree and it came to him on its own. He came to the border of total unbelief and absence of any kind of hope, and he passed this zone too.

How to untangle the psychological knot

You can become aware of something in yourself only by doing it yourself. Nobody can do it for you. As a rule, the investigation continues until the moment when you get stuck in a conviction that you don't want to let go of something. If you don't want to see it, the investigation is stalled.

The investigation is something that helps us to approach the limitations we built for ourselves. At this point the investigation can only continue if we are ready to see the fence we installed. We collide with our deep conviction, with a certain important belief.

In the process of reading this book, you will approach your main convictions. If you wish to see them, you will see them. The vision is action. If you will really see them, all the falsehood related to them will disappear forever. When I say "vision," I mean holistic vision. It is a vision of both sides of a given phenomenon.

A vision of both sides of your relationships will allow you to encompass them wholly. Only in this case will the ball of knots of your problems untangle.

What are these knots? For example, I take a rope and tie a knot, and then another one, and one more. Why do these knots hold? What holds them together? It is a force of friction. If I were to remove friction, the knots would untie by themselves. What is a problem if not a knot? It is the knot, which collects multiple ropes and nodes of opposite convictions, opinions, and beliefs.

In making efforts to untie a psychological knot, one frequently ties it even further, to the point where it is impossible to find from which side to approach it. But a professional, to whom one turns for help, will say, "I know how to untie it." This professional will start pulling on one "rope" or another, depending on which concept or theory he operates on. And here you go. He starts pulling one end out, at the same time entangling the knot further. He pulls and pulls, and because of it, the knot gets tighter.

This "psychological knot" can be untied only when the problem is seen as a whole—all the sides simultaneously. At this point friction disappears and the knot unties on its own without effort. Any effort just makes the knot tighter, and entangles it further. Any given effort produces a further pull, at least in some aspects of a knot. But if efforts are strong and chaotic, the entanglement gets stronger in all parts of the knot.

You have probably seen a bob used for fishing. It is usually marked with two colors: one part is the underwater part, another part stays above the water. A fisherman throws a line. The bob dangles on the surface of the water, one part in the air, another in water, and somewhere below there is a line, weight, and a hook. A fish pulls on the hook. The bigger the weight of the fish, the stronger the pull and the deeper the bob submerges in water. Sometimes the whole air part of the bob submerges in the water. This bob represents the state a human being is in.

If one does not know anything except one's personal desires, we can say that one's personal attachments are constantly activated, keeping one constantly under water.

Multiple hooks-desires constantly aim to catch and keep the prey. These desires drag the bob deeper and deeper. That is why not only the submerged but the air part of the bob is constantly hidden deep under the water. For such people, the state when they happen to be in the air may be very infrequent, fleeting seconds. At all other times they are deeply submerged in water. What if one were to cut the line underneath with the weight and the hook? What would happen? The whole bob would pop up to the surface. When nothing is dragging the bob from below, it ascends to the surface completely. Now the bigger part is in a different environment—in the air. That is the analogy.

It all depends on a human being. If one really wants to be free, one will discover it; if not, there is nothing to talk about. There is no guarantee here and cannot be. In the process of self-investigation, everyone will approach the "internal fences." What will happen next depends on one's willingness to see them. Is one ready to see what is hiding behind them or not? These are not happy encounters, because these are the fences one is constantly running away from. Now one is being offered a chance to see them and to return; this is the only way to return to oneself.

The return route will be exactly the same route you took to escape. The route you took to run away from yourself, now you will have to take to return to yourself. One will use the same roads and intersections. Many want these roads to be beautiful and to pass through arches of triumph, flowers, and congratulations. Perhaps somebody has already offered you this road. This is a trick. On your return, you will have to use the same road you used to escape. Walking this road, you will encounter everything you were running away from. This is the only way to yourself. The speed of your movement will depend on your readiness.

The road back toward yourself starts from a 180 degree turn, as no other turn will allow you to return. It is possible to flip 360 degrees and to start running in the same direction.

The road home is a hard road, but at the same time it is a happy road. It is impossible for the way to be universal, to fit everyone, as each and every one used different escape routes to run from themselves. The return will not be collective. What is universal for all of us walking Home is this 180 degree turn and a walk without turning back. Each will use his own road, walking to wholeness.

CHAPTER 5:
TOWARD AWARENESS OF SELF

•◆•◆•◆•◆•◆•◆•◆•◆•◆•◆•◆•◆•◆•◆•◆•◆•

Who will buy the ticket to reality?

Is there anything outside of what we know?

There is an external reality that we know. If we were to turn to our inner reality, we would see that what happens inside us is exactly what happens in the outside world. The problems we observe around and far away from us, with people close and not so close to us are all the same and exist in every human being. Is there an exit from this closed circle of common problems? If so, **where is this exit?** All your attempts to solve these problems and conflicts lead nowhere. Years pass by, but nothing changes. What can be done? Can something be done? If there is nothing else there, then irrespective of time passing—ten, twenty, or fifty years—the same situations will continue to recur.

Is there anything else there aside from all these problems? Is there **some other kind of Life, some kind of different perception of Life?** If there is some other Life, **can one get to know it here,** in this body, not after physical death? What kind of Life is it? Some people say there is a material side to life; others insist there is also a spiritual side. They start to argue, trying to find out which one of them is more spiritual and which one is more material. We are constantly confronted with divisions, partitions, and dualities: this life—that life, this world—that world. Can a man that exist here, in this physical reality, **be simultaneously present in some other reality?**

Some philosophers have come to the conclusion that there is no meaning in this life. Perhaps, we should look for an exit using a different, unusual method? This exit cannot be found using the mind. One needs to use a different organ.

Where is this organ? Does it exist? If you were to tell your friend that you are searching for an exit and the organ that would help you find this exit, how would he react?

Are you ready to see something new, something unknown? One may investigate and ponder different things, different fragments and different aspects for a long period of time. What if there is nothing behind all of them, but just an interesting intellectual game? What if there is no exit? What if our only option is to change candy wrappers, to change certain forms? What if you just plow one field after another? You may say, "There are many fields out there. I will plow them all, one by one. That will at least occupy me. One has to do something anyway as long as one is alive. I will plow these fields, and cultivate them. I will consider all possible perspectives."

This is not a philosophical, but a practical question. If there is nothing else, nothing new and different under the sun, then why are we here? Why do we need all this mess? But if something else exists, then **how can we get there?**

Who are these people that stop on their Way to themselves? These are people who could not or decided not to taste That Life.

Can your mind help you in this endeavor? No. The mind can only prepare you to get as far away from That Life as possible. That is not the life the mind can or wants to live in.

The mind will never buy a ticket to That Life. If we were to discover That Life, it would happen not because but despite of the mind.

Then the question arises: if it happens, **not thanks to the mind but despite the mind**, then what do we attribute this to? This is not a rhetorical question.

I cannot say. I do not know when, how, or who with it may happen. In my opinion, this is something that is impossible to plan. Yet, I see that some people walk toward it and some get off the track.

Why do some people continue walking this path? What is it that guides them? Whatever it is, it is not the mind. The mind can only take you away from the path. It is something completely different that guides you.

Perhaps, it starts with an understanding that you don't know anything about yourself, about other people, about the world.

When you suddenly understand that you don't know anything, when it really happens to you, it is a shock. It comes with pain. The mind wants to define everything. It wants to foresee and to explain everything. But you need to see this activity of your mind on a daily basis.

The mind clings to different things, and each one of us clings to something different. **There are no two people with identical hooks of the mind. That is why our pathways are not the same.** One can let go of one's first, second and third hook, but will hang on the fourth. It is precisely this fourth hook that his personality will find comfort in. He will say, "Okay, I don't know this and I don't know that, but I know for sure that at seven o'clock, I will come to a place I call home, and nothing will interfere with my evening cup of tea."

One keeps something for himself. That's something he wants to be sure of one hundred percent. For example, he says to himself, "These people do not respect me, but I have one friend who, I know for sure, respects me."

The mind will never buy a ticket to **That Life**, because **That Life** is completely different—you cannot define anything there.

To get in touch with That Life means, for just a moment, to not know anything, to not know anything at all.

But because our heads are filled to the brim with knowledge, to not to know anything, to be empty is something incomprehensible for the mind.

It is not just unusual and terrible. It is something totally incomprehensible in the sense that it is impossible to imagine. You let go of one thing only to find out that you are attached to many other things. One says, "How much farther? I am so tired. Do I really need **That Life**? I have renounced so much, but it appears I am still attached to other things." There are people that have such strong longing, they go till the end. Others don't have such longing. **It is longing, great longing that may help you to get there.**

What does a man usually want? For example, if he studies, he wants to get a diploma. Having a diploma he will get a good salary, status, and weight in the eyes of other people. Look how good it is. A man's life is aimed to get something for the personality, something that will aggrandize and reinforce it. We acquire knowledge, things, relationships, and respect. **We invest our energy only in what later would provide a visible return to our personality.**

Here, on the other hand, we have something completely different: great fervor aimed at letting go of everything, the **complete opposite of** something that the mind does. To let go of everything that was stored! We are not talking about material things. We are talking about the disposal of your attachments to all of your convictions. If you are **really**

serious about this work and understand its necessity, you will not hold on to anything you had before. You will not try to hold on to the old knowledge. You will let go of all your attachments, convictions, and believes. You need to let go of them all. Your mind will not like it. It will get resentful. It will say, "Enough of this game. I don't like it anymore." The mind plays these games until the mind gets something for itself, but as soon as it stops getting something, it stops wanting it.

So, where is this passion coming from, the passion of the one who lets go of everything he has?

It comes from the passion that is bigger and stronger than the mind.

It is thanks to this passion that one can touch something real—That Life. This **great opportunity is given to every human being**. If you have never touched That Life and don't know the taste of it, it will only be words for you. Intellectual conversations will lead you until your intellect is interested in them, but if you get a taste of That Life, real life, **you will not be able to walk away from it**. Then the longing is born which can overcome everything. This longing, this fervor is akin to a drowning man who extends his hand to catch a tree branch to save himself. He is taken by the current, but still strives to save himself. That is the longing, the **longing for Life**. When he starts to drown, when he sees death, the great strength, the great longing is born in him. It helps him to extend his arm and pull himself out. That is the longing I am talking about.

The majority of people only show this fervor when they are about to lose their bodies. I am talking about fervor of a different kind. I am talking about fervor which develops while the body is in a normal state. The majority of people will say, "What kind of fervor are you talking about? I am fine. I have a nice house, and I drive a good car. Why would I extend my arm?"

Where is this longing coming from? Where is our man going? **He is fighting for Life. He wants to Live.** Someone may find it strange when a man who is physically well develops fervor to Live. But for the one in question it is similar to the **rescuing of the drowning man or the freeing of the prisoner.** Whoever takes a breath of **that air** will always strive for it. **He will not be able to live without that air.**

So, what kind of life is it? Why does one, having once tasted that air, develop such fervor for it? What is there? Can it be explained to one who has never experienced it? How can you explain it? To explain it mind to mind is impossible.

This can be explained only by giving a man an opportunity to catch a breath of that air on his own, if, of course, he wants to. When he tastes it, the necessity of explaining anything will disappear.

Someone **caught a breath and touched That Life,** and someone did not. That is the only difference. The one who never did will simply talk about it.

But is it possible to enter it using the mind? Will the mind buy a ticket to travel there? **Does the mind need That Life?**

In this life, the mind is commander in chief. Science and new technological developments are carried only through the mind, and the mind can do a lot. It is a tool that can create amazing things: cars, airplanes, robots. This is its sphere, its turf.

But over there is something different. Over there, none of this is necessary. **What is there?** We say "That Life," and "over There." It is very hard to understand this using everyday language. **We say "over there," but in reality, this Life is Here."**

It is just as if we were blind. We don't see it. We don't notice it. It is inside each and every one of us, but one does not see it.

164

Investigating your internal world, you will see that you have created it based on an image analogous to the material world, where the mind is king. **But in fact, the mind is just a servant**. It can be a great servant, but it should not be a master. **To acquire a real master** means to remember oneself, to return to oneself. That is the most important reason for our being here.

Life, the breath of which I am discussing, is **so loving**, it cannot be compared to anything else. It gives one a chance, a great opportunity **to know oneself.** It provides everything a human being needs. But personality prevents one from seeing it.

Where is That Life? It is everywhere. Everything is saturated by it. **It is the essence of all things**. That Life pierces everything, everything we see, hear, sense, and everything we don't yet see, hear, sense. Everything is pierced by it. **It is everything**.

But how can one get to see it? How can one get there? What kinds of circumstances would allow one to see it better? **We are these circumstances**. The lives of every single one of us are filed with circumstances, which provide an opportunity to become aware. Animals do not have this opportunity, plants do not have this opportunity, and minerals do not have this opportunity, but human being does. An animal does not have a personality; it has instincts, reflexes, pleasures, pains, laws it lives by, laws of nature. But an animal does not have the opportunities a human being has.

Have you ever paid attention to **the eyes of household animals**? They are not in the wild, yet not in a human world. There are dogs with very sad eyes. Wild animals do not have this sadness in their eyes. What is it that separates these animals from others, who are similar to them but wild?

Domesticated animals have come in touch with something that they do not understand. They have come in touch with a human being. Perhaps they start to feel something completely unknown to them, something related to the human world. Maybe some impulse develops in them in relation to this, an impulse they do not have an opportunity to realize. They are in a tragic state. **They feel an impulse that is beyond their understanding,** but lack the ability to realize it.

A human being has this opportunity. He can realize it. And this opportunity may be realized, not in some laboratory, not in the Himalayas, not in a monastery cell, but in ordinary conditions. **We are already living in the necessary for us conditions.** If we really want to take a breath of that air, that's where we need to start; from the spot we are in right now.

I don't know why some people strive toward That Life so much while others do not.

That Life is Life where one constantly meets the unknown. That is why the mind constantly resists and denies it. It does not want to accept the presence of something it cannot know, its **inability to plan**, to be the master. This is the most complicated, but also the basic moment: **to live not knowing, not thinking.**

I am not saying I don't use the mind at all. When I cross the street, I perform a certain mind operation appraising my environment. I use a computer and I contemplate how to position the text. I am engaged in multiple technical questions. I do not deny the mind's functionality during these multiple actions I perform. These are important and necessary functions of the mind. I mean something different when I talk about "Life without thinking." I really want to make this clear, to somehow pass it on.

If one is involved with technical questions for a long time, the mind takes over because it is very active. Some people

166

become workaholics? Why? It happens because their mind is constantly active, constantly working at full speed. When this full speed is not used in some action, one starts to feel bad. That is why one **constantly needs to do something**: read a newspaper, move stuff from place to place, or talk to someone. One has to constantly occupy himself. When the mind is continually doing something, solving all these problems it created itself, you can, after a while, forget that there is something else, something you breathed in before.

The Way is similar to walking a rope. If you are far to the right, you fall. If you are far to the left, you fall; **you need to walk the rope straight**. You have to **use** the mind and at the same time you have to **turn it off**. This is a movement on the border, **life on the border**, movement on the rope.

Fall into the "material," and you will have nothing but the mind, there is nothing else there. You are solving your technical problems very successfully, but you are already down.

Fall into the "spiritual," and it is impossible to say whether you live here or not.

How is one to walk this rope? Have you ever asked this question? This question is not theoretical or philosophical, but a practical one. If one walks on the left side, one has certain questions. If one walks on the right side, one has different questions. If one walks in the middle, he has completely different questions.

When I was in elementary school, I studied aviation models. Students were making gliders—airplanes with wings but without a motor. At the end of each year, we would have competitions. A student, who has made a glider, would give it to a friend, while he himself held the line attached to the glider. Then both would start to run. In a few seconds, the glider would start to rise. As it ascended, one had to run along and drag it. If the pull was too weak, the line would sag and glider

167

would start to fall. You needed to allow the glider to get very high. It would get into an air current and start to ascend on its own. At that moment, you would feel the glider braking out of your hands, and precisely at that moment, you would have to pull sharply on the line. The end of the line, attached to the glider, would detach and fall down as the glider would continue to fly on its own. It would glide. It would glide free now. Take a look at this analogy. You bring a glider to the peak, it forces itself higher, and you don't need to hold it any longer; you let it go. There is quite a big difference here as in compared to movement on a bike or a car—activities that are related to contact with the Earth.

It may seem that air is the same everywhere, but take a look **how differently birds fly**. Look at how an eagle flies. An eagle flies and flaps his wings, and then suddenly he freezes, his wings expand, and he starts to glide in circles. He uses no effort, applies no force; he simply glides. He is in an air current and may glide for a long time.

There is another bird called the albatross. The albatross may surmount big distances. It is a strong bird. But even this strong bird cannot fly applying effort for a long period of time. It finds air currents and glides there. Is there a difference between **effortful movements and effortless movements?** When one walks or runs, especially uphill, one overcomes the force of friction, due to which he gets a repelling force. He pushes the Earth and the Earth pushes him back. And the harder he pushes, the harder it repels him.

This is an analogy of the life of the mind—always with effort. I push, and I am being pushed. The stronger I push, the stronger I am being pushed, and the farther I will be able to run. But a **bird just glides—effortlessly, in total silence.**

Observing these **analogies** we can understand something and touch that Life. Both birds and a glider follow the laws of

That Life when they glide. When a bird makes an effort to catch prey, to pick it up, and to fly away with it, it is different. The eagle is very powerful. It can catch a big prey and lift it in the air. But the same eagle may drop everything and glide. Can a human being drop everything and glide? Can you do it?

An eagle may catch a sheep and lift it into the air, but an eagle cannot force it to fly. **If a sheep were to grow wings**, it would not be a sheep anymore. If an average sheep were to try to fly, it would climb a high mountain and jump. There is a probability of dying during this process, but the sheep would experience something that is close to flying. How do young chicks learn to fly? Some birds simply throw their chicks out of the nest, and **they are forced to fly, learning in the process that they have wings and what flying is. Do you have wings? Wings do not appear by themselves. Why would they grow if one never wanted to fly? To get a taste of That Life is to taste the unknown. You don't know. You don't try to explain anything. You just live.**

Holistic vision and the predestination of a human being

What is wholeness? Let's take the closest wholeness to us— **our body**. The body represents wholeness. It consists of a multitude of cells. These cells create certain organs that perform certain functions in a human body. Why can we walk? Because we have legs. Why can we breathe? Because we have a respiratory system. Why are our cells supplied by blood? Because we have a circulatory system. Why can we think? Because we have a brain. We can view any organ, any system comprised of these organs, from the point of view of certain functions necessary for the wellbeing of our body.

A human body is something amazing. It is really amazing, because it is whole and harmonious. It comes into disharmony from the constant interference and meddling of the fragmented mind. But if we were to bring the mind into accord with the rest, with body and feelings, a beautiful **harmony of the organism** may be restored. The organism itself is very harmonious and beautiful.

Every human being is part of wholeness. Humanity is also part of another, **larger wholeness.** Every part enters certain wholeness. What kind of wholeness humanity enters into? The wholeness itself is a part of some other, larger wholeness, and it is infinite. What kind of wholeness does a human being enter? **A human being may enter into different wholenesses**. For example, a human being can enter into a nation, into a country, into humanity. A human being is a representative of humanity, a certain part of it. Humanity is a part of the Earth. If we look at the Earth as wholeness, we can see it as a being, in which humanity performs a certain function.

Every single human being has a certain task. As an organ of a human body has a task, so a human being has a task as a part of humanity. He may understand it or he may not understand it, but he has to perform it. A part may not work against the whole. If a part stops performing its role in this wholeness, it becomes unnecessary for this wholeness. It can be simply useless or detrimental. For example, a cancerous cell may destroy the whole organism. Then either the organism throws out this cancerous cell, or the cancerous cell enslaves the organism.

How does each part, comprising certain wholeness, perform its task? A human being has a brain comprised of a myriad of interconnected cells. If we see a human being as a part of humanity, and humanity as a certain organ of a creature called the Earth, then every human being has his task. One may think of humanity as a nervous system of the Earth.

170

We were investigating how the mind works, how it creates the sufferings we live in. **To know oneself means to exit the borders of the mind, but first we have to clean it.** One needs to clean one's memory of the emotional information recorded in the cells of the brain. But **the same can be said about the Earth**. The Earth is an evolving creature. Similarly to a human being, it goes through the process of growth and transformation. Each one of us represents a cell of the Earth's brain, and performs his own task. We view the Earth as a creature, but the creature of a completely different scale as compared to a human being. A human being enters this creature as a small part. This creature communicates and interacts with creatures of its own scale. How exactly does it happen is unknown to us, but we can extrapolate certain things by analogy, observing them in ourselves.

A human being is a part of some big wholeness. As a part of this wholeness, he performs certain tasks. Every single one of us performs his own task. **How well do we understand our tasks?**

If we were to ask an average guy, **"What is important to you?"** he may answer, for example, that it is important for him to make money to feed himself and his family. It is possible that he created a company and its success is important to him. Maybe he is a member of a certain political or community organization and performs certain functions there. **He sees himself as a personality** with definite responsibilities toward these entities to which he belongs. These are **responsibilities** of a **personal sphere**. The entire life of the personality consists of such obligations toward different organizations and people. Now I want to touch upon the question of the greater predestination of a human being.

Does a human being have a greater predestination? A human being is not just a personality; he is something

much bigger. A personality is just images and convictions programmed inside the mind. But if a man were to exit the borders of the mind, he might be able to become aware of something else, some kind of predestination which is outside the borders of usual notions of what he has to do and not to do in his life. But in order to get there, he needs to taste that other life himself. Then, possibly, he will move to some other aim with greater awareness, **to the aim not limited by** notions of family, economic and political organizations, etc. Maybe at that point he will start to understand his predestination as a Human Being with a capital H, not just a personality. Perhaps, the holistic vision he acquires will allow him to become aware of the task he came here to fulfill.

A human being can be compared to a musical instrument, like a **violin**. By itself when it is encased, it is just a piece of wood and a number of strings. But if a good musician takes it into his hands and starts to play, it comes to life. From the instrument that just a few minutes ago appeared to be just a number of mechanical parts, beautiful music starts to flow. Can we separate this music from the violin or does it become one with the music and a musician that produce it? But when the music ends and a musician puts the violin back into the case, it turns back into a wooden part and a number of strings. Just a moment ago it was something amazing, and **it is precisely during that moment it turned into something whole**. Is it possible for a human being to experience something of this nature?

The personality of a human being is a collection of habits and character traits related to the duties he performs and responsibilities he has been assigned. What kind of instrument can we compare it to? What kind of melody can this instrument perform? The melody of guilt? Debt? Grievance? Indignation? Hatred? Anger? Jealousy? These are the melodies performed by a personality. That is how its inner strings vibrate. But can one perform a different melody, which has no relationship to jealousy or fear? Can this instrument change and start to play a **beautiful symphony of Eternity, real Love, and Wisdom?** It seems to me this is the most important thing. This is an expression of the fervor that some people, who attempt to exit the limits of the mind, possess. This is a fervor to **become concordant with the Great Melody of Eternity. When a human being turns into such an instrument, and his strings start to vibrate in resonance with this great Melody**, he becomes simultaneously a performer, an instrument, and the melody itself. If there are a few such people, then something is expressed through one of them, something else through the second one, and third thing through the third.

What is the difference between the performance of beautiful music by one musician and an orchestra? One violinist comes on stage and plays. It may be delightful. But if the same melody is performed by an orchestra, where not only the violin, but multiple other instruments bring in something of their own, it turns into something completely different. Even though it is the same melody, now it turns into amazing, **magnificent consonance**.

The one who Sees, who understands and feels his task, performs this melody. But imagine he is not alone. Then we get an orchestra composed of a few people performing **That Great Melody**. What if it is not five or ten of them, but one thousand, two thousand? If more and more of these people were to appear, then **the melody from these spheres would penetrate deeper and deeper**, and even the deaf would hear it.

That is precisely how the unknown enters this sphere where everything is already known, where everything is circling the same circles. Can the deaf hear anything? And what if everyone were deaf? Does the question of something unknown, something different even arise? But if some people who long to hear were to appear between them, and if the number of these people, as they started to perform what they hear, were to grow, the melody would start to spread out into the world. People, who may never have heard anything, would begin to hear some unknown melody. They would stop and listen to it. This is a good analogy of a predestination of a Human Being.

Here is another good analogy. A human being has learned to use electricity, but it does not mean he understands what it is. **What is electricity?** To understand the essence of an electric current is to understand a lot. Perhaps, a human being is that **conductor between this and another world.**

Let's take a look at an electric bulb. Inside of it there is a small wire of a special quality, and when the difference of potentials exists between its ends, electric current starts to pass through it, and to emit light. There is a difference of potentials and something that we call a conductor. Certain changes occur in the conductor, and it starts to shine and to warm up. Is not a human being also a similar conductor, one end of which is present here in the material world and another end is situated in another, nonmaterial world? If one were to fall on one of these sides, what would happen?

For example, imagine we were to take a battery and some kind of a conductor—a wire. One end of this conductor we attach to 'minus,' while keeping 'plus' in the air. Will an electric current pass through this wire? No. If we were to apply it to 'plus' only, nothing will run through it either. Only in the case if we were to apply the electric current to both 'plus' and 'minus,' will it run through. **So, if a man falls into the "material," a current does not pass through him; if he falls**

into what is called "spirituality," a current similarly does not pass. But if he is simultaneously present in both, this voltage appears, and a current starts running. Perhaps the essential predestination of a human being is to conduct that current.

Conductors can be very different. What are the characteristics of a conductor? Resistance. If the resistance of a conductor is very high, the current passing through it, heats it up. If connections are bad, or the wire is broken, sparks appear. These are analogies which help to explain what happens to a human being.

When some people start to experience this current, these vibrations, not understanding where to direct this energy to, who to interact with, how to transmit it, they can develop a short circuit. I have seen cases of an electric current coming from human beings and burning some nearby objects. Why does it happen? It happens because their structure have not yet developed the necessary connections, and does not know how and where to conduct this energy. Everything is interconnected. This is not just a phrase. **It is extremely important to direct this current correctly.**

What is the task of a human being? How can one get to understand it? We can see the tasks are quite different. These tasks are usually well defined on the personality level, and if they are not clear to you, someone will help and define them for you. It could be your wife, husband, supervisor, politicians, relatives, etc. You will not be left without a task. But are these really the tasks you want to perform? Are these really the tasks you came here with? In order to figure out **the tasks of a different, non-personal scale,** one needs to see them, one needs to have Vision. In order to do so, it is necessary to complete the work we do here. We need to remove many obstructions for this vision to appear.

Consciousness—awareness of humanity

What do I mean when I say—**the Mind**? There is the **Mind** which is **holistic**. As we can see the consciousness of a human being and humanity is not whole, it's fragmented. Otherwise we would not have these horrific wars, conflicts, contradictions, daily fights, internal and external. So, if this Mind is absent, then everything is meaningless, because everything ends in separation, pain, and suffering. But does this Mind exist? And if it does, can humans perceive its influence? Can it change the consciousness of humanity?

If we were to assume that this Mind exists, how can it enter a human being? What kinds of conditions are necessary for it to enter and to influence an individual human being and humanity at large?

Is it possible for it to **enter the consciousness of humanity**, not touching each human being separately? It seems to me it is impossible, as the consciousness of humanity represents a sum of the consciousness of its entire people.

Perhaps the Mind can only enter certain minds for now, minds which are ready, waiting, and eagerly desire it. And if the Mind will enter these minds, and if we were to have more and more of these minds, perhaps the consciousness of humanity would change as a result of it, but not from large to small, but **from small to large**.

People are waiting. They say, "The consciousness of humanity should change. Something has to happen. Someone will come and save me." Is it possible to receive **the Mind on account of or from other people**? Perhaps, the only possible option for us is to create the necessary conditions in ourselves? Can the Mind enter the fragmented mind of a human being where different parts are in constant conflict? Is it possible for something mindful, something whole to enter such a mind and stay there?

Can it enter not at once, but in small portions? Can it enter into a small fragment, into a part of the mind? No. In such a case, it would not be the Truth, it would be a fragment. The Truth cannot enter this way. It can only enter a human being who has **become a clear vessel**. Therefore, the question of the Mind, Truth, and Wholeness is a question of a perceiving instrument, i.e. the question of a human being healed of fragmentation. It can happen only when one becomes a clear vessel, capable of listening and hearing.

We need to long to hear the call of the Mind—to hear, not to define or to classify it. The only thing we can do is to listen and to hear it. One may only be able to hear it when one is completely empty internally. Only then can something develop; only **into the emptiness of a cleansed mind can the Mind enter.** We can prepare ourselves for it, but a strong longing is required. A strong longing can appear only when you really see what is happening in the world and what is happening in you as part of this world.

To see reality and to passionately wish to hear what you cannot know, but what you can experience is the most important thing. A philosopher wants to make his existence meaningful, but his "meaning" will only last for a few years. **Meaning is the pleasure of the mind;** it is an infinite repetition of the same thing, in order for the mind to substantiate the necessity of its presence.

How many people are willing to take a look at their own mind objectively, from the side? People got identified with it and ceased to understand what moves them. But if you were to **observe your mind** and to see its mechanisms, you would come to similar conclusions. Then you would ardently desire to get out of the unlimited influence of your mind. Perhaps then, you would develop longing for the Mind to enter you.

From clear vision to a proper action

Holistic vision is action. Take a look at people who have a fragmented vision. They perform multiple repetitive actions. Yes, they are doing something. They are doing something every day. They spend a lot of energy. But where are we moving to? What is happening? People usually move in circles. **Every one of us has his own cycle, inside the limits of which each one of us moves**. At the same time, we cannot say that we are doing nothing. There are people who are very active. They fidget a lot. All these actions, feelings, and thoughts lead to circular movement, while a clear vision of reality manifests itself in a correct action.

I am going to use an analogy, which will possibly help you to understand this, even though one can fully understand this only through personal experience. Let us imagine that someone wants to get to a certain city. Let's say Almetevsk. He thinks, and someone confirms it, it is situated up north. He spends a lot of effort trying to get there. It is difficult for him as he is short of money. He walks and hitchhikes. He spends tremendous amount of energy, and finally he gets there. When he arrives, he realizes that it is not the Almetevsk he wanted to get to. It is a different city with the same name. Meanwhile, the city he really needs happens to be down south and very close to the place he started from. **So, this human being had an incorrect vision and performed multiple operations, which, in the end, happened to be useless.** If he had had a proper vision, he would not have to perform all these unnecessary movements. This example shows that **correct vision prevents many unnecessary actions**. As we discussed before, if we were to look impartially at a man's life, we would see him perform multiple actions, all of which in the end lead to the startup point.

To see something correctly means to get into holistic essence of life, where everything is interconnected.

There is a river in front of you. It flows. Let's assume you know that the current will bring you to where you want to go. You have vision and you know it is really so. If you were to walk into this water and relax, the current would take you to your destination. You have a vision, and you do not act forcefully, you do not try to apply efforts to swim anywhere. You just relax, and the river brings you where you want to be. Someone else does not have this vision and considers that in order to get where, as it seems to him, he needs to go, it is necessary to overcome the current. He spends a lot of energy expecting to arrive where he wants to arrive. However, he will not get where he need to get. But the one, who had the correct vision, will be taken to a right destination by the current itself. One needs to see it. **When one finally sees it, he does not need to fidget any longer.**

Usually one sets up certain aims in order to satisfy the desires of one's personality. In order to fulfill those desires, one starts to apply efforts, believing one will have to compete with other personalities to achieve them. The more one wants it, the more effort one applies. What happens when one finally achieves what one wanted to achieve? Many people may never achieve these aims during their lifetime. They set up aims that are impossible to reach. Some continue to apply more and more efforts, even after their goals are achieved. For example, one decides to become rich. He gets $500.00 a month. Then he wants to make $5,000.00 a month. His perception of what rich is changes in accordance with an increase in his earnings. He wants more and more, and this continues indefinitely. It applies not only to money, but to everything else personality may desire. It is a non-stop race, non-stop efforts. They are connected to his vision. It seems to him that this needs to be done, constant effort should be applied. We see that the majority of people do not want to change their vision. They simply act more or less actively inside the harsh brackets of society's views. To understand that vision is action is possible only for the one who is ready to change the habitual point of view. **The correct vision shows to you what you really need**. Seeing it, you get into a sphere where the laws governing life are completely different. You do not need to apply any effort in order to get what you really need. In reality, a **human being needs to apply very strong efforts in order to receive what he does not need**. The more effort he applies, the more he aims toward something he really does not need.

This is quite a paradoxical and unusual point of view. Not many people will agree with it. This is a view from a holistic world. If one has a holistic point of view, one can see how wise life is. Life does not require any effort in order for something to happen. That particular human being represents life itself. He is what happens and to whom it happens. **Is there any effort required on the part of a violin a musician plays?** Do chords need to apply any effort to create a melody? No, they don't. A violin plays. It creates these sounds and no effort is required on its part. The violin is what it is. This great melody is performed by the violin the way it is. Who is the great musician performing this great melody? It is Life. **Life is music, and at the same time Life is the instrument on which this music is being played.**

Someone may say, "But man is not free from society. Man is not free from its laws. How can he play this melody of Life?"

The only melody one can play is the melody one's instrument represents. One can produce only what one lives at the moment, i.e. the emotions one currently experiences. If these are the emotions of jealousy, fear, achievement, or aggression, then these are the only melodies one can conduct.

That human being is not capable of swimming the current of the river of Reality. That is it. The river we are discussing is not a usual river. One cannot simply undress and jump into its waters. In order to step into this river, one needs to change. In order to see this river, one needs to change. Only the one, who developed desperate longing to become whole, can see this river and enter it. These are the areas not seen by usual, physical vision and, therefore, cannot be approached by everyone. This river cannot be seen by many, not because they cannot see it, but because they do not see it. There are people who have pushed themselves to such a state that they cannot see it. Unfortunately, there are many of them.

There is a certain state that precludes one from getting there. I don't mean a certain episode or situation, but the state of one's organism at a given time. **Some people destroyed everything inside themselves, beyond a point of repair**. If you were to take a violin and smash it against the wall, it would be easier to make a new violin rather than to repair the one you broke. Some people are in a state of such complete disarray, that it is impossible to compile them into something whole. **Others are damaged less,** some of their strings are not tightened, some are ruptured, but it is still possible to heal them, to make them whole.

But the master who will make this beautiful instrument, the master everyone awaits, will not come. **Only the human being himself may become this master,** and in order to do it, great longing is needed—the longing to turn into an instrument that the melody of real life can be played on. Many may say that certain melodies are already being played around, and ask why would they need to attune themselves to some other, unknown melody? They may be afraid to become an instrument that nobody here needs.

True, if you are attuned to something else, you will not perform old melodies, melodies of pain, sadness, hatred, anger. Your instrument will not perform them any longer. This music will not be produced by you. People will ask, "Who are you? Why are you there and not with us? Why are you here, but do not participate?" If you stop playing the part accepted here, some may find it to be strange. Imagine a musician who comes to the orchestra where everyone plays a military march, and starts to play a waltz? However, this waltz may be so beautiful that **other musicians would want to switch and to start playing the new melody.**

A human being wants to have both the usual and the unknown at the same time, but this is impossible. If one is faced with a choice of what to sacrifice, one is likely to sacrifice the unknown. You can easily see whether one needs the unknown or not. **When one turns into an instrument that attunes itself to unknown melodies, one stops seeking the old, the known.** It was Socrates who said, "There are so many things in the world that I don't need." Yes, there is an infinite number of them. There is a great variety of things out there. You will not learn all of them in your lifetime. However, when your instrument attunes itself not with this **horizontal diversity and quantity of things,** but with a different quality, all these diversity will become monotonous and uniform.

It is difficult to explain how a man can refuse something he has always used. It is practically impossible, especially if he does not know anything else. He needs to feel the taste of this new unknown. It is impossible to describe this in words. I can repeat ten times, "Try not to think. Try to say it without thinking," but these are just words. This does not happen right away. In reality, it happens instantly, but in order to get there, one needs to have a very strong longing to live in the unknown. It is a state of not knowing. **To live in a state of not knowing is to live in a state of knowing everything**. It is a state outside of the mind, and the appearance of such a state is shocking to the mind. To be in such a state for a certain period of time is not simple for a man who is used to living by the mind. In this state, you do not know anything and do not want to know anything regarding to what will happen to you.

And what does the mind do? It plans constantly. It plans in minutes, hours, and years. Everything is being planned, counted, and calculated. It appraises: is it pleasurable or not? But I am discussing something else. I am talking about the vision of life, devoid of any planning. We can talk about it, but one can only understand it by experiencing it. One can only feel, see, hear it for himself; one needs to be in it. **How can you explain to a man who has never submerged himself in water how to swim?**

I have already talked about global stereotypes of human consciousness. It seems to me that one of these stereotypes is the **conviction of the necessity of efforts**. Perhaps, you have noticed that practically all your work is done in an atmosphere of effort. Why? If you are convinced that everything can be gained through hard effort only, a certain atmosphere develops, a strong voltage develops, and a very strong current passes through. A lot of energy is discharged and wasted. You may have felt it already.

In what situations and how often does this approach toward work show up in you?

Act, do not ruminate

Is it possible to act without thinking? It is very unusual. This is something that for the majority of people is impossible to understand. A number of books are written on the subject of how to plan properly, books with titles like, "You are going deliver a speech! Think thoroughly through your speech! You are applying for a job! Think how to present yourself! You are about to get married! Think and plan carefully for this event!" However, it is possible **to do all these things without planning**, without calculating every single step. One's action can stem from the mind or from a clear, holistic vision, which by itself is already an action; the one who **sees—acts**.

One comes to a psychologist and says, "I have a problem." They contemplate and discuss it for a long time, trying to decide how to do something better. And the client says, "Now I understand. I see the situation, and I know what to do." He goes and performs a certain action. **What preceded this action?** It was preceded by thinking through the process step by step and discussing it. This is a usual method, used by everyone.

I ask, "Can any other method be used?" As soon as you see something as a whole, it becomes action. Vision by itself is action of great power.

I have a problem. I try to solve it. I try to think it through, I try to force it. I try to investigate all the nuances of this problem. Next, I start to act. It seems to me, I am solving the problem, but in reality I am creating multiple problems stemming from the one I started with.

Suddenly something happens to me, some kind of insight makes me realize that there was no problem, **that everything was created by me and by my vision of the situation alone.**

Is something that was not a problem, and was created by me, require any kind of solution? Do I need to spend psychological energy on it? Do I need to spend time in order to transfer from a state of problem to a state of no-problem? No. What allowed me to figure it out was vision—correct vision. I saw what it is in reality. I don't need to do anything. The **problem disappeared. It disappeared instantly**, without any time delay, without any work. Vision solves everything instantly. There is no time there. It is timeless. Over there it is instantaneous. It is "Here and Now."

It is impossible to change gradually; it is only **possible to change instantly**. And this is a result of clear vision. Everything else is an illusion of change. Where time is present, no change is possible. There is endless repetition under the name of "change." Vision is action. Having this vision, I can act without thinking. I will not perform useless steps, turns, movements that would waste my energy. I act the way I need to act. I don't think these actions through. I don't try to figure them out. I live in this vision. I am this action. There is no intermediary. There is no mind. There is no thought. Is such a life possible? Is such a state possible for a human being?

Are you capable of doing something without thinking how to do it? You know now what you need to do. Do it today.

CHAPTER 6:
WAY TO ONE'S HEART

Search for understanding deep in your heart

If a real understanding is to be born, it can only happen through the heart. But in order for it to happen, the heart should be cleansed. Only in the heart can real aspiration be born. Only in the heart can the truth be found. Only in the heart may the wholeness appear. The heart is what should become a major part of a human being. The mind does not want to get outside of its own sphere. It wanders around the labyrinth of its own thoughts and conceptions, not even understanding where in reality it happens to be. Only the heart can lead you to the exit and show you the way.

There is a physical heart and a spiritual heart. A physical heart is under the influence of the conditioned mind. It is contradictory in its feelings. It wants one thing and it immediately wants something else. It exists under the hypnosis of the duality of the mind. Deep-deep down, there is another, spiritual heart—it is whole and it is free. To feel that heart means to awaken. When that happens, everything falls into place.

How does this awakening happen? I can only describe my own experience because there is no universal path for everyone. Every human being is unique, and there is no technique, no universal system using which everyone can be guided through one path. Of importance here is personal experience, one's dedication, and one's desire for liberation. Here one has to jump, walking is insufficient. Walking is a method of movement of the mind. It wants to move slowly. It always tries to predict what lies ahead before taking the next step. Here one needs to jump. The mind will never jump, but the heart can jump.

The spiritual heart is an unlit candle. Do you want to light it up? Until you bring it to light up, only what has already happened to you will happen again, you will not be able to touch the unknown. You can become a famous philosopher or a psychologist, but that does not mean that you have come to understand. These are just the games of the mind. I speak about that serious aspiration, really serious aspiration, toward the unknown.

If the sensitivity of the heart was lost, the possibility to move toward unknown, toward freedom, is ruined—one will continue to wander inside the mind. But when the heart is sensitive, it senses all the contradictions of the mind. It senses all the contradictions of the life one lives. Friction develops in the heart. It is not a friction of the intellect. One conviction of the mind rubbing against another conviction, not infused with the energy of a feeling, is insignificant. Only real sufferings of the heart can produce a spark capable of lighting the candle of the spiritual heart. But, in order for this to happen, a man must look inside himself.

There are sufferings real and unreal. Unreal suffering is created by the mind. It uses feelings only to suffer over some pretext. For example, some people suffer because their favorite soccer team lost a game. Do you think it is a real suffering? One goes to a game of soccer not to find himself, but to forget himself. People have worked up a number of methods to forget themselves. All these methods bring up certain emotions. These are not real but superficial experiences. **Real experiences are situated deep inside a human being. But, in order to experience them, you need to direct your attention inside, to the depth of your heart, and see all the contradictions of your mind.** When you see it, a friction develops. This friction can produce a spark that could light a candle. And when the candle is aflame and burning constantly, everything changes inside. Then it is not the mind anymore but the heart that is of most importance. Only in the heart there is wholeness, only in the heart there is understanding. But the mind does not want to surrender. What kind of a king will step down from the throne on his own? It will resist. But one should not fight it, because the more one fights it, the stronger the mind gets. I offer you to observe it. Observe the games and vagaries of the mind all the time.

The majority of people occupy themselves with something that leads them away from themselves, away from reality. During childhood, everyone has periods of seeing reality clearly. A small child is care free. A child walks barefoot on the grass and sees a bird. It may seem unimportant to an adult, but to a child it is everything. It is the whole world. A child sees with the heart, and flies with the bird. A child feels expanded as the whole forest, as the whole sky. A child and life are the same. There is no observer or observed—they are united, and they are one.

Why did a human being stop feeling?

The mind needs to classify and put everything in its place. It can reduce everything to a scheme and, in the process, strip of life everything it comes in contact with. The mind castrates life. An understanding of life comes from personal experiences and from the heart. It does not come from the mind.

How does a baby learn to perceive the surrounding world? A baby is taught language, i.e. certain concepts expressed in words. These concepts have a dual nature, and therefore from the upstart carry an internal conflict. What is a conflict? It is found in duality. **Where there is a conflict, there is always duality. Me and you. I say this, and you say that. I want one thing, and you want another thing. We have a conflict. There is always one and another, and there is always a conflict between them, i.e. separation. The essence of the mind is separation, duality. You will see it, and you will know it when you start to observe**.

The mind, being in duality, transmits it to the heart. That is how a duality of feelings and a duality of experiences are born. Love and hate. Want and don't want. A duality of experiences is established in the heart by the mind. And then the real sufferings begin, because the mind requires the heart and emotions in order to exist. Conduct an experiment. Observe how a feeling develops, how it acquires strength, and how it disappears. In the beginning, an image of a certain event develops. Next, a feeling you used to experience appears. You continue to develop this feeling with an associated thought. You hold and extend it. Pay attention to this. It is precisely with a thought that you evoke and regulate the intensity of the feeling.

189

That is how the mind starts to dictate its duality to the heart. From here a duality of feelings that leads to suffering is born. If you were to observe your thoughts and feelings, you would see that not a single feeling is born before the thought. In the beginning, a thought appears. A feeling follows. A feeling will not appear until the mind approves of it, until the mind determines what should appear.

You will see that not a single feeling can appear until a thought calls it a name. This is very important. One wants to experience certain feelings. One tries this and that, but nothing happens. Everything stays the same, because feelings do not appear by themselves in a human being in whom the mind prevails. And that is the majority of people. So, the mind is not only the jail for the thoughts, it is also the jail for the feelings. If there is something in a human being that wants to escape to freedom, it is the heart.

What are feelings? Where are they born?

For the majority of people feelings are the products of the mind, and that is the tragedy. Working with groups of people, I asked them what they feel. They named different feelings but, in reality, did not experience them. This was quite a shock for someone to discover that he is not feeling anything, and what he used to call feelings were just words. It is the mind that talks about feelings, not the heart. **There are many people who do not feel anything. And why don't they feel anything?** Take a look at what happens when the mind starts to assign its duality to the heart. A child's heart is still open when duality of the mind starts to enter it. A strong suffering develops. Every one of us has been in such a situation and experienced a duality entering the heart. The pain was so severe and unbearable that feelings started to deaden and the heart closed. That is how the heart would protect itself. It would stop feeling. Then the feelings would be exchanged with thoughts *about* feelings. That is how many people live. They do not feel anything, but they talk about feelings. They write romantic novels, poetry, act on TV and perform in the movies, but they have forgotten the real feelings because what happened to them in the past has closed their hearts. There might still be something there, some left over energy, but this energy is enslaved and used by the mind.

Why are people so eager to have sex? For some people, orgasm is the only instance when their mind shuts off. It is the only moment when one can be outside one's mind. As soon as it is over, the mind starts to recreate what happened before, what was written previously. The mind wants to have pleasure and avoid displeasure. All its activity is aimed at repeating the pleasure it experienced and not to repeat the displeasure it experienced before. **When you start to observe, you will see how hand in hand, like a bride and a groom, pleasure and suffering walk, and how suffering is born from pleasure**.

What does a human being want? A human being wants to have pleasure and to not have suffering. He believes it is possible, and this belief feeds his mind. **The mind aims toward pleasure all the time. It does not seek new pleasures. It wants to repeat old, familiar, and habitual pleasures.** If you experienced something pleasant, then from now on you will try to repeat this experience all the time. You will see that you attempt to recreate the same experiences.

In the past you may have experienced pain and unhappiness and now you are constantly trying to move away from repeating that situation. It is not here in the present moment, but if suddenly something reminds you about it, the mind reproduces and repulses it. That is where the fear is born. **Fear is a result of the unwillingness of the mind to experience something unpleasant. It drags it from the past into the future, sees it and gets scared.**

Your spiritual heart is the only alternative to the mind. One who does not save his spiritual heart and his feelings turns into a robot. There is only one organ that may know the truth—it's the heart. It is the spiritual heart that will object to phony life in its own way—through pain, emotional dramas, and sufferings. But through these sufferings one may come to find an alternative to the mind—a real owner of the human being—yourself. The mind is similar to a house with multiple servants constantly fidgeting and running around, fighting for power, unable to do anything while the real owner is the one who will come from the heart, from its very bottom. When the real owner comes, you will have no doubts that he is the real owner.

Some people are searching for enlightenment. They try different techniques and finally come upon this question: "When will this enlightenment come? Where is the criterion?" There are no criteria. One says one thing, and another one says something else. And the mind doubts. The mind is always in doubts. Here you have this "enlightened one" walking around; he is enlightened now and un-enlightened the next minute. There are no intellectual criteria appraising how enlightened he is. But when it happens, one cannot doubt any longer. One's heart knows what it is, and no confirmations or prof are necessary because one's heart has found the Truth. It is impossible to describe, and no one can ever explain it to you, but if you were to experience it, you would know, and would never doubt again, as that old merchant who gave up all his treasures for a single emerald.

Suffering real and unreal

Many people suffer from pain that is unreal. They imagine something and then they suffer because of it. The unreal pain is impossible to transform into awareness. You can become seriously disappointed on behalf of certain theoretical presumptions you do not like, but it will not be a real suffering. It will be imaginary suffering. But every one of us one way or another gets in contact with reality, and these contacts lead to pain, real pain. You can only push away from that pain. Only through that pain you can understand what is really important and necessary. It is precisely from that pain that you can return to reality. Every one of us will have our own encounters with reality.

Perhaps you have been in the situations when you could not restrain yourself, and that lead to pain. This encounter with pain led to an impulse to understand what was happening and what is happening with you in reality. You wanted to change something, to take away that pain, to free yourself from that suffering. Then you tried to change something in yourself. Is that correct?

How can you free yourself from negative emotions?

What is your relationship with your negative emotions? Do you try to suppress them, or to observe and investigate them?

If you completely suppress all emotional manifestations, nothing good can happen. You have died while still being alive. You should not suppress emotions, but become aware and see them. You can try not to express and to slow them down, but only in order to be more aware of them.

Why do we constantly recreate negative emotions? We do so, because we do not understand what they lead to. We cannot see the whole picture of what is happening when we express them. **We do not see the huge amount of energy leaking out of us while the negative emotions are being expressed**. We do not see how our relationships with other people change. We do not see multiple negative consequences of negative emotions. If we were able to see all the negative consequences, we would stop doing what we do.

A butterfly flies toward a fire and gets burned because it does not understand what this action can lead to. It is an instinctive behavior. A toddler puts his hand into an open fire not because of the desire to burn himself, but because he cannot comprehend what this action will lead to. A human being expresses negative emotions because of lack of understanding of what such a choice can lead to. Become aware of what you are doing. When you start to become aware, you will be unable to do something so harmful to yourself. You simply will not be able to do it. If you say, "I am aware" but continue to be irritated, nervous, jealous, and envious—you are still not aware. Awareness is a great force. When we really become aware of ourselves, everything we do not need leaves us.

There is an old story about the thief of Baghdad visiting an enlightened man saying, "I have heard a lot about you. You are an enlightened one and you know a lot. Do you know who I am?"—"Yes, I know. You are the thief of Baghdad."—"Yes, I am really the best thief of Baghdad. There is no thief better than me. I plan to rob the Shah himself and steal all his jewelry. It is not proper, but I am going to do it anyway. What can you say to me?" And the enlightened man replies, "Do it. I am not against it. But while you are doing it, be aware of what are you doing. Constantly be aware of everything you are doing." The thief replies, "I will do what you ask me to do." Later on, the thief comes back and says, "What a sly man you are. I was unable to steal. When I became aware of everything, I was unable to steal."

Emotion is energy

A man says, "In order to be strong and to have energy I need to be thrifty and economize." He does not run. He does not

194

even walk. He stays in bed all day long. I am exaggerating, but try to see the analogy here. Something atrophies in him. It is quite difficult to talk about certain things and encompass them in their wholeness. Every single thing has two sides to it. When I talk about one side, I am omitting the opposite side. When I am talk about the opposite side, I skip the first. This man asserts one of two extreme positions. That is why I am going to answer him by showing the opposite position. He says, "I need to save energy. In order to do so, I have to suppress my emotions. I should not express them." Where can this lead? He starts to suppress emotions and, in the end, stops feeling anything. His feelings and emotions are not expressed. They are not expressed because he transformed them into awareness, but because he suppressed them. Let us take a look at the old oil lamp. I turn the lamp on and it throws a huge flame up. I don't need such a big flame. What can I do? I can turn it off completely. Then I will not have a big flame, I will not be afraid to burn everything around me. But, I also lower the flame.

What do you do with your emotions? You can suppress negative emotions, but by doing this, you will suppress positive emotions also. You will suppress all your emotions.

Painful experience and perceptions

Do we see everything or do we see only what we allow ourselves to see?

When an adult explains to a child what is what, when to every single thing a certain name, definition, and notion are applied, a child is being educated on how to see the world and himself. He is being told, "This is good, and that is bad." What is it but not the education on how to see the world? Then a child encounters life. He experiences suffering and pain, and as a result of being afraid to experience these feelings and sensations again, he forbids himself to see things that were connected to these experiences.

The mind is designed to watch out for its own survival. Truth does not interest it much. It is the smallest part of the mind's interests. The mind is interested in one thing only: self-preservation, and if a threat to its well-being arises, it will do anything to protect itself. It may completely or partially turn off some of your functions and prevent you from seeing, hearing, or feeling holistically. You will become partial, incomplete—you will hear partially, you will see partially, you will feel partially. For example, something you saw, heard, or touched brought you severe pain. It was fixed in your mind as something you should not touch again—not with your eyes, not with your ears, not with your skin. **But then, what do we have?** We get to the point that we don't want to see anything, because everything around us cause pain. In reality, if you were to see this way, you would see that everything around you causes pain. **The mind strives for pleasure, but pleasure causes pain**.

Can you **see pain and pleasure simultaneously?** For example, you want something, some **pleasure** attracts you, but **at the same time you see the pain** that will undoubtedly follow should you indulge in this pleasure. If you were to see this pleasure and pain simultaneously, your **perception of yourself and the world would change**.

Consider something that gives you pleasure? Now think about how this pleasure brings you pain. Consider closing your eyes and doing it now if you are ready to see it.

Let us take a look at brain physiology. The brain is made out of cells. What happens inside these cells? We have processes of excitation and inhibition. We may envision all these cells as units—capacitors of information. They record everything that happens to a human being. That is their function. This is the experience fixated in memory. The experience, fixated in memory, is material because it is fixated in matter, in cells. Inside these brain cells feelings are also recorded. Information that is brought to these cells also carries feelings: pleasant, unpleasant, painful, etc. Try to remember any fact of your life, a time when you were hit or hurt yourself hitting something, for example. What does your body feel now? How does it react to these memories now?

See how strong your memory is. Recall a past experience now and you start to somatically recreate what happened then.

What is written inside these brain cells is not simply information. It includes all feelings and sensations you experienced in the past.

What kind of sensations and feelings do you experience bringing back an event from the past? Become aware of them. How does this memory reflect on your perception?

The mind tends to see what causes pleasure and not to see what does not cause pleasure. If feelings and sensations you felt in certain situations were not recorded in your neurons, you would not have memory of them as pleasant and unpleasant. Memory would contain only facts and information, and not be colored emotionally at all. But that is not how it happens. Memory records information, feelings, thoughts, and the sensations associated with them. That is why one perceives everything he sees through the prism of memory, through the prism of the pain and pleasure he experienced in the past in connection with certain events, things, people, etc. That's how strongly our perception is conditioned.

How does the memory of a past event you just remembered influence your perception of yourself and others? Become aware of this right now!

The mind is a mechanism that records everything that happens to you during your lifetime. This recording starts as soon as you are born. Every single thing that happened to you when you were a child, a toddler, an adolescent, and up to a present moment is written inside your brain.

Recall the most painful situations of your life. Do it right now. Become aware of all your thoughts, feelings, and sensations connected to these events. Free yourself from the painful memory of the past. It is long gone already. Stop transferring your past into your future.

Cleansing of the past

When people open themselves to each other, they exit the limits of the norms and rules, and what appears then is something that can truly happen between people, something sincere.

Why is it that we show this natural side that exists in every one of us so seldom? Someone expresses his "love" because he is obliged to. Another expresses "hatred." But these are two sides of the same coin. Can you see and feel them simultaneously? Can you exit the borders of duality, and get in touch with something that is inside of you?

If you are to **observe non-selectively (impartially)** what happens in the mind, to become aware of it, **not trying to stop it**, not trying to silence it, **but just observe**, remembering that what you observe are just thoughts and images—perhaps something very important may open up to you, something very important specifically for you. You may see precisely what currently happens in you. You may see these closed zones and territories that exist in you and increase the fragmentation of your consciousness. To see these fragments is **to open up one more forbidden territory, to bring light into the shadow**

territories of your mind. Opening these zones is painful as they contain painful experiences. They contain things you do not want to see. But you can see these things. **Illuminate these territories with the light of awareness, re-live and release these painful experiences.**

You will see the **illusory nature of your suffering.** You will see the **illusory nature of your pain.** True, some time ago it was a real fact, but now it is nothing more than memory of the past event. But inside of the mind it is contained as real pain, which can jump out and hurt you again. Clear the mind of this pain. You may discover many zones in your mind that need to be illuminated with the light of awareness in order to be cleared. Every cleared and illuminated zone will increase your wholeness.

Awareness opens up certain zones and instantly illuminates them. More and more clear space appears in the sphere of the mind. I don't want to describe it or give any kind of explanation of how it happens. **One can only find this out on one's own.** It is the most important thing—the understanding that comes from oneself, and about oneself. What is the movement toward oneself? It happens simply, but quite painfully as dark zones of what you did not want to see open up. The understanding comes later as a result of expansion of wholeness, as a result of opening and reclamation of these zones. Without this work you will not understand anything. How can you understand the truth with the fragmented and bedimmed mind?

Release from a painful past experience

Let's take a look at **what memory is after all.** What happened to you during your lifetime is recorded in your memory as specific information, similar to the information about a city you visited last year. Moreover, this information carries an emotional load, connected to what happened to you. Let's say you were beaten up as a child, or you got seriously sick and spent a long time in the hospital during your ninth grade. The memory of that period of time of your life will carry this information with the superimposed emotional color that you have assigned to these events. **Memory turns on** information about the events as well as your emotional reaction to them. Can we remove the emotional reaction, but keep the information. Can we only keep the facts?

Let's say you are watching a movie and what happens on the screen strongly affects you emotionally. You experience it very painfully, or on the contrary, you live through the whole movie laughing and feeling pleasure. Imagine you are watching this movie for the thousandth time and emotionally you are not touched by it at all; you know precisely what the hero will say, where he will go, what will happen, but you experience no emotional reaction. Can you imagine this? Then the question is, "Can you have the same response to past events of your life? Is it possible to free yourself from experiencing the pleasure and suffering caused by them?" It is precisely these positive and negative emotional attitudes to different events, people, and facts that are being fixed and reproduced by the memory of the mind. The mind is not attracted by the facts or the events of the past. The mind is attracted by their **emotional overtones**. If it was pleasurable, the mind wants to repeat it. If it involved suffering and pain, the mind wants to escape it. That is exactly what the mind is occupied with. It is its main job.

Are you ready to **see your past?** Are you ready to quietly observe it all?

And what does it mean: to quietly observe? It means to see it without emotional overtones and coloring.

Feel the main question of your heart

The majority of people occupy themselves with intellectual games to **escape** and not to see their own mechanical nature and not to feel the pain of their hearts. Until the moment you decide to get in touch with this pain, you will continue to occupy yourself with these cheap intellectual games. If you were to **allow yourself to get in touch** with these painful experiences, your main question would arise—your **chief enquiry**. This enquiry may lead to serious self-investigation and **deep understanding of yourself**. Investigating the mind, you will see that it cannot escape its limits; it reproduces only what it already has. This applies not only to a specific human being, but to humanity at large, as the consciousness of a human being is part of the consciousness of humanity.

You may say that you are not very interested in where humanity is going. You may say that you want to be good and live your life safe, but your consciousness—is part of the consciousness of humanity. **Everything is interconnected.** If a war is going on somewhere, and a Muslim is killing a Christian, or a Jew is killing an Arab, it means that every one of us has contributed to it. "How is that possible?" you may ask. What causes a Jew to fight an Arab? This fight is caused by the separateness and fragmented nature of man's vision. But **is not this fragmentation present** in the mind of every one of us? Don't you think that it is the fragmentation of our consciousness that gives birth to fragmentation of the consciousness of humanity? Then why are we surprised that there is so much fighting, war and hatred around us? Until the time every singly human being understands his role in all of this, no **real change** is possible.

Intelligent, serious people get together and contemplate serious questions on how to regulate different conflicts. If you were to look carefully you would see that these initiatives do not solve anything. At best they achieve a **temporary truce**, but then everything **starts all over again**. That is the history of humanity. We can see that all prior and current attempts to find a way to peaceful coexistence have not led us to peace. This is a serious, not an abstract question. This is a question of vital importance for every single human being and humanity at large.

The mind will eternally debate these questions and **pretend that it can solve them**, but the fragmented mind only gives birth, reinforces, and thrives on these questions. But there is also the **internal essence of a human being,** which can see reality and which **does not want to live in the hell of separation** we all currently live in.

It is important to see reality, to have a strong desire to get in touch with it, because only through this contact some **real feeling can be born**. And from this real feeling some **real enquiry** can be born. If that feeling is absent, nothing will happen.

Some people have a more intellectual mind which is imprisoned in a bigger sphere where it pounds as bird in a cage. Other minds are smaller, and their birds pounds in smaller cages. But the result is the same. It does not matter whether one flies five feet or twenty feet to hit the fence. **But does the bird want to see** its own cage?

There are many minds that do not see and do not even want to see and feel the constraints of their cages. If we don't see the borders, we believe they are absent. We believe that the mind is limitless. Until it is understood, a man will not have any desire to exit the borders of the mind. He will constantly look for some kind of exit inside the borders of the cage of the mind, using old, and as we can see ineffective methods. He will say, "If I don't understand, it means I have not read enough on the subject. It means I have not attended all the courses, and not heard all the smart people on this topic." He will soothe himself with the hope and belief that he can fundamentally change something. **A hope and a belief are the attributes** that keep the mind in a state of fallacy. Without real question, without real enquiry your self-investigation will not be real. It will be illusory.

What is your chief enquiry?

Sincerity—Possibility of hearing oneself

Why is one afraid of being totally sincere? Why does one say certain things and hides other things? When one says something, actually by pronouncing it, one can see himself as if from a side. It is true, many speak not hearing nor seeing themselves from a side, but that opportunity is available to everyone. When you say something sincerely, you can hear what is deep inside you. You can see and possibly free yourself from what burdens you. Unburden yourself from certain misbeliefs that something is not right, horrible, or shameful. The majority of people carry these misbeliefs inside. In such case, it is extremely difficult to see them.

A sincere conversation is a possibility to see something inside yourself and to release a certain misbelief. Why are you afraid of saying something? Is it because you think that it is inappropriate, uncultured, or not smart enough? This is just the appraisal and conviction of your mind. When you say something sincerely, you become different, you clean yourself. If you don't accept something within yourself, it does not evaporate, but gets stronger.

Perhaps, some friend or a family member starts to irritate you, and an aversion develops to him. These thoughts and feelings scare you. You start to deny them. You are afraid to acknowledge them even to yourself. But this is what it is. You may not want to see it, but it will not disappear because of it. It will disappear only when you see and acknowledge it. For some it is best done during a sincere conversation with another human being. Verbalizing it, you will see that it is not something that belongs to you. It is not yours. Sincerely let it out, and perhaps you will see that what you kept and saved from yourself and from others for so long is not yours and has no relationship to you. It exited you and left you. But until you stop keeping it as some horrid secret, you cannot separate from it.

And what kind of secrets do you keep?

Two sides of one love

Love and business are incompatible things. Attempts to reconcile them lead to prostitution.

The family life of many people represents a similar prostitution. The principal is the same: I will give you something, and you will give something to me. Is there any other principal that governs the relationship of two personalities? Let them use the words they want. Let them call it love and pretend it is something beautiful. But if you were to look deeper, you would see what is, in reality, behind this word. But who wants to see reality? We want to delude ourselves with pretty words. We are under the hypnosis of our own words. Only exiting the limits of personality can lead us to real love. And then, there are no questions: who do I do it for, and what I will gain?

Why does personality fail to understand that it is possible to love everyone? Try to discuss it with a group of people. You will be instantly accused of being a sexual pervert. What do you mean everyone? Are you not satisfied with just one partner? But we are discussing completely different things here... The love we are discussing does not choose. It is expressed to everything around you. It is like air, which is necessary to everyone, not just one, two, or three people. Imagine if the atmosphere of Earth were to decide to start selling its air. Some people would be deprived of air. Imagine what would happen in the world if the Sun were to love this way—selectively. But that is precisely how people love. They choose someone, call him or her a darling, and send him or her some surrogate of love. If the Sun were to love this way, what would happen to humanity? The Sun does not separate good from bad. The Sun does not consider who to give more light and warmth and who to give less today. It shines equally for all.

Does a flower choose when and for whom to bloom and to smell? It blooms for everyone. If it smells and blooms, it does not do so based on who is present here and who is absent. But can a human being bloom and smell? No. I will bloom for you because you are dear to me, but for him I will not smell because he is bad and disgusting. If a flower blooms and smells, it blooms and smells for everyone. But this is something that is extremely difficult for personality to comprehend. It is That Blooming, That Love.

There are quite a few people who, based on certain religious concepts, say that it is necessary to love everyone. But let us take a look at how they live in reality. Do they really love everyone or simply say that they love everyone? Do they really love just one human being? If you think about it, to love someone, to love like this means to love everybody. This love is devoid of fear.

Some spiritual groups frequently use the word "love" as some magic word. The more frequently this word is used, the more these people think they are where they are supposed to be. It is possible to parasitize on this word quite a bit. This word may be used as a slogan, similar to slogans politicians use: progress, freedom, equality… These are magic words which easily hypnotize human beings. One starts to repeat and to believe them.

The word "love" is also a magic word, similar to words such as god, equality, liberty, truth… But what hides behind these words? This is an interesting and subtle question. If one has already hypnotized himself and others with these words, one starts to react to these words only. One does not want to think where these words are pointing. And they are pointing toward something that cannot be expressed with words. One reacts only to form, not seeing and not wanting to see the essence.

A formal intercourse using words is extremely superficial but quite satisfactory for the personality. Only the superficial, the external side of things is available to the personality—only forms. That is why the personality is not interested in true love; it is satisfied with words alone. And it uses them in its own interests, in order to get something for itself, to reinforce and assert itself.

Look how many drama movies are played in the movie theaters. These movies are very popular. These movies show "love." They form the general presumption of what love is and how it should be. These movies are created by the directors who have a subtle and deep understanding of human relationships. They clearly show the whole tragedy and inconsistency of such relationships and society reactions to them.

Not many people allow themselves to exit the limits allowed by society. Society mandates you to abide by certain rules, but pleads against strong feelings and passion. Society's morality is a compilation of certain convictions that attempt to keep feelings in certain brackets. If someone leaves these brackets, society retaliates. Usually it is dramatic and quite frequently tragic.

The real drama is usually tragic. A strong passion develops between two people. As a rule some circumstances not allowing them to be together interfere. This is a very important moment because desire is strengthened by resistance and opposition. The more difficulties these people face in order to be together, the stronger their desire. The desire is born, nurtured, and strengthened in this state of opposition produced by external circumstances.

Romeo and Juliet is a good example. External circumstances do not allow them to be together. Their desire grows because of it. As a rule, this desire ends in tragedy. The relationship of these people exit the limits of usual, the limits of what is called normal, socialized love. Their relationship becomes a challenge to societal norms and notions of morality. They become a topic of conversation and condemnation.

As a rule, these people take it very hard. Feeling obligated to overcome certain norms, they start to ignore them. Their unacceptable behavior displeases many. People who experience this frequently do not understand what happens to them; they are being carried by a fast current of a mountain river, inevitably dragging them toward the waterfall.

What is this? Where does it come from? Quite a lot has been written and said on the subject. People talk about fate, destiny, supreme bliss or suffering. Usually, it is a very strong attraction, frequently sexual. What kind of an attraction is it? What is this sexual energy? What is the attitude of a society to this energy which escapes the control of the mind? The attitude of a society fluctuates between two poles: total puritanical suppression and a total permissive orgy. Society and the superficial mind are afraid of this energy, attempt to control and suppress its manifestations. But no one has ever been able to do so. It breaks violently in, sweeping away everything in its path. For rigid moral convictions, it is quite a serious threat. The mind cannot possess this energy and is therefore afraid of it. The mind wants to have control over everything. It has a strong desire to stop it. But with certain people it is so strong that their minds are unable to do anything. These people become, in a way, insane. They do not act based on the logic of the mind. They do not consider important something that many other people consider to be very important.

A smart behavior, from a standpoint of many people, is taking into consideration certain rules and norms. A smart man will say, "Get your pleasure quietly and safely. What are you going crazy about, what are you doing?" But people in such an "insane" state do not accept anything except what happens to them. The mind, naturally, is in a state of great discontent.

So, what is it? What kind of an impulse is it? What kind of a call? Is it a "call from above" or a "call from below," if we may use these terms? A call from above is like a breath of fresh air. It comes from above, and encompasses everything. It does not separate anything. The Sun shines for everyone, and wind blows over everyone. So, where is this call coming from? Is it coming from bellow? It has some kind of characteristic we already discussed: a strong sexual passion. Where does it come from? Is it related to a man and a woman? An impulse from above can come to anyone irrespective of sex. It comes frequently without any connection to anybody or anything. It comes, and it enters and permeates everything around. A sexual passion comes like lightning, a thunderstorm, a hurricane which develops between two people: between a man and a woman. It is like a hurricane which destroys everything, or a high voltage tension which is impossible not to feel by the people nearby. Is there a similarity between these two impulses? What do you think?

What happens between a man and a woman is related to sexual energy. The mind cannot enslave this energy when it is so strong. It cannot cope with it. It pushes through the borders of societal norms. It is analogous to a river which overflows its banks—no one is able to predict what where it will run to.

The mind constantly tries to control everything, including sexual energy. Sometimes it leads to excess. Monks of some orthodox religions, where sexual relations between a man and a woman are forbidden due to their sinfulness, fight this attraction all life long, tormenting their bodies. Some of them castrate themselves.

I recently read about such a case. One monk after castrating himself enquires, "What did I do? I fought myself for many years, considering body sinful. Now I did it, and what do I have? I don't feel alive anymore. I feel dead. Energy has left me. Life has left me. What did I achieve by having done this?" He did something incomprehensibly horrible, as he later comes to understand. This energy should never be killed.

If you kill this energy, you kill something very important in yourself. You kill this life in yourself, as all the living things in this world are driven by it. Without this energy animals would not be able to reproduce, to live, to survive, and to evolve. The same can be said about human beings. But human beings are sly. Human beings have a mind that wants to use sexuality for its own personal purposes. The mind wants one thing only: to increase its own pleasure and to decrease the obstacles to it. The mind intrudes into the sphere of this energy. It wants to conquer it. And in the process of doing so, it starts to muddle and distort it.

What does the mind want? It wants to obtain the energy. There is the energy of feelings and the sexual energy. They are both very strong. How can one master these energies? The mind can work only through images and thoughts, convictions and beliefs. For example, a monk fighting evil in the image of a woman is under the control of his own superficial and conditioned mind which creates these convictions. And, in such a way, his mind enslaves this energy, holding it inside these convictions. And what happens to this man? He torments himself for many years and nothing changes. Instead, life leaves him.

There is something that cannot be destroyed. One may kill one's body, let the life energy leak out of it slower or faster, but it is impossible to kill life itself. It is possible to kill one of the forms through which life manifests itself, but it is impossible to harm life itself. For plants and animals, there is no division of love. They do not divide it to sexual, godly, or some other kind of love. They happen to be in the current of one love, not even understanding it. In reality, everything is pierced by it; it is the essence of life.

The problem of the human being is that the conditioned mind does not want to submit and accept **what is** as it is. It constantly superimposes its convictions of how it **should and should not be** onto everything else. That is where all human torments and sufferings come from. We already reviewed some of these.

One may ask, "What do you offer? I can't just simply release control and accept everything as it is. It will lead to chaos. What will happen if we were to take away all the bans, norms, and regulations of the mind and the morals the mind created? Devil knows what will happen."

Yes, this energy is very strong. In a sense, this is the energy of chaos. That is why in some religions women are considered to be unworthy to be accepted by God. That is how these religions understand God. A woman is frequently viewed as a carrier of this chaos, this tremendous energy. A man is unable to not experience the influence of this energy, but at the same time a man is afraid to lose himself in it.

Do you have any questions? Does anything resonate with you? People talk about "Earthly love" and "Heavenly love." Animals know only the first kind, which is instinctive, instinct that forces them to unite and to continue their breed. A man also knows that, but he also knows another side of love which is unknown to an animal.

But, in reality, are not these two the same? Maybe it is precisely the joining of these two poles that will allow us the possibility to understand what we discuss all the time and are unable to name. The problems of a man and a woman develop as a consequence of separation. All the contradictions and all the conflicts are the result of this duality, this separation. The world of form is dual. It contains multiple dualities: light and darkness, cold and heat, affluence and power

A sexual energy appears only in the presence of two poles: a man and a woman. It is similar to electricity—a plus and a minus cause the current to appear between them. A current may only develop when the difference of potentials is present. The stronger the difference, the more masculinity is in a man and the more femininity is in a woman, the stronger the passing current. As a rule, these people are unable to understand each other at all. Because one pole is strong in one, while another pole is strong in the other. Why is this love usually so very tragic? It is because the assumptions about the nature of life of these so called "real men" and "real women," are very different. They are opposite of each other.

It is precisely the interference of the conditional mind that creates this tragedy. The notion of tragedy itself is a notion of the superficial, dual mind. Without the mind, there would be no tragedy. The tragedy of the situation appears precisely when the mind tries to resist its being overthrown. The insanity of love is that in a certain sense it destructs the personality. This passion, this attraction becomes stronger than the mind and the personality. A man appears to be insane.

But take a look at what this destruction of personality can lead to if one is to understand it only from a personality standpoint, if no other understanding is available. We already discussed how in the body of a human being, on the base of the superficial mind, the personality is formed. It means that a human being has a body with its animal instincts and the personality with its social instincts. When such a strong passion overtakes a man and a woman, it may lead to the destruction of their personalities. But if they did not find or learn anything else, if we may say transpersonal, what is left? What is left are just two animals, experiencing mindless passion. That is why society condemns it so severely, because it is something that can destroy it.

True, people overwhelmed by strong sexual passion may simply turn into animals attracted to each other. It does not mean that anything superior to the personality entered them. There are no guarantees here. It is possible for something old to be destroyed, but no new understanding to be developed.

We have talked about the "call from the top" and the "call from the bottom." In both cases, passion develops. In both cases, very powerful transformation occurs. The personality gives in, and the mind steps down from its throne. But what does it gives in to? Does it give in to passion coming from an animal instinct or to something else, to the true owner—to the Essence?

In the first case one just turns into a body with animal instincts, while in the second case, one acquires himself in a total fullness and wholeness of his being.

Yogi talk about Kundalini, a certain "snake-like" force that is concentrated in the coccyx and can be released as a result of some special exercises. Some try to do it. There are known cases when the body was simply extinguished, burned to ashes as a result of releasing this energy. This is a tremendous force, tremendous energy. Possibly it is that Earth energy, energy of the female essence, that tremendous energy of chaos. This energy can destroy anything. Indian mythology talks about Goddess Kali. Her power is destructive, but at the same time, without her there are no changes, no transformation.

How can spirit and mater unite? What can happen as a result? What is god's creativity? It's an entrance of spirit into matter. What we call and perceive as material is born from the spirit. It is just a form for the expression of the spirit. It is a form through which spirit can manifest itself, and a form should correspond to the spirit's intent. If the form does not correspond to the spirit's intent, then it is not needed, and spirit destroys it. But matter may pretend to be the way it is in order to preserve its form. Spirit wants to change these forms. Spirit strives to express itself through forms. It needs neither permanency nor stability of forms. Matter, on the other hand wants to maintain defined and constant forms.

A man and a woman

Look around. They say that man is a head and woman is the neck that turns this head in the direction it needs to face. A man may have a very high societal status, may have multiple accomplishments, but at the same time there is usually a woman next to him who may be completely inconspicuous, but who determines many of his decisions. You may easily see it in historical examples.

Some are convinced that the enlightened human being unites both male and female parts within himself because one without the other is not whole. But when confrontation is in process, a man wants to use a woman, and a woman wants to use a man. Quite frequently a woman is more successful in this fight.

A woman is stronger than a man. Notice that on average women live longer than men. They are more resistant to challenge and misery. They stand stronger on the surface of the Earth; they are closer to Earth. How does a woman use these advantages? Having these advantages, she can lead a certain man where she wants to.

So, where will she lead him? She may direct the facilities and strength of a man toward achievements to benefit some circumstances she needs. Have you ever seen a woman use a man and his energy in order to get not what she wants but, on the contrary, to give him her abilities in order for something extraordinary to happen, something outside the habitual notions of "normal and happy" life?

A male's energy requires a female's energy exactly as a female's energy requires a male's energy. But usually, we see them in confrontation, and as a result, one starts to lead the other in the direction of one's choice. But who knows where to go? Who can know that? If we were to investigate this question impartially, perhaps we would be able to arrive at another question—what is the predestination of a man and a woman? Idea, plan, intent—are they more intrinsic to male or female?

We can say that a man assigns a direction and a woman creates the conditions that allow the opportunity for moving in that direction. Moreover, they should move together. But most often this is not the case. Everyone pretends to assign the direction and as a consequence one suppresses another, one energy suppresses another. Unity is impossible, because where there is suppression, there is no unity. Without unity there is no realization, only constant confrontation and resistance. Everyone tries to use available advantages but in the process kills an opportunity to receive what is only possible to receive during the **fusion** of one and the other.

Full realization may happen only during full fusion and unity, but does the personality aim toward such a fusion? The personality has its own desires. The personality of a man has its own desires, the personality of a woman its own, and the forces of these desires collide and oppose each other. In the process, they fight each other, attempting to get more. Each one of them presumes it can get more on its own. The personality only wants to take, to achieve something on its own. But is the full fusion we are discussing here possible in such a case? Is a full understanding possible? Is it possible for two personalities to unite and to fuse? The personality always feels its separation from others. It constantly attempts to snatch something for itself.

If we say that the realization of a man and a woman is only possible with their complete fusion, then what are the prerequisites for this fusion? Purely physical fusion of two bodies may occur with both animals and humans. This is something I presented in our discussion on sexual passion. Complete fusion of two personalities is impossible. If it was not for the sexual instinct, which attracts people of opposite sex, it is doubtful they would want to be together at all.

If a human body was devoid of sexual instinct and had only the personality, it is hard to say whether people would even want to touch each other. Most likely, they would keep a certain distance from each other, and negotiate how to get something for themselves. A body, having sexual instinct, is attracted to another body, but their fusion is incomplete. It is just a partial rapprochement, rapprochement of the bodies. But rapprochement of the souls, the complete fusion may only be known when all the false convictions of the mind are thrown out. It is precisely the personality that does not allow one to see and to feel this full fusion. The personality is an unnecessary intermediary between the body and the spirit, which does not allow one to see that these two forms of love—"earthly" and "heavenly"—in essence are one.

CHAPTER 7:
WHAT IS THE POINT OF GROUP WORK?

• ◆•◆ • ◆•◆ • ◆•◆ • ◆•◆ • ◆•◆ • ◆•◆ • ◆•◆ • ◆•◆ • ◆•◆ • ◆•◆ • ◆•◆ • ◆•◆ •

Beginning communication or readiness to see oneself.

Everything that can happen here depends on your readiness. For example, I knocked on your door as a guest, but you are not yet ready to answer my call today. Moreover, you don't even want to open the door to me. Next time, keeping the door ajar, you may take a quick look at me. The third time, you may allow me into your hallway. Then you may lead me to your kitchen. And one day you may allow me into your room. It does not happen instantly. Sometimes people spend years talking through a closed door. One can be allowed into the hallway, but then, as the owner reconsiders or gets scared, one can be thrown out. There are different levels of communication.

What leads to this unwillingness to have a deep communication? It is the internal overload—overload of an emotional, intellectual, or another character. Let's take a look at my room as a representation of my internal world. If it is overloaded and there is no space left for anything new, neither for new furniture nor for a new feeling or a new thought, I may

217

talk forever about my desire to have something new, about my desire for a change—it is all words. People just juggle with words.

Frequently the word "love" is used. Look around. "Love" is everywhere. People do not know what Love is, but everyone talks about it as if they know what it is. They come to church, and they are told, "Love is God." In order to come to God, you need to pray every morning and read the Bible. They stop next door and someone tells them, "Love is a political party. You need to love your party and its leaders." People do what they are told and think that they love. This is fiction—equilibristic with words and images.

A human being can be easily deceived. It is easy to do anything to a human being because one does not know who one is, does not know one's essence. One is afraid to look deep inside. We are not going to achieve much here unless we allow something unknown to enter us. It is a risk. The unknown is always a risk. Otherwise, it is just a repetition of the known. Someone approaches me, and I don't know what he is going to say to me. I don't know what he is going to do to me. I don't know what is going to happen. If I know, then it is nothing new. It is just a repetition of what I experienced before: apprehension, fear, desire to increase the distance, etc. There is nothing new.

How strong is your desire to have something new? Not simply to talk about new, repeating the same thing again and again, but really learn something new. How much are you willing to risk? Are you ready to allow something new to come inside you? How ready are you to renounce something you consider to be true? How ready are you to see in yourself, under a new light, something you consider to be right or wrong? Those are the questions that are going to arise during our meetings. I may send certain vibrations on certain levels, but you may either accept them or not. You may simply close yourself up, making it useless. You may open yourself up, and have a possibility of a change. How deeply we are able to open ourselves will determine the result. We will define and establish a certain depth to our conversation. It will be very superficial or very deep, and it will be established only by us. We will decide on it together. There are no teachers and no students here. We have an atmosphere where one is a teacher and a student for oneself. How far we will be able to get in this study will depend on our readiness and ability to open ourselves to this process. It will determine everything. We can repeat smart, intelligent words, but what is behind these words will be determined by the level of our sincerity and honesty to ourselves.

We will not be able to achieve anything without opening up. The essence of this work is sincerity, and primarily sincerity to oneself. Only the one who is sincere with oneself can do something here. So, let's try to be sincere. One needs to learn to be sincere. One really needs to learn it because nobody ever taught us how to do this. Moreover, we were taught to lie. We were taught to lie to ourselves.

Can a newborn child lie? Does a child know what a truth is? Does a child know what a lie is? Does a child know what good and evil are? No. **So, how did a child learn these concepts? Why did a child become dishonest? Who made a child dishonest?**

Your main question

You need to figure out what you really want. Understanding what you want and what happens to be a problem for you is very important. I am well aware that this is not simple, especially if you do not know how to do it. You need to formulate your main question, i.e. what is of utmost importance for you, and why. The majority of people are occupied with a completely different business. If they are discontent, they may go to a casino or a pub, or have a glass of beer. You, on the other hand, want something else. It means you have a certain impulse. What is it and where does it come from? Every human being around you has problems, but not everyone wants the same thing you want. **Do it right now. Write down and answer this question: "What is my main problem?"**

What is a conversation? Right now we are communicating through this book. Did you notice there are different atmospheres of communication? Sometimes this atmosphere may be very tense, and sometimes it is light. What is it now? Do you pay attention to it?

But how is this atmosphere created? What happens or does not happen between us? Do you have an enquiry? If you have a very deep and strong question, I call it enquiry, something develops between us, something similar to an electric current passes between us. It is not just a transfer of information. This is something else. Everything that surrounds us can be reduced to the transfer of information, but this is not the main thing that is happening here.

Understanding may happen, or it may not happen. It depends on every one of us present here. It does not depend on me alone, because if you do not know your life enquiry, reading this book will not be of much help.

I ask you to formulate the most important question for you—your life's most important enquiry now.

What is life's most important enquiry? You know what it is when you look at someone and see that what he says concerns him deeply, that it is vitally important for him. It comes from something buried deep inside. There are many people we see around us and on the TV who talk a lot, talk beautifully, but what they talk about does not touch them deeply.

Look for your enquiry deep inside your heart. Get in touch with it right now.

Write down your questions. Take a look at them from all sides.

Perhaps some questions arose in you after having read this book. For example, "What is personality? What is essence? What is the chief feature of your personality?" What do you do with them? You take them one by one and ask further, **"What does it mean?"**

Why do you ask? You want to understand how something that is named with one word is connected to something that is named with a different word. So, what is the problem? Is the problem in your inadequate understanding of what is behind a certain word, and as a consequence in your inability to connect different words and different notions, or the problem is in something else—specifically in the one who is asking these questions—in you?

We are conducting an investigation of the mind, inquiring into the structure of consciousness. And what do we see? We see that many questions have fragmented nature. It means they come from certain fragments, from certain parts of our mind. Questions themselves reflect and graphically show separation and the fragmented nature of the mind of the questioner.

Are you capable of seeing the fragmented nature of your questions?

Where is the question coming from?

What question do you want to get answered now? And who is it in you that want to receive the answer?

Why do I keep returning to this? If I were simply distributing some information, it would be a strange action on my part. Why do I constantly return to the same thing? **Why do I ask all the time, "Who is asking this question?"** One may get an impression that I repeat myself. **From the point of view of acquiring and storing knowledge** this question may seem to be completely irrelevant, but somehow I keep doing it. The way I see it, it is extremely important.

It is imperative **not to forget who** within us **asks** the questions. If we forget who it is in us who asks these questions, we start **to accept** many things **at face value, to accept them to be true,** even though **they are not**. This is a very important point. That is why I frequently **switch** from the question that is asked **to the one who asks** the question. It is essential to know who asks a question.

We can talk for very long time, but in the end we realize that what we discussed is not worth a dime. That is what I want to avoid. Therefore I **return your question to you** and ask, "Who is asking this question? Who wants to know?" It is extremely important—who is it in you who wants that, and what does he want. **Is it really important and necessary for you?**

Usually one is interested in hearing something new and interesting. But I would keep asking you, "Who is it that wants to learn and feel something new? Can this someone see, learn, or feel something new?"

But how often this question is being asked by someone who bought the book and read it, or came to hear something, see something, and understand? Does he see himself as an apparatus, with a certain spectrum of perception, attention, seeing, sensing?

Is the question of **our own tuning** important or is it enough to simply ask **some kind** of a question and to receive

some kind of an answer? You can say: "How come? It is my question, I asked it and therefore it is important for me." But I am not sure that this is the case. **First,** I am not sure you ask the question that is truly important for you. **Second,** I am not sure you are ready to receive an answer to this really important question of yours. We can be submerged in an **illusion of a certain communication,** certain change. So, in my opinion it is quite important to understand: "Who asks the question, what kind of a question is it, and how ready and tuned in you **really are to be able to hear the answer?"**

Impartiality—the base of self-investigation

True contact develops between people when they talk about something that comes from their depth, from their essence. Our communication is a many-sided process. Observe yourself. Pay attention to what is going on inside of you. You may observe quite a few different things. Someone says something to someone, but in reality it is being said to you. Someone answers a certain question, but in reality your question is being answered. A thought pops into your head; you suddenly experience a desire to talk but you do not, and it disappears. Be aware of what is going on in and with you all the time.

Do you think that what I do, pertaining to myself and to you, is the main part of my work? I am occupied with self-investigation. I investigate myself all the time. What is necessary for the conduction of an accurate and effective self-investigation? Is it possible to get a different result if you already have a pre-conceived assumption of what you want to receive? Is it possible to open something new if you already have an idea what you want to receive? If you already have an idea about what you want to receive, you would receive only that. What is even more interesting, – you would receive exactly what you expect.

If any of you been to academia and were involved with science, you probably know how PhD theses are written and defended. There are quite a few recommendations on how to speed up this process. When you define your thesis, you are asked to prepare the conclusions you expect to present at the end of the investigation. So you write up the results and then shuffle your data to fit your results. That is how many scientific investigations are conducted. If this strategy was only applied to science, I would not discuss it here. It applies to everything. It applies to life in general. For example, I am going to a meeting with someone. I already know what I want to get from him. Let's say I get what I want, but I don't receive anything new. I only receive what I already had. In order to receive something new, I need to say, "I am going, and I don't know what I will get. I am ready for anything." **The characteristic of a real investigator, as I see it, consists precisely in the fact that one says: "I am going, but I don't know what I will get. I cannot know that."**

In which situations are you capable of being impartial, and in which are you not?

Request—direction of your movement

What kind of a topic would you like to investigate? What interests you now and why? It is not hard to find a topic. There are quite a few of them. But many offered topics are speculative, castrated, **dead convictions of the mind**. Someone said something, invented a model. Someone likes it and adds something of his own to it. That is how a certain something, a certain image, notion, conviction that originated with one person starts to **become bigger and to acquire**

weight. And when a man is told that it is **accepted by everyone** and it is very important, he starts to **respect** it. This scientist has not one, but thirty students. He is a PhD, and they are all on their way to getting their PhD's. His work is probably very solid and real. He becomes more significant, authoritative, and important, continuing to accumulate more and more students, notions, convictions, etc. That is how all scientific, religious, and psychological schools **grow**.

Of course, something in this concept of his is valuable, because everything in this world has a certain value. There is a certain kernel of truth in it, but people throw so much stuff around it, that it is not visible anymore. There was once that original spark, **that light**, but **no one remembers** it now. This light was coming from a human being. He was saying something and light was shining from him. But then the words he was saying, the acts he had done, were recorded by someone. In time these records were rewritten and corrected, and what is the result? Do we still have the light of such people as Christ and Buddha, or do we have something completely different? Why do I speak about it for so long? It all depends on the question you have right now, because something really true is being born out of the given moment and not from the past. If I were to pre-plan, pre-think, prepare something, what would I really contribute? I would contribute something outdated, not related to the given moment.

But that is precisely how all the meetings and lectures are being prepared. That is how books are written and movies are made. All of this was already done. It was once real for someone, but now it is just a repetition and recreation of the past. **That is why ultimate value is found precisely in what is happening right now**. You are currently in a certain state— **this and only this is a fact**. And it is precisely from this fact, from our common presence here, that something new may be born. The closer we are to **the present moment,** to the awareness of us at the given moment, the more interesting our investigation will be, the **closer** it will be **to reality**.

What is collective self-investigation?

The most important thing for you is to take an active role in self-investigation. If I were to complete it for you and show you the result, it would not receive your resonance. If you are only interested in receiving predetermined answers to certain questions, you would not be able to self-investigate. Look, why did you come up with this question at all, and is it possible to have a ready answer to it? Perhaps, you would see that your mind is not interested in self-investigation at all, but only wants to ask a question and pacify itself with a ready answer.

What is a dialogue? What is a conversation? What are we doing? We are having a conversation, we are having a dialogue. I am aiming toward you and you are aiming toward me. If this aim is present, if there is a strong desire to investigate and understand, then something develops. The results we may receive during our investigation depend upon the level and the depth of our aim. I do not offer any premade formulas. I do not talk about systems. I offer one thing only—investigation.

What is a handshake? One offers one's hand to someone but is not offered a hand in return. Is this a handshake? No. Only when two people extend their hands to each other, a handshake occurs. Here is my hand…

How do I differ from a book?

What do you think about now? What do you feel?

Perhaps you play the same record over and over again. You have done this many times.

226

Do you want to see that you are doing the same thing again? Why do I remind and bring your attention to this again? I keep reminding you because awareness is the essence of our work. You cannot get it from any book. **I would direct your attention to this as many times as necessary, until changes occur, but this change will only occur when you really want it. I will create conditions for this opportunity to always be present. I create this opportunity for you. Whether you use it or not—depends only on you.**

Every one of us is made up of others. You are present in me, and I am present in you. Everything exists in each one of us, and until we accept the fact that everything is present in every one of us, it will be difficult to understand, to see, or to hear something new. You have an image of yourself, and you say, "This is me." I show you another image of you, and you say, "No, this is not me." Every one of us has something we don't want to agree with. I speak about this because this is the essence of the process that is happening between us here. Why do I say, "Learn to learn?" What does it mean to learn to learn? Not just to learn. If it was simply learning, I would present you with a certain system. We would discuss it and experience the intellectual pleasure related to it. But that would not help us here. It is just a repetition of the same thing. The majority of people who attend different spiritual schools and seminars, in reality, do not want to change anything inside themselves. They want to follow someone. They want to have a certain image of themselves as a followers of some big knowledge, some great teacher. Then they believe, "I am a big student. I am very important. My teacher is so and so, and I am such and such." One does not want to change, one wants to follow what one likes. "I am familiar with Gurdjieff's system. I know. I agree with everything. I know we are all asleep. I know this and I know that." You will repeat it again and again, but why do you

227

say that? You want to prove to yourself that you are knowledgeable and smart human being. That allows you to live with this image of yourself, but nothing changes. You do not allow anything new to enter yourself. As soon as someone encroaches upon it, and I do encroach on this image of yours, you get scared and stop feeling anything at all.

And how do you react to what you just read?

When the mind is overloaded with knowledge

It is a scary thing when one's mind is overloaded with knowledge. Look what we start doing when we have just read something. When we have a certain baggage of a classification, we start to put both human being and life into the brackets of this classification. We do not see a human being. Did you observe this peculiarity in yourself? When you have learned a certain psychological system, you start to approach other human beings from the point of view of that system. Do we even see a human being when those classifications, those convictions, are applied?

Yes, you know quite a lot, but this is precisely what precludes you from seeing the most important thing. This is applicable to almost any human being. So, I am not the one who would give this very important thing to you, as nobody can give this. Not a single authority can give this to you. It may happen, but how, when, and whether it will happen to you is not known. What can I do? **I can only clean up something inside in order to allow for this to happen. If it is not cleaned up, nothing new can enter. If my room is occupied by the old furniture, and I buy a new set, then in order for me to set it up, I need to remove the old furniture. This is my job. I clean up the internal world from everything old and dead.**

You can resist, but then you will not be able to receive anything helpful. People save knowledge as they save old things, to demonstrate it to themselves and to others. First of all, we demonstrate it to ourselves. But if something is present in me, it would manifest itself in my relationships with other people in one form or another. In one form or another, it will obligatorily manifest itself. If you experience pleasure and respect yourself more because you know more, would not you count and show it in your relationships with other people? Would not you experience pleasure when someone says to you that you understand more, and you are more knowledgeable now? Is it not a reinforcement of that trait of a personality that wants to save and possess knowledge?

What about you? Does your personality have this trait that wants to save knowledge and brag about it?

Where is your inner attention pointing to?

Your attention is constantly directed toward the outside world. We are constantly occupied with external things. So, let us turn our attention toward our internal world. Usually one turns one's attention inside when one is in pain or something is not connecting in one's mind. I, on the other hand, suggest you turn your attention inside and to become constantly aware of what is happening inside of you. We can see that it is not so simple; even when you assume a posture which is not habitual for you, it is still difficult to be aware of anything more than a sensation of discomfort. But if you are comfortable, you would completely forget that you wanted to become aware of something.

Do you want to see how much and what you are aware of?

Right now, place yourself in an unusual and uncomfortable position. Stay in it for five minutes. Then pick up a book you have been reading and start reading it again where you left off.

Our experiment lasted five minutes. During that time your feelings changed. Your sensations changed. Many thoughts have passed through your mind. Where was the vector of your attention pointing? Was it concentrated on the body, on certain parts of it which experienced unusual sensations, or did the vector of your attention travel toward feelings, and you became aware of what you were feeling; or toward your thoughts? Where was it pointing more frequently? Write down your observations. Where was your internal attention pointing to during our experiment?

What were you observing more clearly: thoughts, feelings, or sensations? What were you able to observe the least? You would be able to discern this better after reviewing the notes you just made. You have just received the slice of awareness of your psychological functions. If your list contains practically no notes on sensations, it means you did not pay attention to your body. If notes on feelings are lacking, it means you stopped feeling. If you did not write anything about your thoughts—you are not aware of your mental sphere. Think about it. Your inattention to certain psychological spheres is expressed in your life. How? Try to see it yourself.

We can meet only now

Just listen. It is so unusual for a human being just to listen, just to be in the Here and Now. You don't need to think. Just listen. Can a holistic vision develop in such a state? Just turn into one **huge attention and silence inside**. Then something can happen.

If something worthwhile happens, it happens in the exact moment of communication, Here and Now, in that instance where something may happen, if one is very attentive, if one has a strong wish to hear. But it can only happen during this moment when it is said and being heard, when the **speaker and the listener, writer and reader become one,** when there is no separation, no fragmentation.

It happens when the one who speaks and the one who listens become one. But it can happen only instantly, only during this moment. There can be no postponement. "I would understand later" would not happen here. There is only now.

It can happen only now. And it depends on how open the speaker and the listener are. This is not a question of time. If two become one, it happens, and it happens instantly.

But in order to get there, to a place of no-effort and no-action, one needs, in the beginning, to apply effort and will; one needs to act. It is paradoxical, but that is how it is. There are people who say, "I already understand it all. Everything is quite clear to me. I live in it." But is this truly the case?

Effort is necessary in order for one to start asking questions, in order for one's mind to get the desire to surpass itself. What we are discussing here may be born out of this effort. When the mind arrives at the point of bankruptcy, it gives up, and then there is no effort. That is precisely when this will occur. This will occur on its own when the mind gives up, when effort stops. Vision does not require effort.

Vision occurs simply and without any effort. **It is impossible to hold on to happiness.** As soon as I start making an effort to be happy, I instantly become unhappy. There is something that is impossible to hold on to. There is something that is impossible to foresee. There is something that is impossible to predict. **It comes when it comes,** but the mind wants to plan everything, to calculate, and to receive.

231

This would not happen this way. It cannot be done through effort.

How do I listen?

I will share with you how I listen. I am very attentive to everything that happens. I am extremely attentive. While doing this, I have no thoughts. I don't think about anything. No questions and no answers appear in me. There is only very focused attention, and from that attention something is born. I never know what is going to be born. It simply flows through me. That's it. Something is being born, and it flows.

Can I be **totally attentive to what is happening around me** if I have a problem, if I think about something, if something bothers me and does not allow me to be tranquil?

How do you listen?

To find reality in yourself

We cannot come to ourselves if we constantly run away from ourselves. To run away from yourself means to be pre-occupied with philosophical and theoretical conversations.

You may say, "I want to understand this problem better." Who created this problem? Until you said it, this problem did not even exist. Try to pay attention to what happens to you, because it is precisely the vision of what happens, the new vision that will allow you to understand reality. Until you started to think that you had a problem, the problem did not exist. If you ask someone a theoretical question, and say, "I want to understand this problem better," it means you have created it and you want to attend to it. Your main jailer is clearly seen here. It is a prison and a jailer at the same time. It is the mind.

The mind lives only when it thinks about the past or about the future. The mind is not interested in seeing something real, because reality is something that actually exists. The mind, on the other hand, works with something that does not exist. It works either with the past or with the future, i.e. it works with something unreal. For the mind to be in reality, to be in the present moment, is equivalent to death. You are reading certain words and phrases right now. The most important thing is not *what* we define, but that internal experience you may *receive*. It is precisely the experience, you living through this experience, which is very important. It is extremely difficult to discuss this. Understanding comes to everyone by a different route. Reading this book is just a preparation that is necessary in order for this to happen to you faster.

I am constantly trying to dig out something real from everything you have in you. To know just a little bit of truth about ourselves is much more important than to know a lot of something that is false and unreal. Many people carry piles of garbage of knowledge, convictions, illusory questions and only a small oasis of something real. The unreal surrounds us. It is being constantly fed to us by media. Most of what surrounds us is unreal and illusory. And if one loses the last grain of reality one has, one discovers himself totally submerged in a world of fantasy out of which there is no exit, as there is nothing to stand upon in order to exit. That is why it is very important for all of us to find this real part in ourselves, to strengthen it in order to stand upon it. When you come close to the reality in you, you will understand why you bought and why you are reading this book. This is the main purpose of our meeting.

Only the real we have in us can connect us, and not only our group, but all the people on this planet. Only the real knowledge of yourself can help.

The intensity of your aspiration

When can a very strong desire to figure something out appear in the mind? In what kind of mind can this desire appear?

The duller the mind, the less energy it contains. Many people, colliding with life and being unable to solve some of life's contradictions, start to dull themselves with alcohol, drugs, work, etc. Many methods can be used to dull the mind.

There are some minds, which have inner passion for the Truth, and these minds start to investigate themselves. All religions, philosophies, worldviews are attempts of the mind to know the Truth. These minds have a strong passion to know the Truth. Whether they get to know it or not is a different question. As a result of the movements of these minds and their attempts to find the Truth, we have all these systems of thought now.

People are very different in this aim of theirs. Some create their own systems, some follow other systems, and some are not interested at all, as they already have certain assumptions about life. Usually it is about eating tasty food, having a country home, a nice car, etc. Usually that is enough; they do not need much more.

The intensity of these aspirations toward the Truth varies from person to person. The character and the results of self-investigation depend on the degree of the aspirations of people performing it. What happens within the group of self-investigators is a result of the joint aspiration of all its members. Love is also the result of mutual aspiration.

The mind wants to possess what doesn't belong to it

Pay attention to what your mind usually does. It wants to usurp everything. Let's say you had some kind of experience, and this experience was outside of the mind, unrelated to it. Take a look at what your mind wants to do. It wants to usurp this experience. It wants to possess something that does not belong to it. It wants to usurp everything. It wants to understand death, which is something outside its limits. Death is a state where the mind is absent. What kind of a trick does it use? It starts talking about it. You start talking about it. It is your mind that is doing the talking. It talks, and an illusion is created that it knows it and is capable of understanding it.

Every experience the mind has had or it seems to have had, it will simply repeat. That is why nothing new happens. The mind possesses only what it had before, what it knew before. This is what it did before many times and will reproduce again and again and again. Look at how strong the mind is. One's personality constantly wants to return to something habitual. Pay attention to your conversations. Most likely you have talked about it many times before, and you will continue to discuss it again and again. You say that you want to learn something new, but where is this desire when you talk about the same thing all the time? You say, "I want to figure something out," but when you try to figure it out you say exactly what you had said many times before. You repeat the same questions. Where is *new* here? Is it possible for something new to exist here at all? The mind says, "I want to change," and an impression is created that certain principal changes are possible. Is it possible for real changes to occur in the mind overloaded with multitude of beliefs and convictions?

Your mind can exceed itself

Usually one walks away from the most important thing. One thinks one can hide it, but what one tries to hide is the most obvious to other people. This is an interesting rule. What one tries to hide from oneself is obvious to others. Have you observe this rule in yourself?

Your readiness for something, for a certain change, for touching something in yourself, for seeing something in yourself, is determined only by you. If you do not allow yourself to move in this direction, to see something in yourself, you will remain where you are. The more you allow yourself to do it, the faster your movement is going to be. Observe, be aware, and get your experience. Observe yourself. Observe your manifestations in different situations. Observe your internal expressions: sensations, thoughts, and feelings. For example, "I am interacting with this guy. What kind of thoughts, feelings, and sensations does it create in me?" You need this experience of self-awareness. If you do not have it, we would march in the same spot. You need your internal experience. Without it there is no self-investigation as there is no material for work. Otherwise you would simply shuffle your previous convictions like a deck of cards, philosophical thoughts that would lead you nowhere. It may be interesting from an external side but is totally useless from the point of view of internal work. So, let's become aware of ourselves more frequently.

In the groups of self-investigators, opportunities are created for everyone to see something inside himself. Everyone is a mirror for everybody else. The mind may overcome itself and see itself. Then, and only then, real vision may appear. But in order for this to happen, one needs to be ready and to have a strong desire for self-investigation. Nothing can happen without it.

If you do not have this desire for self-investigation, you would probably be better off somewhere else, somewhere where different images are being offered. Here is an unhappy human being. Where can he go? Perhaps, he would go and see a psychotherapist who would create different images for him. He can go to a church where he would be offered different images: the consolatory Jesus-Christ, comforting Buddha, or peace loving Krishna. All these images create an illusion and allow a possibility of escaping reality.

If you meet Buddha—kill him

Look what happens. A child picks up a cup and breaks it. Is it real? It *is* real. This is something that happened. It is simply a fact. If no one were to tell him it is bad, no one were to punish him, what would he feel after breaking it? Would he get frightened? No. It is natural for him. A small child is living in reality. A child has not yet been taught the notion of good and bad, right and wrong. Here he is, lying and seeing some spots on the ceiling, something is happening out there, some sounds are reaching him. What do you think he is thinking about? Does he think, "Mom said this. Dad said that. Mom and dad are fighting. Stroller is being moved." He does not think this way. He has not been trained to think yet. He does not know the words yet. He sees and hears only what is present in reality. But can we see what is real?

When we look at something, what do we see? And don't forget it is not even we, but a certain part of us which at the moment pretends to be a leader. Let's just not evoke any authorities. **For as long as we continue to appeal to authorities, we will never understand what we ourselves**

know. The education of the child is done through authority; authority of mother, father, adults in general, etc. A child internalizes their convictions and subsequently follows them all his life, suffering because of them. His entire struggle with himself comes down to the fight with different authorities, contradictory opinions and convictions present in his mind. That is why authorities are very dangerous. I, for example, don't want to be an authority for anyone.

And you, do you want to be a student of some famous authority? Maybe you want to become a "spiritual authority?"

Spacious thinking

There are people with very harsh convictions. They always have a set point of view on everything. Other people have multiple points of view. They are more flexible. I allow myself to have multiple points of view on everything. In order to do this, I don't need to affirm anything. I just have to presume and tolerate.

What are we doing during our investigation? We consider one point of view and then another. We could say something and insist that this is the only right thing, throwing everything else away. That is not what we are doing here. We say, "Let's allow this point of view and let's allow that point of view." **We look at the situation from many different points of view**. We always remember that everything is allowed. We never affirm, we always allow. Everything is relative. Then the **spacious thinking appears inside the limits of the mind**. If the mind is flexible enough, we can see quite a lot.

Different people—different minds. One man allows a different point of view; another will not allow more than one. So, the minds are very different. We see this. One's mind maybe as flexible as a wind—it flies around looking at the situation from every angle. Somebody else's mind is like a stone; if it hits, it hits in one place and it hits strong. Some minds are not capable of performing these investigations at all. For them, it is something incomprehensible. Yet other minds are made for it. The mind can also develop.

It is impossible to bypass neither the mind nor the feeling and the sensation in our work. Everything needs to be developed. If something is underdeveloped, you will not be able to come to our discussions, as they require a certain **development of all the functions of a human being: motor, sensory, and intellectual.** The mind that is underdeveloped will not even be able to understand that it is jailed inside its own convictions. Our study requires a **harmonious development of all psychological functions of a human being.** The mind requires development. Feelings and sensations similarly require development. But sooner or later, when all three spheres develop to a point when you start to become aware of yourself, to see something in yourself, **questions start to arise of how to get outside the limits of these spheres.**

Have you experienced such questions yet?

"Profit" can be extracted from everything

I support philosophical conversations only in order to use them for practical work. I frequently have to redirect conversations in order for them not to turn into mindless philosophizing. **In reality, everything can be used. Everything can be useful.** If you lose interest in work and submerge into sleep, it is because you don't want to understand the integer behind all those seemingly multiform and different themes, opinions, and ideas. You see them through the prism

239

of your stereotypes. Everything is interesting because everything may be used as a material for impartial investigation, practical work, leading us toward ourselves.

No guarantees

Quite a few seminars and trainings sessions are being offered today with a promise of **fast change,** but what guarantees can they offer? In reality, nobody knows what a human being is capable of.

There is an old joke about a former president of the USSR, Leonid Brezhnev, who was known for awarding himself with a medal every year. The medal he particularly liked was awarded during World War Two for exceptional bravery, and was called the Star of the USSR Hero. One day, wishing to get another Star, he called on the supreme forces.

"What do you want?" the voice from above asked.

"I want the Star," he answers.

"OK." And suddenly, he finds himself, grenade in hand in front of a German tank.

"Here you go. Go get your Star."

How does one think? Imagine I am sitting in this chair with five medals attached to my shirt. Give me another one, and I will sit in the same chair with six stars. This is the approach many people have toward all the spiritual and psychological promises of change. Those that offer fast and cardinal changes make their business precisely out of this attitude. Those offers are being advertised as something completely new, unique, and proven. We do not offer it here. We investigate what gives birth to the possibility of these beliefs and the seduction of these offers, i.e. we study the mind. Notice that any system represents a stereotypical thinking pattern. **Why do some people get involved with one system while others get**

involved with a different system? People with certain types of thinking, corresponding to the stereotype of a given system, are attracted to it. That is why people who gather around any given system are somewhat similar. This reflects the stereotypical character of their thought process. They are satisfied with this particular theory or system because it is concordant with their own stereotype of mentation. That is why they don't doubt the main postulates of the system.

Any system promises something: self-improvement, better life, spiritual advancement, salvation. Any system has to promise it. **I, on the other hand, don't give you any promises but offer you to find what is of utmost importance:** Who you are at this given moment, i.e. to connect with reality.

Contact with reality is extremely unpleasant for the mind and for the personality, because it is a contact with one's own mechanical nature. It is a contact with the illusions, convictions, beliefs that every one of us carries, grows, and nurtures. **This contact shows our own "love" to our own self.** Personality is a collection of these convictions. I love myself, therefore I love my convictions. While doing this work each one of us can see our readiness to do it, and our advancement in practical investigation of ourselves.

What is your reaction to the fact that the School of Holistic Psychology does not offer any guaranties?

To name is not to understand

Your mind wants to receive a description of what enlightenment is in order to reproduce it. Due to its predestination and nature, the mind cannot understand what it is because enlightenment occurs in a state of mindlessness, a state which is outside of the mind. But the mind wants to prove

241

that it is capable of achieving the enlightenment. Why does the mind constantly try to learn something? Once learned, the mind would recreate what has been learned with the help of the images and say, "I already have it. Enlightenment. Nothing is simpler. I know. One enlightened dude secretly told me everything. I have already experienced it hundred times." Do you understand what I am talking about?

What kind of enlightenment can we even talk about? If that will happen, it will happen. But in order for it to be possible, we need to see the nature of our mind. Because the only thing that precludes us from seeing clearly and holistically is the mind and its games. Here we are occupied with uncovering the mind and showing its games to everybody. We also observe how it reacts to being exposed. Until this is done, it is impossible to move forward. Please understand, nothing new will happen until the mind operates using the habitual scheme. Listen to what everyone said today during our meeting. Was anything new said, or was it something usual and habitual for each one of you?

- *For me it is the same: "What is the mind?" I don't know...*
- That is what everyone here is talking about. Repeating the same thing over and over again. One has a question, and one keeps asking the same question again and again. That is what happens here. Look at each other. Look. It is difficult to understand it in oneself. Look at your neighbor.
- *I don't understand anything. I doubt anyone understands what the mind is.*
- Sad that it is not being videotaped.
- *Is the audiotape finished?*
- No. You still have a chance to ask your main question.
- *Would anyone be able to explain to me what the mind is?*

242

- Two minutes left. You can ask this question five more times. Who wants to ask his main question?
- *What is your opinion of Castaneda's techniques? Let's talk about the mind.*
- Write down your question and then look at what you have been doing for the last twenty years. It is interesting what one can spend one's life on.
- *No, not twenty years.*
- Five years.
- *Yes, for five years I am asking myself this question.*
- What you have been doing today is precisely what you have been doing all your life.
- Write down your questions and answers, and you will see what you have been doing all your life, and what you are going to do for the rest of your life. One does not need to go to the fortuneteller. Everything is here. All your current actions show everything you did before and what you are going to do forever. What a variety. Look at each other. Where is the unknown? After couple more meetings we will know each other thoroughly. No one will say anything new. As soon as one will open one's mouth, everyone will laugh, because everyone knows what one is about to say. That's how it is.

Everything you say is meant for you

The most interesting part is that everything we say, we say to ourselves. We do not say it to other people, we say it to ourselves. Redirect the arrow of your attention inside yourself. Usually we are totally identified with other people and

243

project everything we have onto them. Nothing is left for ourselves.

Try to talk boomerang style now. Say something to another human being, but always remember, you do not say it to him or to her, you say it to yourself. Why is this so important? **It is important because, and I repeat again and again, there cannot be any teachers in the matters we discuss. There is and will not be anyone who will take you by the hand and lead you to God, Nirvana, or Enlightenment. One should become one's own student and one's own teacher. But in order to become one's own teacher, one has to learn how to learn. Once that happens, one no longer needs any teachers. One has his own life to perceive and to learn from.**

Some people say, "Teach me this and teach me that," because that is how our educational system is built. You come to school or university. You pay money to be taught something. I say: "Let us learn how to learn." That is a completely different position. **People do not know how to learn. They simply want to learn, i.e. to know something about a certain subject. Learning how to learn is the most important thing. Awareness is the ability to simultaneously see all your thoughts, feelings, and sensations.**

What is written here is just an invitation to an investigation. There are no rules and regulations here that you need to memorize and comply with. I invite you to investigate yourself. What I do and say may help you to discover something very important in yourself. But it will only happen if you will lean on and push off the internal experience of your own self-investigation. If you don't have it, there is going to be nothing but a philosophical discussion. I am talking about your experience of being aware of your own patterns of changes of thoughts, feelings, and sensations depending on the situations you are in. But in order to achieve this you need to learn to see yourself from the inside. Start very small. Try to separate thoughts from feelings, feelings from sensations, etc. You need to learn to see inside yourself and to understand your thoughts, feelings, and sensations.

Life in and by stereotype

You will be able to see your own stereotypes through another human being. It is this knowledge of ourselves that we try to procure. In reality, knowledge of your stereotype must be dug out. You can look for it in books, but those who write them are also inside the brackets of their stereotypes. The concepts they offer are the thought stereotypes they have. Any given work carries an imprint of the personality of the author unless he previously get rid of it. If it is a famous writer who possesses certain abilities valued by other people, they, while reading his books get into the stereotypes of his feelings and mentation process. It may be a fashionable and up-to-date concept: psychological, religious, philosophical, etc. What do we observe in different fields: cultural, political, economic, and others? Take any particular field and you will see the stereotypes that exist there.

The mind of the average human being does not want to hear anything except what it **considers to be right** and insists on affirmation of what it knows. It wants to pass through the same circle eternally, insisting it says something new, something you did not hear completely, something you did not understand.

What is the personality of a human being one is so proud of and constantly wants to affirm? It is just a fixation on certain stereotypes. It is enough to take one singer, one politician, or one administrator, and we can see what kind of thought stereotypes take place in their milieu—in the milieu of singers, politicians, administrators, etc.

"But not all administrators are the same, they are not all carbon copies of each other," you may say.

Yes. **There are different stereotypes**. There are stereotypes inherent to the mind of a given human being. There are stereotypes innate to that particular slice, that particular way of life one is following. Let us take a human being who is in politics and who considers the role he plays in it to be important. The stereotypes accepted in a particular political system he works in become stereotypes of his mentation.

Perhaps you have noticed that not every single human being fits into a certain life style, into a certain sphere of life. You may have also noticed that if he does fit in, the mechanisms start to work and condition him, in a certain way confirming the stereotypes characteristic for this particular sphere of life. One turns into someone who has been worked up by this mechanism. Of course, there are certain **individual qualities** of the mind, and intrinsic to it stereotypes and thought patterns, patterns of emoting, patterns of feeling which are unique for this particular human being. But when one enters a certain life style, tries to join in, so to speak, one gets a definitive "work up and processing" characteristic for this particular life style.

Take a New Russian, for example. It is a certain stereotype of mentation and behavior. You can see the stereotypes of behavior that are present in the mind of this human being, but he himself is unable to see them. This is something one can see easily in his neighbor, but not in himself. This is something that is easy to see in your friend, but very difficult to see in yourself. If you are told, "This is you. This is about you," you would get angry. Similarly, the behavioral type of a city dweller and a villager can be determined. Nations can be similarly separated. They all can be differentiated based on various stereotypes they fit into.

Let's consider the stereotypical behavior of a man and a woman. What is allowed for a woman may be forbidden for a man, and the reverse also holds true. Certain circles maintain very harsh stereotypes, while others are more flexible. But those are also stereotypes. Flexibility is also a stereotype. We accept this, and you accept that. In one country, you may be sent to jail for speaking about a particular topic, while you might freely discuss it in another country. This is called a stereotype of democracy. A stereotype is something born by the mind. We study the stereotypical and mechanical reactions of the mind.

"But it is impossible to walk away from stereotypes," you may say.

It is impossible to walk away from something you don't yet see. Life consists of stereotypes, so **let us see at least some of them in ourselves**. Let's see our own personality and the stereotypes of which it is made.

To see your personality is to see your stereotypes. Perhaps, you will not be able to see all of them now. But if you do not start seeing them, you will not be able to walk away from them? You need to see them first. It is difficult. Some people see one stereotype and they don't want to see anything anymore.

Do you want to see yours right now?

When one starts to see his own mechanical nature, the stereotypical pattern of one's life, one says, "This is terrible. I want to live differently. I am ready to do anything." And then life itself creates conditions which make it possible for him to see what made him unhappy.

But how many people do you know that want to change their mechanical nature? Many talk about it, but don't do anything. There are quite a few who are ready to talk about the philosophical or religious aspect of this, but who really wants to see one's **personality as it is in reality?** Even if one agrees, how far can one progress in this study? Let's say one pulled out a harmless stereotype, one out of thousand, maybe two or three. Will he want to go further? What will he say face to face with **the most important stereotype**, which is a cornerstone of his personality? He would protect himself with many shields. He will have such a strong defense reaction that no one within a radius of a mile would be able to approach him.

So, does a human being or humanity itself really want to change anything, to change its stereotypes, or is it all just talk, talk, talk? How can we talk about what will happen when we don't yet know what *is*? The only thing that makes sense to do now is to **reveal and to see** the **stereotypes** that are intrinsic to us. Otherwise, everything we discuss, everything we try to move toward will be just another stereotype.

Of course, you may say it is all rubbish. Or you may say, "Yes, there is something to this, but there are also other things. Why make it so dark? Yes, I have some stereotypes. Yes, I can take a look at some of them; it is even somewhat amusing, but one can't spend a lifetime doing it. I have other things to do." What do you think about this?

A man who sees himself in others but does not want to accept himself, starts a war against the image of himself he sees. That is how all conflicts and wars start. A man does not want to see something in himself; he projects it and sees it in somebody else. He does not want to accept it in himself, and he starts a war against his neighbor.

"So, how do we get rid of it?" you may ask.

The question "How?" is a question of the mind, which is not used to living with a holistic understanding. The only thing that can bring one to one's true self is a clear vision of one's own stereotypes. It is extremely difficult to allow oneself to see them. It is usually accompanied by an emotional outbreak. Where do I run now? What do I do now? How?

And what kind of questions do you have right now?

Definition instead of understanding

Would we be able to **understand each other better** if we were to provide definitions for everything we discuss here?

For example, at a certain age every one of us probably asked the question: **What is love?** Perhaps you heard a lot about it at the time but you did not know what it was. In order to understand it better you started to read books that described certain situations and provided certain descriptions and definitions of love. As a result of this work you became a professional in this field, but you have never experienced it practically. **Who**, in your opinion, **understands more about love**: the one who has read a thousand books on the subject or the one who experienced it?

So, what do you want? Do you want to create a huge library about life and the mind, or do you want to experience it?

We have already discussed that the only thing that interferes with our life is the mind, because it lives its own life. The most important thing for the mind is to define everything it comes in contact with. It is also important for the mind to save certain information. Until the mind gets tired of its own definitions, nothing new can begin.

Sometimes one needs a few hours, a few days, or even a few years in order for the mind to become exhausted with itself and then, something new can happen. In reality, in order to see

249

and to understand something holistically, **not much time is needed**. It just seems that multiple things need to be covered and studied. It is an assumption of the mind used to accumulation of knowledge. In reality, understanding occurs **instantly**. It does not require time. What requires time is the assimilation of knowledge, because **thought is time**. More knowledge means more time, and therefore more thoughts are needed. A flash of understanding, on the other hand, happens instantly. Everything we are doing now is just a prelude, a preparation to a possibility of the flash of this understanding, i.e. **instant understanding**.

Meetings between words

When two or more people get together, they **create** a certain **atmosphere**. Every single one comes in a certain state, everyone with his own question: conscious, unconscious. When they get together, **something starts to happen**. The atmosphere of the meeting is defined by the degree of interest of each one of the participants, their desire to feel and understand others.

For example, two human beings are talking and boredom surrounds them. Around others there is fear and aggression. But around some who may just be silently and quietly sitting together, the aura of love, acceptance and trust is felt. Why does it happen? Is it possible to understand this by paying attention only to the words they say? **Is there something beyond words that is being present here**?

So, what is the most important ingredient? Is it the words or something between the words? **The words or pauses**? What do you consider to be the most important? Where would you **want to find the points of connection**? Where can we meet? Can we meet between the rounds of the words we fire

250

at each other? Is it possible that meeting may happen in some **other dimension?**

What role do our words serve? Do they serve to open us up or to close us? When we talk, do we want to defend ourselves or do we **allow ourselves** to be defenseless? Do we use the words we pronounce—the machine gun rounds—to clear the space around us, to protect ourselves or to open a **sincere communication?**

What can one **insert** into a **word?** A word is just a certain form. A word is just a package we transfer to and from each other. What do we really insert in it? What is inside this cover? The packaging may be beautiful or ugly, but it is just a cover. The factory producing all these is a human being himself. So, what does one fill them up with?

And what do you usually react to? Do you react to the **package** or the **substance it contains?**

Do you think these are important questions for self-investigation? That is precisely what we are doing. Someone transfers something. Someone receives something. It is similar to **breathing in and breathing out.** For example, as a result of a certain communication you may feel like someone who is constantly breathing out, being unable to take a breath in. You may say that you are not being heard, you are being constantly interrupted, you are not being able to breathe out when you are overfilled. Another may say, "Here we go. I constantly breathe out, and I can never take a breath in." It is important to understand how this happens. **How does it happen in your case?**

Looking at people, I see **someone asking for water**, screaming, "Give me water, give me water." He is running outside. A small cup in his hand is filled up to the brim. A rain is pouring, and he is screaming, "Give me water, give me water."

So, what do you hear when you listen; what do you perceive when you read?

Every one of you has been to a park and has seen hiking trails. The mind is a big park with its own trails for the thoughts. A human being has a few well-worn **trails for thoughts**. There are couple highways—major thoughts. If one started at point A, one would be obligated to come to a point B while walking a certain trail. It is possible to make a **map of one's mind**. It would contain the **trails of thoughts, trails of feelings** one constantly walks on. These are well maintained, frequently used trails one does not want to get off.

So, what do you hear when you listen, what do you perceive when you read?

Look, but can't see

A child that does not know words is in reality. Later, when the child learns the words and what they depict, the child does not simply look, for example, at a table and see it, but calls it a certain word, a notion. The child names it. Have you ever paid attention to how you look at objects and people around you? How do you look at your husband, your wife, your children, at a passerby on a street, at someone who is being introduced to you?

Who do you see? Between you and another human being there is an image. Every time we look at something, irrespective whether it is a table, a human being, a societal event, a political leader, or an ice-cream in a store, between us and what we are looking at there is an image, an image that was created by us. Describe your image of someone close to you. You do not see him; you see your own image of him. And because of that, a conflict may start, related to him doing something that is incongruent with your image of him. This incongruity starts an internal conflict.

So, between us and what we are looking at, there is an image. How is this image created? In reality, this is precisely what our child was taught to do. The child lost his vision of reality. And how did it happen? The child has lost it by learning words, notions, and convictions. To everything that surrounds him he now reacts with certain notions. He does not need to get into an essence of things. He simply calls them names. That is it. You say, "This is a table," and lose interest to it immediately. You said it and you calmed down. The mind calmed down. **The mind is disturbed when it collides with something incomprehensible and unknown to it, with something it cannot name, define, and classify.**

Have you been in situations when you came in contact with something unknown and incomprehensible? What happens?

A possibility you can easily miss

A path of human development goes through multiple crises. Certain knots develop. It is precisely those knots that **create the biggest opportunities**. Some take advantage of those opportunities, some don't.

There are certain periods of time in the process of the development of a human being, and humanity when **this opportunity may be realized**, when certain conditions develop for the realization of this opportunity. Will **another opportunity** of this kind **occur again** if this period passed and this opportunity was missed, overlooked, not used? **When?** It may not happen very soon. It may never happen again.

For example, one did not understand and did not see the opportunity for which a set of certain necessary conditions converged. Will he be able to recover this missed opportunity later: in a week, in two weeks, in a year?

Some opportunities appear very seldom. A human being cannot create them by himself, because they appear as a result of global processes.

I am not talking about such thing as, for example, grocery shopping for a pound of cheese. Today you were unable to find it in this store, but tomorrow you would buy it somewhere else. I am talking about opportunities, origination, appearance, and the realization of which depend on global processes and on a combination of a multitude of different factors. If one, coming in contact with this opportunity, does not see it, one loses it and it may never appear again.

One is offered a chance, albeit not in a beautiful wrapper, not in a form of something pleasant and familiar. It may be completely unexpected and it might even be quite tragic. One usually wants to run away from it. One tries to think it through, but this is a chance one cannot approach with one's mind. The mind will never understand it, but you can see behind this something big, something very important, something that you cannot miss. **But it is not going to be the mind that will tell you that**.

The mind will tell you something completely opposite. The mind wants to show that it is in charge here and decides everything. So the mind rejects the opportunity. It leads you away from it, not toward it. One must see this opportunity. The art of seeing is very important here—one's ability to see reality, not the illusion.

The role of a teacher on the Way

I don't think there is a universal path here. Every single human being has his own path. I cannot and I am not asking you to follow my path. Every one of us sets forth somewhere he wants to go to, and this movement comes from **his own quest**. The speed of this movement is defined by the **power** of the **question**. Direction of this movement is defined by the seeing of a given human being at a given period of time.

Your desire may be very strong, but your seeing may be very fragmented. In such a case, wanting to get out of the forest, you can circle around the same tree. You may pass many trees but get lost between three of them, or circle four trees, calling it a fourth way.

We can say that the first thing is your desire to get out of something or to move somewhere. The second thing is a clear vision that allows you to perform this movement and to see what happens. Otherwise, you would constantly walk in the same circle, calling it The Way.

You are not walking behind me, you are going with me. It is **presence, not leading**. I see my role as a role of the one who is **being Present**.

Is there a difference between a leader and the one who is present? Of course, there is and quite an essential one. **I differ from a leader. I do not take any responsibility to lead you anywhere**.

We do not sign agreements here. You may walk by yourself. Where would you arrive? You will arrive where you are going to arrive. On the other hand, you may happen to be in the presence of someone who has walked many different roads.

Let us say I know the woods very well. Someone is lost, and I am sitting by the fire. He runs to me happy, "Finally, I found someone. I was walking here for the last ten years unable to find an exit. Can you help me?" I say, "Okay. I would be near you, and you would go as you want to go. You can talk to me, you can ask me questions." He says, "I need to get out of the woods." The one who is present asks, "And where do you want to go?" "It is not very important to me where to go, I just need to get out of these woods." "How can I lead you out if you don't know where you want to go?" And he replies, "It is irrelevant to me; I just want to get out of these damn woods." "Let's do it this way. I would be with you, but you will have to decide for yourself where you want to go. Otherwise, I will take you somewhere and you will say you did not want to go there. You may find a new place to be even worst that the woods you came from."

It is a big difference between **one walking in the presence of someone** and one leading someone. First of all, the one in question does not even remember how he got into these woods. Secondly, he is unable to say where he wants to go, because he does not know anything except these woods. He only sees these woods and does not know what is behind them. What will he like better: the woods he came from or the new terrain he is standing in front of? He does not know the new terrain he is about to enter. He might come to a city full of angry people or to a place where his feet are going to be washed every night. He may like the second scenario and remain in a state of bliss for ten days. Day eleven comes, and he says, "That is so boring," and starts a fight. City dwellers ask, "Where did he come from?" "Here is the guy who brought him." "Why did you bring someone like him?"

What about the movement itself? Let's acknowledge that some people have a desire to move somewhere. It might develop out of their dissatisfaction with the place they currently occupy. That may be a sufficient reason for them to start moving, but the impulse might be weak. For example, a man sleeps somewhere in a wetland. Led to a dry place, he is happy and does not have any desire to go further. He sits on dry grass with the sun shining, "It is great here."

A lot here depends on the strength of one's impulse, on one's question. A man may take ten steps and stop. Cuckoo is cuckooing over there. He sits listening to the cuckoo and asks, "How many years do I have left?" Cuckoo cuckoos at him. He asks another question and the bird cuckoos something else. He may decide to stay there.

That is why I say that **the answer depends on your question**. Everything depends on one's stockpile of desire: ten steps, twenty steps, twenty miles, or hundred miles. If your stockpile is good for ten miles, you walk it and stop. If your stockpile is bigger, you can walk more.

When you take a few steps forward, a mirror appears in front of you. **You see yourself in this mirror.** And here the most interesting thing happens. These mirrors for different people appear at different moments. Someone sees his first mirror after the first step, another sees his mirror ten miles down the road.

Let's say the **first mirror** appears. He sees himself in it, but he does not recognize it as a mirror. He does not realize he is seeing his own reflection. He thinks he is seeing another human being. He starts to interact with this human being. He may get angry, upset, and fearful. He may get aggressive and physical, but what appears in this mirror has a very interesting peculiarity—it acts in the same fashion. If he acts as he acted previously, the mirror continues to support him in that interaction. The chain of interactions develops, leading him through the same recurrent circles.

If he is unable to see that he is dealing with his own reflection, the situation repeats itself: the same thoughts, the same emotions, the same behavior. This will continue until he realizes he is in front of a mirror, i.e. his own reflection, some part of his own image. It may take a long time.

What does the one who is Present do in such a situation? The one who is Present says, "What you just met is your mirror. Stop. Make sure you **pay attention** here. Observe and see it. Everything you say, feel, and do is being returned to you through this mirror. It gets you into a loop. Look at it. Pay attention to it. Hear it. Feel it." That is the role of the one who is Present.

What can a leader do here? A leader can grab our man by the neck, and force him to go forward. A leader can join our man, stand in front of the mirror and try to communicate with the mirror.

The one who is present will remind our man that he just encountered a certain part of himself, and the external world, **as a mirror, reflects this part back to him**. If he is capable of seeing his own reflection, he will pass through it, similarly to Alice in Wonderland, and walk further.

More and more mirrors will appear in front of him. He will recognize some people as mirrors, others he will not. This will continue until he gets to know himself fully. The one who is Present will accompany him on this journey, showing and explaining to him what he encounters, reminding him that **he sees his own reflection everywhere**.

Someone may stop in front of a certain mirror and say, "No, this is not a mirror. Please, do not fool me, don't mix me up. And, you know what, I like it here a lot, and I will stay here." The one who is Present will continue to wake him up, reminding him of what, in reality, happens here, as long as he wants to be woken up, but if he says, "No. It's enough. I am tired of it," the one who is Present will walk away. It does not mean he will stay away forever, but the conversation stops. It stops until the desire to wake up and to see reality resurface in that human being.

"May a man clash with his own reflection and not understanding it, walk through the mirror?" you may possibly ask.

No. One either continues to stay in front of the mirror with his habits, or one walks through the mirror. But the only way for him to **walk through the mirror** is to become aware that this is a part of his own image. **Mirrors happen to be very different.** There are small mirrors and there are big mirrors. The further one goes, the bigger is the mirror that appears in front of him. Finally, the mirror may appear that reflects him all. In the beginning, the mirrors that appear only reflect him partially, one fragment at a time. It will be impossible for the second mirror to appear if the first one has not been passed through. It is impossible for the third mirror to appear if the second one has not been passed through. How many mirrors he will have to pass is not known. Where and how will he meet them is also unknown, but it is essential for him to understand that the second mirror can only appear once the first one is passed. **It is impossible to bypass the mirror.**

There are **curved mirrors and straight mirrors**. The one who likes to philosophize usually collides with the curved mirrors. One can never see oneself in a curved mirror. It provides only distorted and falsified images. It is a mirror that reflects the illusion. One only sees one's own illusions. That is why I am constantly reminding you about the difference between philosophizing and a real question, a real conversation.

The one who philosophizes meets curved mirrors, which take him further and further away from reality.

One's aim is determined by what kind of mirrors appear along one's way: curved or straight. These mirrors appear regardless whether you come to our meetings or not. Your whole life consists of these mirrors, but not many people can

259

see them or understand them. The one who is Present may point out these mirrors for you.

One can **live amongst the greatest opportunities** and yet not see them. In such a case, the most important thing is for him to recognize them. One walks a road and sees a pointer with the word "Prague." That does not mean that he knows what Prague is. However, seeing the **pointer**, one may **move in the right direction** and find out what Prague is later. On the other hand, if one comes to a pointer that is a curved mirror, it would direct him to a completely different place. The most interesting part is that one will see this Prague, but it will be the illusory Prague, a false, distorted, fictitious city, carrying the same name.

When a man have lived his life, when he lived not one but many lives in these distorted mirrors, the pointer showing **an opportunity to meet a straight mirror** can play the role of a ship for someone who spent five days in the ocean, drifting in cold water without food or water. It is similar to a sinking ship receiving the answer to its SOS signal. The ship with its crew and passengers is sinking. They will probably not survive if the SOS signal is not returned. Therefore, the question of them being heard is not a philosophical question. It is a question of life and death. When the **strength of the question** is so strong, a man would go through not one, not two, but all the mirrors he has to go through. If the question is not that strong, he may not even want to see these mirrors as mirrors.

Life is an opportunity. If we understand it, we use it. If we don't, we don't use it. What kind of an opportunity is given to us during our meetings? Our group is an organism. All organisms either grow or die. Some people think that an organism can live neither developing nor degrading. This is fiction. This is self-deception. Everything in this world either develops or is subjected to degradation. There is no other option. Any given organization or association of any kind (human beings in particular) either develops or dies. No intermediary state exists. The development itself also goes through death. The enlightened beings are said to be **born twice**. What does this mean? It means one has died at least once being in the body, but the body did not disappear during the process. How can one be born if one did not die? He dies, but the body remains, and then he gets born again. The body may die differently, not decomposing physically. It pertains to one human being as well as to a group of people, as well as to humanity at large.

I feel very good when something develops or something dies. In both cases I serve as a **catalyst**. May what needs to die, die faster, and may what needs to develop, develop faster.

What I say is very simple...

A few words on my vision about what happens in the groups of self-investigators. First, I ask what kind of question you have today. Usually one has a very hard time expressing it. Let him say it anyway. He may not ask exactly what he wanted to ask, but it **starts a dialogue** between us. Let's **start an interaction**. A certain channel opens up. One says something, I listen, and other people listen too. A certain channel develops between us, a certain interaction. And through this channel, something can be transmitted. A **connection develops.**

Using these channels, I try to carry something to people who are present, and they in return try to carry something to me and others. But if one starts to resist to what is coming one's way, if something is touched that one does not want to see or hear, something very personal, something harsh, then **one starts to transmit some hard schemes through this channel**. These are his convictions. These are the thought patterns, and usually they are quite hard. Imagine some stones that fell into a sink and clogged up a pipe, and water has a difficult time passing through it now. This is analogous to what happens when one aggressively vocalizes his convictions and does not want to hear anybody else. These hard thoughts and convictions start to obstruct our channels of communication. I try to blow air through them, but quite frequently the intensity of these hard convictions start to increase, sometimes clogging up the channel completely. I experience it as an **inability to breathe out.** One brought in certain questions, certain inner desires, but certain parts of the personality resist.

What happens between us is an **interchange of energies**. These energies generate certain transformations. I don't want to discuss what it is and how it happens; one may create multiple hypotheses in regards to this. This process **is not knowable, but it is very active**. Its action is such, that the mind cannot comprehend it. It is understood differently, through the vision of the body. The **mind over body control is lifted**. The fact that the mind does not understand something or does not want to understand something does not mean that it is not happening.

The more we unplug from the mind, i.e. try to understand and classify less, the more our body starts to see, sense, and feel. It happens imperceptibly, very quietly. **Which one of you can hear the wind**? Who notices and hears birds singing? They are constantly singing. Actually, they are singing right now outside. The wind is also a melody. **It is a melody of life, melody of nature. Who notices it?**

One would pay a lot of money to listen to and to see a famous actor or actress. One spends a lot of money to get a front row ticket at the opera. Now one sits and enjoys it. This is the result of one's effort. One can enjoy it now. This is traditional, stereotypical **assumption of a human being on how to get pleasure.**

The same human being walked the street and had the wind blow in his face, birds were singing, and all this was natural and inconspicuous. Who paid attention to this? Who pays money to stay under the tree and listen to a nightingale? The bird does not ask for money, it just sings. It is natural. **It is self-explanatory. That is precisely why the majority of people are not interested in it.** What is self-explanatory is not interesting. People are interested only in what requires applied effort and needs to be achieved.

How often do we look up at the skies? How often do we see sunset, sunrise, clouds. One considers himself an esthete and lover of the arts, attends expositions, checks the paintings of famous artists, pays enormous amounts of money and hangs them in a bedroom and looks at the painted skies and clouds, and shows it to others. One explains what an artist wanted to say depicting skies and clouds, and one is respected as a connoisseur of the arts. The skies are there all the time, but who lifts his chin to see it? Who gets up in the morning to hear a nightingale sing the sunrise?

One may say, "You know, I went out today at four am to listen to a nightingale." People would say, "You are nuts. We went to see Michael Jackson. That was real! That was something! I was listening to Michael. He was dressed so… and he just went through the latest plastic surgery. His nose is completely different now." This can be discussed forever, the music forgotten.

But what can you say about a nightingale? How can you describe it? That is why it is not interesting for most people. One cannot describe or talk about it; therefore it is not an event. **A nightingale sings, the wind blows, and who cares?** Do I discuss something one may think about? What is

263

there to think about? **I say simple things. What is there to think about?** Many people do not find it interesting. "What is there to say about nightingale? Describe and explain to me your philosophical system. That would be interesting!"

The mind wants to create a technique out of everything, even out of hearing birds sing. But this is not a technique. Someone may say I recommend listening to the birds for ten minutes before and for twenty minutes after dinner. Another may say that nightingale should be listened to before meals and chickadee after. This will be conducing for enlightenment. One can create a whole system around it.

When you listen to a bird, you do not appraise anything. This is a taste, a smell of That Life. A certain **pause** develops in our habitual hurry-scurry. One was running before and will run afterwards, but presently one touch something, something outside of one's habitual worries and convictions. Asked what one thought about at the time, one would probably say, "Nothing really; I did not think about anything." At the time, one listened and one heard something.

Prior to that, one also listened to many different things: radio, TV, some people on the phone during the workday. One listened, but did one really hear anything? Someone calls you, but you are thinking your thoughts. Someone talks on the TV, but you are thinking your thoughts. That is why there is nothing unusual, everything is the same: your own thoughts, emotions, and problems. **Unusual enters one in a completely unusual way.** That is why it is unusual. Unusual cannot arrive in a usual package; it comes in a different, not habitual way. But this something that comes not in a habitual way, one either rejects it or simply fails to notice.

By the way, listening to the birds singing may also become a habit. Any method, any system turns into a habit after a while.

264

Then there is no movement, just a repetition that a human being receives pleasure from.

To *live differently*

What is the intent and the meaning of our meetings? What is the intent? How is it being realized? How do we become aware of this idea that unites us, and how do we become aware of the meaning of it as applied to each one of us in particular? I think these are very important questions. For me, these are essential questions. They are constantly with me. I view everything that happens to me and others through these questions.

Are there ready answers to those questions? I don't think so. **No one would ever say, "You came here for this. This will happen, and then that would happen."** We are not dealing with an astrological prediction here.

How can one find the answers to these questions? There are no premade answers here. **This is the Way, and these questions are the Pointers along the Way.** It is a movement. I hear, feel, and see that I need to act. I have to act, and as a result of my action I will come to understanding. But this is not a usual, directed toward a certain material aim, action. At the same time, any activity requires an aim. If one does not understand one's aim or does not see it clearly, one is unlikely to achieve a result. One has to understand what one is doing, what one is doing it for, and how one is to do it. This can be defined as a "competent approach" to business.

So, what we are discussing and getting in touch with here is not "this" and is not "that," because our **habitual approaches to setting aims, doing, and acting are not useful here**, even though we don't exclude them. **To do by not doing. To move while at rest. To be in That world and**

in This world. This is a rope you walk on. You have to see very clearly what is on the left, and what is on the bottom, and what is on the top. This is the balance that is created early on the way by some kind of strong inner tension. I call it a cross with the top, the bottom, the right, the left, and with you in the middle. It is a **combination of incompatibles**, the unification of certain polarities and dualities. The Way of the mind goes through a plane where duality is present, but you can exit its limits and arrive where everything is one.

How is one to walk one's path? Again, there are no premade answers here and cannot be. One is constantly facing questions and facts. **What is a fact?** Let's take facts of the outside world. A fact is a real event that has taken place in the outside world. For example, it can be a bus being few minutes late or some event which happened in the world far away. It is something that really happened, really took place. It may be an event totally unimportant from the standpoint of usual perception. More often than not, one's usual, habitual vision will not notice it. It may be a combination of fallen leaves. It may be a certain weather pattern. You may be able to see it or not.

In order for you to see it, you should be **tuned into seeing** it. It is a very unusual point of view. One living in the rush of the mind will not notice it. That is why cleansing of the mind to have an opportunity to see something unusual is mandatory here. Without it, this way of vision and this way of life is impossible. But it is precisely this way of seeing things and this way of life that create an opportunity for understanding the questions we discuss. A lot depends on **what kind of a perceiving apparatus a given human being has.**

If it is a usual, traditional perceiving apparatus, it will perceive the usual things and facts which are considered to be important from the point of view of that usual life. But these are not even facts, but the interpretation of certain events by others. One joins this interpretation, but in reality does not see anything new. But an opportunity to look at what is happening in reality impartially and with a view free from intellectualization of the mind is a mandatory requirement here. Without it nothing can be seen.

Sometimes a fact may only be noticed thanks to the people possessing a vision. On the intersection of different points of view, a point of focus appears in which this fact can be "caught" and seen. Next, this fact can be discussed by these people, and it may become a pointer to them. Perhaps it may not be understood right away, but what is very important is for it to be noted and fixed. Then they may see another fact, and then another one. And when these facts become visible simultaneously as a result of them being "caught," discussed and understood, they may align in a certain mosaic of vision, which will provide an answer to a certain question, which might have also appeared as a result of a certain vision.

It is not easy to explain this in words. It is a completely unusual way of life, but it seems to me it is exactly the way of life that provides an opportunity to understand the spheres of life we are discussing. I would repeat, it is **impossible to read about this topic anywhere.** Nobody will tell you anything on this matter. It does not mean one should not read anything. I do not say "yes" or "no" to anything because sometimes a fact or something of importance may come unexpectedly from any source. It may be a book or a movie. It may be a simple walk in a park. These facts-pointers come from the surroundings one occupies, but they don't come to everyone. They come to a certain human being or to a group of people capable of seeing this fact and connecting it with other facts they have.

Why is a group of people so important? A group of people represents what I call **different flash lights, i.e. an ability of**

multiple or different visions. This work cannot be done alone. This work is done by a group of people. Each one of the group possesses a possibility of seeing certain things that others don't see or have difficulty seeing. Getting together, discussing these visions together, these people start seeing more. The way I see it, this is precisely the main task of people belonging to what we call "a group of self-investigators." Moreover, everything is so intertwined here that it is impossible to separate one thing from another. This deep inner work of entering yourself provides cleansing of the internal mechanisms and an opportunity for clear vision. The same work creates favorable conditions for questions to be brought up by one member of a group or by everyone. On the intersection of these moments the real questions are being born that point to the direction of investigation. This happens only during group work. That is why the internal aim and everyone's passion is so important. This unity provides an opportunity. It is something alive, something that cannot be born any other way. **This is living through the real meaning of experience by each one of us separately and as a group together.** These are the specifics and the peculiarities of the work of self-investigation.

It is the investigation of oneself, through oneself, and with the help of oneself. A human being represents the investigator and the laboratory in which the investigation is conducted. He is the one who gets the result and the one who uses it. And all this is in the human being himself. No special equipment is needed—everything one needs is already present either in the investigator himself or in a group conducting the investigation. All the conditions required for an experiment are not planned—they occur spontaneously, i.e. life itself is that special laboratory where everything happens. A change in internal states of each participant and group as a whole, leads to the appearance of those special conditions in both external and internal spaces that allow us to carry on the necessary investigation. Everyone in this group is a creative individual. He or she must be an individual, because it is only through the conjunction of those individualities, united in their aim and at the same time individual in their manifestations and peculiarities, that the opportunity is created to lead such an investigation.

What we are doing here is not a religious practice. There are no beliefs and no authorities here that represent a necessary part of a religious cult. It is an art. It is a science. It is a religion. But all these terms carry a somewhat different, uncommon meaning.

The division occurred. Religion, science, culture, economics became separate fields that practically do not interact with each other. Inside each one of these fields a number of small "gardens" divided by "fences" exist. We are attempting to unite them by combining religion, science, and art.

We are entering a completely unknown field where the usual, habitual methods used by science cannot work. Science is built on experiments, on repetition of those experiments, on an ability to receive consistent, reproducible results. We are unable to do so as we are working with ourselves. Reproduction of external repetitive conditions leading to external repetitive result is impossible here.

We are developing a completely new methodology, **a new method of knowledge, where the investigator and what is being investigated are not separated but exist as a whole**: an investigator is the investigated. This is a science of a **human being of the future**. We investigate life of the humanity through a group of select people. Our work is going to influence everything that happens to humanity. Currently, this work cannot be perceived with the usual vision. As a result, it either goes unnoticed or is interpreted inadequately. But it continues. So, we are starting to produce an influence that is not yet well understood. What we are doing here creates an opportunity to understand it and possibly to translate it to language that will be understood by people who are just starting to experience it. Perhaps this process will get stronger and a lot of what people do not notice or do not want to notice now will develop so strongly that it will be impossible not to notice it any longer.

KEYS TO ENTER OTHER DIMENSIONS
OF ONE REALITY

• ◆ • ◆ • ◆ • ◆ • ◆ • ◆ • ◆ • ◆ • ◆ • ◆ • ◆ • ◆ • ◆ • ◆ • ◆ • ◆ • ◆ • ◆ •

Awareness, Vision

Only our own consciousness brings to life everything we look at. If we do not spiritualize our world, it dies. The world dies and gets reborn within us.

* * *

A state of consciousness may be characterized by its duration, frequency of appearance, and depth and width of penetration. Those parameters change as a result of our work of self-investigation. The goal of our work is total and constant awareness of oneself.

* * *

What is important is not what others know about you, but what you know about yourself.

* * *

Awareness ties everything together. Awareness is a force which holds and unites all parts of a whole. Awareness is not a thought, a feeling, a sensation, or an action. It is something that unites all four of them. Awareness is a primary source of everything within us.

* * *

271

Awareness is not the content of what you understand, but a moment of understanding and the experience of it.

* * *

Awareness is an instant broadening of the borders of your perception. It is a holistic vision of what is happening as an interlinked current of events.

* * *

Awareness is never repeated. It is always new. Knowledge gets rusty as soon as it appears; awareness never.

* * *

Awareness is impossible to store. It is impossible to share. It is impossible to describe. It can only be experienced again and again.

* * *

Awareness is always alive. Knowledge is always dead. There is no awareness, no life in knowledge.

* * *

Awareness is a rapidly flowing stream of water, not a river-bed.

* * *

Perhaps, you are aware of your thoughts, but not aware of your sensations and feelings. In such a case, inconsistency between what you think and say and what you feel and do may be characteristic for you. For example, you insist you like your work, but somehow you are not very happy to be there. You can say you love reading, but you do not read. Perhaps you are better at being aware of your feelings or actions but are not aware of your thoughts. Then you will constantly have internal and external inconsistencies. Every single one of us is plugged into a mental, emotional, and physical channel irrespective of the fact of whether or not he or she is aware of it. A complete awareness of oneself as a constantly moving and transforming energy channel is necessary for the one who wants to be healthy. Becoming aware of oneself is a direct Way toward a healthy and harmonious life. To be aware means simply to observe without a choice, not to define or explain.

* * *

Awareness is freeing one's perception of the world.

* * *

The state of awareness is either present or absent. There are no intermediate states of semi-awareness.

* * *

Awareness is not a thought, not a feeling or action. It is an impartial vision, not plugged in observation of newly appearing thoughts, feelings, sensations, and actions.

* * *

Awareness of oneself is an understanding realized in spontaneous actions.

* * *

There is nothing impossible for the Soul that is aware of itself.

* * *

Awareness may be characterized by the magnitude of energy of free (unidentified) attention.

* * *

A sentient being is capable of entering and exiting any process or an event without identifying with it. One who is not present is unable to not get involved in certain processes and events and is unable to exit those at will. Processes and events in which one gets mechanically involved are determined by the characteristic conditioning of one's mind and personality.

* * *

To free perception from limitations, duality, and the fragmented nature of the conditioned mind is possible only through one's own awareness. A sentient consciousness is capable of perceiving and acting in different worlds, and corresponding to the level of consciousness of these worlds.

* * *

The connection to supreme "I" is made through the aware Soul. A presence of free attention is an indicator of Soul's awareness of itself.

* * *

A vision is an observation without a choice, i.e. impartial, uninvolved with the observed event, attention.

* * *

A vision determines what should be said and done and how it should be said and done.

* * *

One's vision is determined by one's body-mind, because the information about the aim of your Supreme "I" is stored in the cells of your body. Every cell of your organism contains information about the whole Universe. By receiving access to this information, which is contained within you, you will know everything you need to know in order to See and to Act in accord with the Plan of the Creator (Unified Consciousness).

* * *

A vision is possible when all three functional centers of a human being are harmonized.

* * *

A vision is a result of practical experience, not of a belief.

* * *

A vision is remembrance of what you already know. This knowledge is encoded in the cells of a human body.

* * *

A vision is a direct understanding without the intermediary of the conditioned mind and thoughts.

* * *

Distortion in vision occurs when one tries to explain, appraise, or judge what is being seen. Mistakes arise due to the interference of the superficial mind.

* * *

Vision has to be realized in the action that follows out of it. This action is what is important, not the interpretation or appraisal of what is being seen.

* * *

A vision does not occur through physical vision.

* * *

A vision is not a manipulation, as it influences neither events nor other people.

* * *

A vision is a direct experience of what is happening, not of thinking it through.

* * *

A vision supersedes any concept, conviction. It supersedes the work of the conditioned mind. That is why one is only capable of seeing in a state of non-thinking.

* * *

To see is to exit the limits of the conditional mind.

* * *

In one object, an average onlooker and a Seer observe: one— an external form, another—its essence. To look does not mean to see.

* * *

Awareness is the change and broadening of one's own perception.

* * *

Sleep and the usual so-called wakeful state are two forms of consciousness, but neither one of them is awareness. Sleep and the wakeful state are the only possible forms of consciousness for an average human being. Wakeful state is just a variation of sleep. Therefore, a human being who is not aware of himself is constantly asleep; he lives in a world of illusions and fantasy.

* * *

In order to see images of yourself, or images of your personality, you have to have free attention, i.e. free energy. If all your energy is habitually spent on your involvement with everything you usually think, feel, and do, you do not have free attention. Become aware of at least one of your habitual involvements, and you will get free energy that you will be able to use to become aware of one more of your mechanical habits. This is the way to increase and to store free energy. It frees you from mechanical functioning.

* * *

Becoming aware of yourself will allow you to perceive everything as a flow of events of mental, emotional, physical, and other planes.

* * *

Consciousness is just an opportunity for awareness.

* * *

Awareness is consciousness aware of itself.

* * *

Awareness is not a mental function. Awareness has nothing to do with thinking, and it is not a reflection with or without a motive. Also, it is not a memory, and it is not a recollection of previously experienced states.

* * *

Awareness is an understanding, a direct experience, and a vision of oneself and what is happening around one as a flow of events.

* * *

Only you can determine whether you are currently aware of yourself or not. Only you can know the real truth about yourself.

Attention

Only through awareness of yourself can the identified attention be transformed into free attention.

* * *

With the help of a free attention, you will be able to create and to destroy anything you want in your life. You will also be able to enter and exit anything at will. It may be an economic, a political, or a social process, a thing, a human being, an event, or a different world...

Free attention is your door as well as the key to the entrance and to the exit. As your attention frees, your possibilities and your freedom increase. The more identified your attention is, the lesser your freedom.

* * *

Fear of total freedom is fear of losing the known.

* * *

Free attention may be directed in different directions simultaneously. Spreading it in three dimensions, you enter a material world. The spread of attention into four, five, or more dimensions is possible. Accordingly, you enter the worlds possessing completely different characteristics and possibilities. Your capabilities are determined only by your capabilities of distributing your free attention.

* * *

Dual perception is simultaneous perception inside and outside of a "soap" bubble of a thought form, an image created by the conditioned mind. It is a perception of an awakened Soul embodied within a human body, capable of dividing its attention simultaneously between physical and non-physical spheres.

* * *

The practice of attention is an ability to simultaneously observe two opposite sides of any event, process, thing, etc.

* * *

An identified attention is energy that helps us to keep and reinforce our illusionary notion of the world, i.e. to maintain the world of illusions.

* * *

Free attention is the energy of awareness you can direct and use. It initiates from the Aim (Will) of your Supreme "I."

* * *

A human being that does not have free attention is simply a mechanism, a robot.

* * *

Identified attention is attracted only to the usual, the known to the conditioned mind and personality phenomena, things, and events.

Perception, attunement, Supreme "I"

Seeing is the perception of something that does not have a form and therefore does not require a thought or a need to be thought through.

* * *

Only the Supreme "I" is capable of correctly tuning one's perception. The correct attunement allows one to see something one needs to see, originating with one's tasks related to certain goals of one's embodiment in a given body, without any kind of mental efforts. The correct attunement of a perception is clear vision and correct actions.

* * *

The aims of the Supreme "I" come from the awareness of its role in the realization of the Plan and Design of the Creator.

278

The Supreme "I" represents one of the multiple aspects of the creative power of One Creator (Unified Consciousness).

* * *

What we see is always a result of attunement of our perception. The ability of seeing in a given human being is determined by the diapason of energetic frequencies (vibrations) of consciousness mastered by him, i.e. vibrations he can catch and understand. The possibilities of perception of a human being exceed current, actualized possibilities.

* * *

Awareness of the Aim (Will) of the Supreme "I" widens the diapason of one's perception, allowing one to see everything necessary for the execution of an Action, born out of the Aim.

* * *

The transformation of energy of personal desires into the Aim of your Supreme "I" is the main result of the process of the transformation of a human being into the Human Being.

* * *

The Supreme "I," in the presence of a good channel of communication with a human being (body-mind), actualizes the tuning of his perception.

* * *

A diapason of perception of the conditioned mind never exits the limits of duality.

* * *

A desire, related to the possession of a certain form, increases the identification, i.e. the attachment to the physical world and fixates one's perception to a very narrow diapason.

* * *

In order to enter the unknown, one needs to abandon the known, i.e. to rebuild the system of one's perception.

* * *

Vision requires the rebuilding and broadening of the diapason of one's usual perception.

* * *

Life is a constant flow of events, a movement of energy. It has no pauses. It has no stops. By perceiving life through the conditioned mind, we create fixations brought up by its attachments and dependencies. A fixation is analogous to a stop-image, i.e. to a film freeze during the showing of a movie. Action stops. When this happens, people in a movie theater start to whistle. They get angry. They want to continue with the movie. In life we constantly stop the perception of what is happening around us. It is the same thing.

* * *

Understanding of any conceptual system requires a certain tuning of a perception.

* * *

Any given perception is relative.

* * *

Global convictions and beliefs of humanity are the major deterrents in the spectrum of perception of every human being.

* * *

What is important is not what you perceive observing the world, but why you are able to perceive so little at present.

* * *

If you do not limit yourself to naming what you observe only, you will be able to see many properties intrinsic to the observed as well as peculiarities of its changes. For example, looking at the rose, you will see its tenderness and beauty expressed in its color, form, and smell… If your attention is not fixed on definitions alone, you will be able to see quite a lot of interesting new things around you.

* * *

Do not define your states, and they will change. If, on the other hand, you define your state as boredom or illness, you will continue to be in it until you define your state differently. But changing one's states by changing their definitions is quite a monotonous and slow process. Just observe your states, and you will see that there is nothing constant in them; they are just a flow of thoughts, feelings, and sensations. Some of them are quite habitual to you, and therefore you do not want to let them go.

Therefore, they recur more frequently than others. Let go of them, and other states will come, beautiful in their unknowingness.

* * *

Everything depends on your perception. You can see this book as something hard and material, but you can also see it as a flow of thoughts, ideas, and images or as energy and information. Everything depends only on the tuning of your perception. Perhaps, for now, your perception is tuned to seeing only material objects and images of your thoughts. Go deeper, and you will see what is behind them.

* * *

By changing your perception, you can turn any material thing into energy, and energy into any material thing. This is real magic. It is accessible to any human being who has become aware of himself and of his real nature of being a creator.

Understanding

Understanding represents a vision of place and of interconnections between a given event, process, thing from the point of view of that wholeness: they all enter as parts.

* * *

Understanding is a perception of a particular out of the general, but not the reverse.

* * *

Understanding is possible only when complete harmony between all of the functions of the body-mind of a human being is achieved. Body, mind, and heart should have harmonious interrelationships. This is a union of rational and irrational, male and female, in a human being.

* * *

If you are looking at something, it does not mean you understand it. Understanding requires a certain state of mind and is possible only during the process of spacious mentation, which does not exclude any, but includes all possible points of view.

* * *

Understanding may have an intellectual, emotional, or physical color. It depends on which function prevail in a given human being.

* * *

Real understanding of something is possible only when you unite with it. When you will become a Unified Consciousness you will understand everything. But what precludes you from doing this? Your persistent desire to become someone is in the way. And for this desire to become someone, you are paying with an opportunity to be everything.

* * *

Vision is understanding without doubts. Any doubt points to the fact that you are still in the realm of the dual mind. Understanding is not dual, and as a result does not have forms of words or images, although you can try to transmit it in certain forms. One should always remember that knowledge transmitted in a certain form is distorted knowledge. In the physical world, we are bound to use a distorted method of transmission of Knowledge. This always needs be considered.

* * *

The only barrier preventing one from understanding is the limitations and conditioning of the mind by its own convictions and beliefs. Understanding does not require any kind of education, as it happens to be a natural state of the Supreme "I." Only one thing is necessary—what interferes with one's ability to be in a state of understanding, i.e. limitations of the mind, need to be eliminated. Every single human being has specific barriers that obstruct understanding. It is a burrow of convictions of one's false personality glued with a cement of beliefs in their truthfulness that create this obstruction.

* * *

Understanding is not given to one who does not seek and have longing for it. The road to understanding lies through deception. Deception is a random walk within spheres of known, not understanding your real position. Deception is temporary; understanding is infinite. Deception is darkness, i.e. the simple absence of light. Light of understanding connects and unifies scattered notions that appear as a result of a conditioned and fragmented perception. Understanding is the knowledge that exists independent of language.

Action

Action, following out of vision, does not require thinking or reflection. It is a direct continuation and realization of vision.

* * *

Actions that result as a consequence of a work of the conditioned mind (appraisals, solutions, choices), carry all the characteristics of the conditioned mind—separation, fragmentation, contrariety. Naturally, these actions will not lead you to real love and wholeness.

* * *

While in action, one gets into constantly changing circumstances, opening oneself up to a flow of events, to life. If action or inaction is caused by fear, this fear will be magnified as a result of the action. Fear is an indicator of a state of fallacy, non-seeing. One should not become afraid of one's own fears but should become aware of them. Awareness of fear leads to its disappearance. To become aware of fear does not mean to analyze its causes. Analysis just makes it stronger as it acknowledges its reality.

* * *

It is only possible to know reality through an aware action. An aware action is vision and vice versa. Vision always leads to action, and action leads to vision. Vision and action are the same thing. Try to understand this. To learn to act correctly is to learn to see correctly.

* * *

Any mechanical reaction strengthens the personality, reinforcing habitual thoughts, feelings, and actions. An aware action cannot bring harm to anyone, as it is coming from the holistic vision of what is happening.

* * *

Any kind of action presupposes a certain consequence of moves that create and make visible what has been done. Operating in the physical world, we are unable to escape doing something. However, our action can be mechanical and devoid of awareness or creative and full of awareness. By doing something mechanically, you perform a stereotypical, rigidly fixated consequence of actions, always producing the same result. This is not creativity but routine recreation of the same process. One is only able to create when one is aware of oneself and acts from this awareness. Real creativity is the creativity of the Supreme "I" embodying the plan of the Great Creator in this world.

* * *

Any choice is a reduction and the throwing away of multiple possibilities for the sake of one. Choosing something to which you are bound forces you to constantly refuse everything else. That is the essence of a choice. To live without choosing means to live simultaneously through all possible variations of development of any given event.

Perception of other worlds

Simultaneous perception of two places or worlds is possible only from the point that is outside of both of them, i.e. from the third one.

* * *

Changing the tuning of perception allows you to perceive other dimensions and worlds. It allows you to be in them, to act in them, and to understand the laws that created them. Some worlds are self-exclusive, and simultaneous presence in them is impossible. Other worlds are susceptible for interpenetration, and it is possible to simultaneously be present in a few of those worlds at once.

* * *

Simultaneous perception of two worlds employs physical and non-physical vision at the same time.

* * *

Sufficient quantity of free attention allows you to move in different worlds and dimensions, and to be simultaneously present in multiple worlds.

* * *

Only an awakened Soul has the opportunity to be present and to act simultaneously in different worlds.

* * *

One who is not yet aware of himself lives only in one room of his own house, unable even to guess that other rooms exist. The unaware human being is doomed to be born, to live, and to die in one of the rooms of his own big house.

* * *

By changing the focus of your perception, you will be able to move to different worlds. The "switch" of the focus of the center of perception is located in the center of the heart. That is why it is only through feeling one's spiritual heart that one is capable of changing one's perception.

* * *

The physical world is not an illusion. It is one of many existing worlds. It is as real as any other world. What happens to be an illusion is the notion that the physical world represents the only existing reality.

* * *

Notions of a winner and a loser, an executioner and a victim are just certain stereotypes of reality that do not reflect characteristics of reality. Reality is outside of any notions.

* * *

In order to be in other worlds, the Soul has to have a corresponding body, allowing it to exist and act in a given world.

* * *

To be present in another world is to learn a basic system of coordinates that create the foundation of that other, manifested, world.

* * *

Aims are manifestations of the Will (laws) of the Great Creator. Awareness of the Aim as of the Will and Laws of the Great

286

Creator (Unified Consciousness) allows a human being to be present in Reality. Presence in Reality allows one to be who he really is, i.e. co-creator. The main quality of co-creator is the possibility of the creation of different realities, i.e. worlds. It is a creation through Love. If you Love, you can do everything you deem necessary. To Love and to Create is an essence of a human being as a co-creator.

* * *

Only your own experience of changing your perception can show you the reality of the existence of completely different worlds, present in different dimensions.

* * *

Complete certainty in reality of one's perception of the world is characteristic both for the one who is fully aware of himself and for the one who is not aware of himself.

* * *

Physical vision totally determines the mentality of an un-awakened human being. Non-physical vision is possible only when a habitual self-reflection of the conditioned mind is turned off.

* * *

Being completely identified with a body-mind, the Soul perceives only the physical world. In case of total de-identification, the Soul does not perceive the physical world. The awakened Soul can simultaneously perceive the physical as well as other worlds. The Soul aware of itself is capable of directing its attention to different worlds, and by doing so can be simultaneously present in different worlds.

* * *

It just appears to you that you are living in a given world. In reality, this and many other worlds live inside you.

* * *

287

Behind every sensory organ a human being perceives the physical world with is consciousness. It is thanks to consciousness that we are able to hear, see, smell, taste, and experience touch. Our consciousness is identified with our physical body and is therefore only tuned into our perception of the physical reality. In order to perceive other realities, de-identification of consciousness from the body is necessary. This de-identification is achieved through awareness of one's own consciousness and its multiple identifications. The ability to identify and de-identify with anything allows you, as a conscious observer, to investigate and experience all the great diversity of the universe. The universe tells us an infinite story about ourselves.

* * *

A word pronounced is a key that allows you to enter different worlds and different realities. For example, in the material world words are used as keys to enter different "rooms" of this particular, material reality. In order to open doors to different realities using words, it is necessary to increase the frequency of vibrations of these words. In order to do so, you need to be able to increase the frequency of vibration of your own consciousness. It is possible to do so when you are aware of yourself, i.e. aware of your own consciousness. Awareness is the light that illuminates the space of consciousness. The more of this light you have, the more of the space of consciousness you have. The light of awareness makes different states of consciousness visible. It reveals in what particular reality your consciousness happens to be now. It also increases the frequency of vibrations of consciousness it illuminates. That increase in the frequency of vibration of consciousness starts to transform the particular reality your consciousness currently occupies. It allows you to transfer to different worlds, realities, and dimensions. Our essence is an observer, in a state of full awareness of oneself.

* * *

Expand your concept of reality. Material is not synonymous to reality. Reality is what you perceive as reality. One may perceive many different realities. Everything depends on your perception. Not a single reality is the absolute reality. They are all relative. Any paradigm and system of coordinates, based on which any given reality is built, is relative. Try to see and understand it.

System of coordinates

At the base of any steady, actualized world lays a certain system of coordinates, a combination of laws accepted as necessary, right, and real. Good understanding of those laws allows one to operate successfully in a given world. Rejection of those laws precludes one from entering the world they operate in as a system of coordinates.

* * *

Any world becomes visible and manifests itself only when a fully formed system of coordinates is present. A system of coordinates is a summary of fundamental laws operating in a given world. Only a full acceptance of those laws allows one to freely operate inside the borders of this world.

One can study the laws only if one accepts them. It is impossible to study something (in a sense, to understand it) if you do not accept it. Unified Consciousness (The Great Creator) is all-accepting and all-loving. The acceptance of something new and unknown is an approach to an all-accepting Consciousness of a Creator. Acceptance is another name for Love.

* * *

Any given human being is a world, a certain world that is based on a certain system of coordinates, on certain fundamental convictions and perception of the world. One's system of coordinates happens to be in his causal body, which, influencing his mental body, gives birth to certain thoughts that are congruent to his system of coordinates. Those thoughts consequently generate certain emotions in one's emotional body. The mental body of a human being is a whole aggregate of his thoughts, while the emotional body encompasses all the emotions he ever experienced. The physical body represents the result of interactions of all prior bodies of a given human being.

* * *

A system of coordinates, i.e. basic convictions of the physical world, contains a notion of birth and death. Anyone entering this system of coordinates accepts this conviction as something self-explanatory. Because of that, in order to be born again, one should die. You may become aware of this notion of life and death as a certain conception, and then it will not have its power over you. This conviction will become false for you. The logic of immortals is different from the logic of mortals. What is true for mortal is false for immortal. To see false as false is to make a step toward immortality. Make this step right now.

* * *

Interaction with a human being is an interaction with the world he is in. Every single human being represents a certain world that has its own system of coordinates. It is possible to understand someone only by totally accepting the system of coordinates of his world. Systems of coordinates of the different worlds of people living on the face of the Earth differ from each other but have many of things in common. Commonality is connected with their common position in the system of coordinates of the consciousness of the Earth.

290

* * *

Nothing, or emptiness, is a potential energy of Unified Consciousness. To be in Emptiness is only possible in a state of the absence of perception of any kind of system of coordinates. Vision of Emptiness is Clear State of being. You can only experience it. It is impossible to perceive it in any kind of form. You can only transfer from one world into another, different world by passing through Emptiness.

* * *

Perception of a physical world is based on a system of coordinates, where one of the major convictions is a conviction that world consists of hard bodies.

External and Internal

External is a reflection of internal. So, do not hurry external events. Everything will come in time as a consequence of internal changes in you. Be aware of yourself and you will see what is of most importance. To summon the external not being internally ready for it is a sign of ignorance. Everything is already here now, but are you ready to see it? That is the main question.

* * *

Everything that happens to you has a symbolic character that shows you the state you are in. Correctly observing what is happening with you, you can understand where you are and where you are going to. Every event symbolizes what is happening with you now. The ability to see and to understand those symbols is the ability necessary to understand yourself. Observing external events, you will see what happens inside. The reverse is also true. Observing and correlating your external and internal changes, you learn to see them simultaneously. The external is a reflection of the internal, and the internal of the external. In reality, those are just two sides of the same coin.

The conditioned mind

Fixating on what it likes or dislikes, the conditioned mind stops perceiving the chain of events, and as a result is always stuck in something that already happened. But there is no life in what already passed. The destiny of the conditioned mind is to always dine on carrion, road kill. That is why it is constantly hungry and as aggressive as a jackal, unable to independently procure his own food. It always depends on others. One, perceiving life only through the conditioned mind, condemns himself to the jackal's existence.

* * *

The perception of the conditioned mind is limited by the soap bubble of its convictions, opinions, and beliefs. It is capable of perceiving its own reflection only. Holistic vision of reality is possible only when this bubble is burst.

* * *

The perception of the conditioned mind is fixated by its convictions and beliefs, preventing it from seeing life as it is, forever changing, flowing, and interpenetrating energy.

* * *

The usual perception of a human being is superficial, fragmented, and dual as it is carried through the conditioned mind.

* * *

A human being is capable of perceiving what his conditioned mind is unable to even imagine.

* * *

Perception, conditioned by strict stereotypes, is attractive to the superficial mind, as it provides a sense of certainty and

292

distinctness. In reality, this is just a harsh fixation. Harshly fixated perception stops one's own life.

* * *

The conditioned mind is able to think only conditionally. If you were capable of thinking at least one of your thoughts to its logical conclusion, you would exit the limits of the superficial mind. Clear thinking is thinking through to the very deep end, to the essence of an event. During that process, nothing is left obscure and not understood. Vision is clear thinking.

* * *

The conditioned mind explains. The Supreme "I" acts. Your constant desire to explain everything does not allow you an opportunity to understand what is happening. Observe what you explain and how you explain it. Investigate the mechanisms of the workings of your conditioned mind. This is the best way to exit its limits.

* * *

The conditioned mind is unable to understand the actions of a whole human being. For the conditioned mind, those actions are not understandable and are therefore dangerous. Observe how your mind reacts to uncertainty, to the unknown. After observing this for a while, you will be able to understand who protects and closes the exit from the prison of perception you are in.

* * *

Perception of the conditioned mind is based on appraisal, comparison, and judgment that stems from the main dualities of a given human being. For example: dangerous—safe, profitable—not profitable, right—wrong, pleasant—unpleasant, etc.

* * *

Perception of the conditioned mind is constant, a never ending attempt to fit what is happening into templates and stereotypes of your habitual notions about yourself, others, and life.

* * *

The main action of the conditioned mind is self-reflection. The major part of one's energy is wasted on self-reflection. Stopping it through awareness, i.e. observing the processes of reflection, leads to the development of free energy (free attention), which can be directed toward the expansion of one's own perception.

* * *

One's conditioned mind overlays one's face with multiple masks and images that one deems to be himself. Only the life-giving moisture of awareness may wash them of, baring the true essence of a human being, his Supreme "I." Take a look in the mirror. What you see there is not you. It is just one image imposed upon you. Wash away the mascara of your social conditioning, turn into a child again, a child who does not know anything yet, but who sees and understands everything.

* * *

The work of the mind is always an effort, which shows in appraisals, comparisons, and opinions. It is something the mind does non-stop doing. If you think there is nothing but your mind, you can spend the rest of your days repeating the same efforts. But you can stop at any time, and see a completely different Life—a Life without efforts and fights.

* * *

The conditioned mind does not perceive a thing as it is; it substitutes it with the name it gave it. It lives in the world of definitions. Looking at something, the conditioned mind recalls its name, and loses the interest. That is why it is always bored; it is unable to see anything new. There are constant changes around it, but the conditioned mind is unable to see them.

Body vision

Reliving the events of your life with a full awareness of everything that happened to you cleanses you. This process frees and transforms the energy of painful experiences into the energy of free attention.

* * *

Recall of the information encoded in the cells of the body, cells that contain the knowledge of all the laws of the creation and plans of their realization on Earth, leads to vision of the body. Awareness of yourself provides you with an access to this information and an ability to act in order to realize it.

* * *

Depth, width, and precision of vision are achieved by the tuning of the perceptual apparatus. This tuning presupposes awareness and harmonization of the activities of all the centers of body-mind. The "switch" of tuning is in the higher part of the emotional center of a human being.

* * *

The body-mind that has harmonized all three of its working centers is constantly tuned in and has an inseparable contact with its own Supreme "I." Therefore, its actions are the direct consequence of the vision of reality and do not carry distortions.

Personality

A human being that has only identified attention is always and constantly involved with his own image. You are not the image you consider yourself to be. You are not personality.

Personality is an aggregate of your convictions, beliefs, and images of yourself.

* * *

Pity directed towards others or toward yourself block any opportunity of real vision and understanding of what is really happening. One experiencing pity does not see anything except his false personality. Pity is the most widespread and effective method of personality reinforcement. Perception devoid of pity is seeing false as false.

* * *

Pity is false compassion. Real compassion is possible only after the elimination of pity. The compassionate shows Love to everything. A man who pities tries to receive Love for himself only, which is impossible. That is why pity is ignorance and incomprehension.

* * *

Personality constantly supports itself internally pronouncing and repeating the same words and thoughts. Obsessive thoughts are a constant, never ending activity of personality that attempts to save itself.

* * *

Personal history is the memory of your convictions in regards to events that happened to you. It is just your own interpretation of what happened in reality. It has no value from the point of view of your Supreme "I." Awareness of yourself is not a remembrance of episodes of your personal history, but presence in a moment, i.e. here and now.

* * *

Importance of an action is usually determined by a way of reflection, i.e. thinking it through. By doing something it considers important, personality reinforces and maintains itself. From the point of view of True "I" those actions represent an illusion, fallacy, and ignorance, the absence of Vision of Reality.

* * *

Personal actions always come from one's own advantage. What is advantageous for personality is determined by the conditioned mind. Personality is only interested in its own benefits, and as a result is unable to see what is happening as a whole. To pursuit one's own personal benefits is to escape from oneself. Holistic action may come only from Holistic Vision, which is in the possession of Supreme "I."

* * *

Personality strives to be unique and original, to be different from others. For the opportunity to be original you pay with the opportunity to be united with everyone. What is most interesting is that it is possible to be both simultaneously. How? It is for you to find out.

* * *

Memory and personal experience create an illusion of the separation between people. Personality wants to preserve itself. It does so by creating and maintaining the illusion of its own separation from everything it comes in contact with.

* * *

An innocent person is not someone others do not consider guilty, but the one who got rid of the feeling of guilt.

* * *

Innocence is non-involvement with any of your own images.

Supreme "I" and body-mind

Action that comes out of Vision carries a Design and the clean energy of Supreme "I." A reactive approach, being a consequence of the conditioned mind, carries in itself ignorance and fragmentation. It is limiting. A limited action, i.e. re-action leads to similarly limiting results. This is a closed circle of karmic events that keeps one inside the confined space of one's own dependencies and attachments. Harmony between Supreme "I" and body-mind is possible only under the clear Vision of the Soul, aware of its true nature.

* * *

Supreme "I" demonstrates itself in unusual occasions. The ability to notice those occasions and correctly understand them is as necessary for the one who walks the Way as a compass is to a sea voyager. Those occasions direct your attention to a side you currently need. By looking in that direction you will be able to see what you need to see in order to act correctly. To See and to Act, in order to See and to Act again is the major rule of the one walking the Way. Only intuition will allow you to notice the signals of Supreme "I" in time. It is impossible to do so using your usual perception, conditioned by the limited mind.

* * *

How can one differentiate between the desire of personality and the desire of Supreme "I"? Any personal desire is fixated on a certain result. When it is not achieved, it leads to disappointment, irritation, and other negative feelings. The will of Supreme "I" is impersonal. It is not self-contained by a limiting sphere of egoistical desires. The will of Supreme "I" satisfies the true interests of everyone, including the one through whom it manifests itself. Therefore, it always comes from the necessity of a Whole, not from some separate parts. The will of Supreme "I" may also manifest through desires of personality. However, personality being contradictory and a plural entity may counteract, minimize, and boycott the Will of Supreme "I." Only awareness of your own desires can provide an opportunity for what is true to manifest itself in order to use the energy of false desires correctly, directing them in a useful way.

* * *

One who knows himself can turn into anything.

* * *

Supreme "I" never sleeps.

Acceptance

While breathing, we exchange (give away and accept) energy with other people. We literally exhale ourselves onto others and inhale them inside of us. That is why it is said about lovers: "They breathe each other." To kiss another human being is to inhale, to accept a part of his or her energy. Acceptance of something is expressed as an inhalation. When you do not accept something you express it as exhalation or by holding your breath.

* * *

You can see two sides of any phenomena: actualized and hidden. The actualized side is a side of phenomena that is obvious for the one perceiving it. The hidden side is the opposite side, invisible, concealed from perception of any given human being.

* * *

Immediate readiness to any situation is an ability that comes from total acceptance of everything that surrounds you.

* * *

In order to realize the positive and negative sides of any phenomena, equal expenditure of energy is necessary. It depends only on a given human being which side of phenomena, i.e. positive or negative, he will realize inside and outside himself.

* * *

Refusing a particular experience that you call negative, you condemn yourself to constant efforts and preoccupation with its possible recurrence in your life.

* * *

By accepting everything that happens to you, you get an opportunity to use everything that exists to create new directions in your movement.

Energy

Vision presupposes an exit from the limits of the conditional mind and requires an additional thrust of energy. This energy may be taken from inside of you as a consequence of releasing some strongly maintained habit. It is also possible to use energy coming from outside, for example, from one having an excess of energy.

* * *

Awareness is the release of your energy, the freeing of your attention. Only the availability of free energy provides an opportunity to perceive something anew.

* * *

Soul (Consciousness) being, in essence, energy, is characterized by the magnitude and individual power. Personal power is the potential energy of a Soul. Perceiving life through identified attention leads to waste and loss of individual power. An aware perception will allow you to return wasted power and to save it, increasing the total potential of individual power of a Soul. Awareness increases awareness. Unawareness increases unawareness. It is an expression of a law of attraction of similar to similar.

* * *

Awareness of oneself is the acquisition of one's energy. The overwhelming majority of people, having energy, do not possess it. They simply throw it away in different directions, not even understanding it. By becoming aware of your thoughts you can direct their energy in the direction you need. The same applies to the energy of feelings and physical actions. What you are not aware of, you cannot manage. You can manage yourself only when you are aware of yourself. Your awareness of yourself may be partial or full.

* * *

A human being is a constantly moving energy. It is possible to separate the energy of thoughts, feelings, and body. Each one of those three energies has its own qualities and characteristics. Becoming aware of those energies in yourself allows you to harmonize them. Becoming aware of the character of the processes each of those three energies is involved in, gives you an opportunity to be in a state of harmony, balance, and health. A human being who achieves a state of wholeness is capable of being simultaneously aware of each of those energies in himself. Usually one is aware of one of those three energies better than other two. Pay attention and become aware of the energies you know less.

Creativity

If you can precisely formulate a question (inquiry), you will surely get an answer. An answer comes in the sphere where a question (inquiry), originated: in mental—mentally, in emotional—emotionally, in physical—physically. Inquiry that one is unaware of gets realized as well as the inquiry one is aware of. Inquiry one is not aware of leads to unaware results. To live without awareness is to create without an understanding of what you are creating.

* * *

301

The creation of love is born while experiencing love. It is not simply a creation of the mind. It is a creation of a loving mind. In this creation, the feeling of love is primary, and it bears thoughts and actions. Not vice versa. In order to create in love, one needs to love. This is the most wonderful thing that can exist. That is how the Great Creator creates.

* * *

It is good not to get attached to any ideas, including those contained in this book. They are all relative. Play with them until they give you joy, but then throw them aside as children do playing with their toys. By throwing away an old idea-toy, you will surely get a new, more interesting toy-idea.

* * *

Every human being is, in his essence, a creator. Therefore, understanding it or not, we constantly create our life. But creating while not being awareness of ourselves, we get what we later do not want to accept. But it is also necessary, if only as a result of such a creation, to ask yourself the question: "What do I create?" One who asks this question starts to move toward an awareness of himself and his own creative potential.

* * *

Life creation through love is an opportunity given to a human being to create worlds and to enter the worlds that already exist. Co-creation is performed by a great power of love, not by intellect alone. Pure intellectual creativity, without love, is capable of creating only forms, albeit quite complicated and sophisticated forms. But form without essence, without love, represents a lifeless body that does not understand its connection with a Whole. Those forms are doomed to suffer. Therefore, the creation of anything without love increases pain, suffering, and illusion.

* * *

Any pronounced word possesses a magical power, as it brings to action energies and influences the flow of events. A word coming from the Heart creates Love. A word, coming from the conditioned mind, recreates the past. A word is also a key that allows entering the essence, which carries a name that corresponds to this word. By pronouncing someone's name, you get in contact with the one who carries it.

* * *

Vision does not require any kind of language. Good knowledge and a command of the language are required only in order to fully describe what is seen. That language should provide an opportunity for a whole, not fragmented, description of events. Usually language does not allow one to do so, as it is made and used by a conditioned mind for its egoistical purposes.

* * *

As soon as you name something, you have lost it.

* * *

Become a painter, writer, and director of your life. Bring a spirit of love, wisdom, and harmony into everything you see. This spirit is your essential "I." So look at everything through its eyes. Those eyes are in the center of your chest, where your spiritual heart is. Look at everything through the eyes of your spiritual heart.

* * *

Only one who understands the true nature of the physical world may enjoy it in all its fullness. The world is given to us for Enjoinment and Creativity, not for suffering and sadness.

Learning

You cannot force yourself or someone else to See holistically. But you can constantly be aware and as a result eliminate what prevents it, i.e. dependencies and attachments of your personality.

* * *

The role of the teacher is to pitilessly and regularly push you toward exiting the borders of the known and habitual, stimulating you to Vision and Action.

* * *

No teacher is able to transfer to you the understanding of your Supreme "I." Teacher can create optimal for you opportunities, to get in touch with what you truly are, i.e. with reality. The true teacher, being on the border of real and unreal, on the border of two worlds, sees everything that happens to a student and carefully directs a student's movement.

* * *

Sincerity and honesty with oneself are main prerequisites of self-investigation.

* * *

Only sincerity allows you to see what is really real, i.e. to see your own ignorance, illusion, fragmentation, and separation.

* * *

Fuel used for the movement on the Way is an individual experience in awareness. Only experience in awareness of yourself and self-investigation may provide an opportunity to stay and advance on the Way to yourself. Everything taken by you without awareness turns into a weight that misleads you.

* * *

Life does not ask questions and therefore does not provide answers. It does not need it. Only the conditioned mind, not knowing any other method of getting information, requires it. Moving with the help of questions and answers is limited due to the limitations of the questions themselves. To live without questions means to know everything at once. One can investigate the woods by walking different pathways, but one can also simply become those woods.

Time

Time determined by usual clocks is linear, but in essence it is spatial and voluminous. A description of the world limited by linear notion of time reinforces the world created within the system of coordinates of duality.

* * *

As time is simply a concept, it can be transformed and changed in many different ways. One of those ways is the compression and expansion of time. Compression of time allows one to have an accelerated experience living through a certain chain of events. For example, one can live hundred years of life in one hour of linear dimension. Compression of time represents a mode of experiencing certain karmic events with the purpose of cleansing one's structure from earlier mistakes and illusions brought up by partial, fragmented, non-whole perception.

* * *

Conception of time is one of the major convictions of system of coordinates of the physical world. Becoming aware of time, as one of the convictions of the conditioned mind, allows you to exit the limits of the usual notion of time as a chronological consequence of events. It is possible to observe everything happening in the past, future, and present simultaneously, as a unified state of being.

* * *

Linear, chronological time is born from a certain mentation of the mind. By changing states of mind, it is possible to change time. In an altered state of mind it is possible to live a whole life in one minute.

* * *

Energy does not know physical time. For energy, there is only moment, only now.

* * *

The true "I" is outside the time of physical world. It exists where time is absent.

* * *

Time is a notion that can be perceived differently, from different points of view. The notion of time can be viewed from the front, and then you perceive it as past. It can be viewed from behind, and then you perceive it as future. One can also look from the place where time does not exist, and then one can see everything as a whole instant moment.

* * *

Time is a method of coding information. By changing this method, you can enter different realities. Time can be compressed, unwound, expanded, etc. In order to do so, one simply needs to get rid of the notion that time and reality is constant and unshakable. Both can be played with and changed according to your wish. If you were to understand that the future is not something given, predetermined, you would see it is simply as a collection of different possibilities. Every one of those possibilities is realized in a certain multidimensional space of realities. Those realities represent a summation of all possible possibilities of development of events. All of them exist simultaneously, and you can perceive any one of them.

Laws, Changes

Only those who know what responsibility is can know the state where it is not needed.

* * *

Any change is the death of something and birth of something else. Change is the essence of life. Life is an eternal process of dying and being born, occurring always and everywhere, with everyone and everybody. Therefore, it is not worth it to either be afraid or to strive toward something that happens independently of how your circumscribed and narrow mind relates to it.

* * *

Any law that is based on Love is a true Law. Laws, rules, and norms created by the conditioned mind reflect only its limitations and do not lead to freedom. Freedom is life in Love. Law, which only regulates the external order, does not express the essence of love.

* * *

When you stop doing something, you remove it. When you stop thinking, ruminating over something, you get rid of it. When you stop feeling something, you get rid of it. We create the world in which we live with the help of our thoughts and actions. By continually thinking over your problem, you prolong it, even though you, perhaps, presume that this is the only way to solve it. Your problems are the thoughts, feelings, and actions connected to this problem. In reality, by solving it, you reinforce it, extending its life. Any of your problems will disappear as soon as you stop thinking about them. But is this what you really want?

Immortality

Life of a mortal is the shuffling of a deck of cards. Many pull out of this deck only one or a few similar cards. Therefore, their life becomes a repetition of one and the same thing. Turn into an aware player, and sooner or later you will pull out the last card of this deck – "Joker." This card is your entrance to immortality.

* * *

What differentiate a mortal being from an immortal one? One considers himself to be mortal while another considers himself to be immortal.

* * *

To be born and to die is just a habit. Get rid of this habit and you will be immortal.

* * *

If your consciousness identifies itself with a body, death is your reality. The body dies, but the soul is immortal. To sell your soul to devil is to identify with your body. A soul that becomes aware of itself as a Spirit and identifies itself with it, is free from the prison of heaven and hell.

Life is a mirror

Everything that surrounds you is you. By meeting other people, you meet yourself. Being in a world of forms, you may talk and converse with yourself as if you were talking with another human being. It is a very interesting game, if you understand its essence. The essence of the game is that in reality, we all are one. Your changing desires attract to you certain new parts of you in the shape of other people and new circumstances. Understand that and enjoy the show.

* * *

The outside view of life reflects Life itself, insomuch as turbulence of a sea surface reflects the sea itself.

Cosmic game

The human being is a mask that the universe puts on in order to meet and play with itself.

* * *

The game of dualities is an amusement for the Seer and a tragedy for the mortal.

* * *

Real and unreal is just a game in real and unreal. Everything exists only in our consciousness. You can name something and in a way summon it appearance. Equally, you can stop calling it, and it will disappear.

* * *

You yourself can create anything and destroy anything. The majority of people are not aware of those processes yet; they simply support what was already created by someone or take part in the destruction of something someone already started to destroy. Only when you become aware of yourself will you be able to do everything consciously, i.e. independently.

* * *

The same thing exists on different levels of being. For example, an automobile on a physical level represents a product you can buy and use for transportation. The same automobile on a mental level represents an idea, an image you can use without paying money for it. Calling up an image of an automobile, you may take a ride in it, but this ride will differ from a ride inside a material automobile. On deeper levels of being automobile cannot even exist as an image; there, it is energy, possessing certain qualities and characteristics. Any material form, in particular an automobile, possesses a certain level of consciousness. This level of consciousness may be characterized by the frequency of electromagnetic vibrations; the higher the frequency of vibrations—the higher the level of consciousness.

Any given product created by a human being has a certain level of consciousness, but unlike human beings, it cannot change it on its own accord. Human beings are capable of changing the levels of their own vibrations. By changing the levels of your vibrations, you can move to different levels of being, i.e. enter different dimensions and worlds.

* * *

Eternity is outside of any qualitative or quantitative changes. When we start to measure time and space, we, as a result, limit Eternity to the scale of our own measurements. It offers us a possibility of living through the flow of events only chronologically or gradually. The difference between Eternity and time is analogous to the free flow of air in the atmosphere and letting air out through a tiny hole, as it happens when air balloon blows out.

* * *

You can participate in transforming the vibration frequencies of the Earth. In order to do so, you need to wish and learn to accept frequencies of a higher order in such a way that they will become natural for you. In such a case you will live those frequencies. By living on a higher frequency of vibrations, you exert influence of awakening character on anything with which you come in contact. By improving yourself, you improve everything around you. Your growth is the growth of the Earth. Unite to create in Love.

* * *

Do not try to define the world. Experience it. Live it. The great opportunity offered by the great Creator to everything that exists is an opportunity to experience being in many different forms. Learn to use those opportunities with awareness.

Accustom yourself to feel and to become aware of exactly what you want to experience at every moment, i.e. your true desires. In reality, in your desire to possess something: a car, a house, a human being is hidden the desire to experience something. Become aware of what precisely you want to experience is, and live through it. If you want to experience the sensation of fast movement, it is not necessary to have a personal car, constantly being afraid of losing it as your possession. Free yourself from identification with the form, because in reality you want new experiences, not possessions.

Human being

Stop storing new information. Become aware that you Already Know Everything.

* * *

Words pronounced by a sentient being are the keys to the information contained in the human body. You know everything, but in order for you to become aware of yourself as All Knowing, you need to ask the right questions. If you ask a right question, the answer comes immediately. It comes from you as you always knew it, but then forget it. You forget it because you acquired a habit of asking the wrong, illusory questions. Real questions bring real answers, while an illusory question leads to an illusory answer.

* * *

Our heart constricts when we are physically hurt and expands when we experience pleasure. The pleasure of the spiritual heart is not susceptible to any fluctuations. Look for it deep inside your heart.

* * *

To See means to allow the world to be what it is. The world is in you. When you fight it, you are fighting yourself. If you are not bored yet, continue fighting. But remember, it is your own choice. At any moment, you can stop fighting and start to enjoy harmony and love inside and outside yourself.

* * *

Eliminate the habitual for you image through which you are looking at a certain human being and you will see him change right in front of your eyes. But as soon as you fix his image

311

again, those changes will stop. Experiment with it and observe what you will discover.

* * *

Every human being is an energy in the "sea" of other energies constantly moving and changing. What you see as material objects is just a result of the work of your fixed diapason of perception of moving waves of energy. Physical vision allows us to see the movement of energy only in this particular way, as material objects. If you are convinced you can see only using physical vision, you will not see anything else.

* * *

The biggest con you can "swing" in this world is to think, feel, and act sincerely. You can play a super con man, but this is peanuts compared to real sincerity. Try it.

* * *

It just seems to you that you live in this world. In reality, the world lives inside you.

* * *

There are many perspectives in one's perception of another human being, from the superficial to the very deep and essential. Superficially, you can talk about someone based on who he is dating, who he is friends with, who he works with, what he does for a living, and what he says in different situations. This is something that can be seen using physical vision. Moving deeper, you can see his feelings, desires, hopes, beliefs, thoughts, convictions, and images of himself. To see this without distortions, is only possible when one gets rid of one's own preferences and conditioning. Going even deeper, you can see the human being as energy, possessing certain qualities and characteristics. But behind this energy is something that cannot be seen—awareness, the essence of everything. Every single one of us represents this awareness.

* * *

312

Learn to save energy. Learn to distribute it correctly. In order to do so, you must sense and feel the Earth as an alive being that loves you. Direct the energy you receive to where the Earth needs it. Become "grounded." If your head is constantly in the clouds, then it is hard to understand what you are doing here on Earth. Only having a good "grounding" you can become aware of your total potential as a being that is simultaneously present in multiple realities. All this multiple realities and worlds you are in are necessary to "tie" to one of the worlds, and in such a way connect all of them together. If you are not "grounded" this awareness of yourself is either impossible or can lead to a serious disturbance of your nervous system. An increase in frequencies of vibrations of your Soul increases the current of information coming toward it. In order to adapt to this huge flow of information and energy you need very good "grounding." Get out more frequently. Enjoy nature: earth, water, wind, sun, and woods. This will allow you not only to collect more energy and information, but also to direct it correctly. Learn to be aware and to operate multiple realities, and through the channel you yourself make, transmit the information and energy coming from them to Earth. You both need it.

WHAT IS NEXT?

•◆•◆•◆•◆•◆•◆•◆•◆•◆•◆•◆•◆•◆•◆•◆•◆•◆•◆•◆•

Perhaps, after reading our book you asked yourself a question: "How do I continue my self-investigation?" In order to do so, we offer you our other books, audio and video materials, and most importantly—our seminars-trainings.

Audio- and video materials

We record all our seminars and webinars. There is no script or program of action. We are guided by internal Inquiries of the participants and the realization of those inquiries only. Each seminar demonstrates solutions to situations that are connected to the imbalance in the internal(and as a consequence, external) world, and describes how this world is made and functions, while opening the connection of a human being to his Supreme "I" and transmitting impulses of Awareness, Unconditional Love, and Unity.

To help you continue the independent practical work of self-investigation, we invite you to acquire audio and video recordings of our school seminars. Every seminar participant goes through same phases:

- Clear cut definition, precise specification of actual internal Inquiry, and exposure of internal conflicts.
- Sharp increase of actual internal Inquiry, exacerbation of internal conflicts. What is hidden starts to become obvious.
- Getting an answer to an Inquiry and exiting the problem.

Moving independently you may spend years to come to the discoveries made by Alexander Pint and seminar participants. You may not be able to attain some of those insights on your own during current incarnation. Watching or listening to a seminar, you can achieve results much faster. That is the reason we call our materials "Catalyst of Awareness."

By listening to the seminar, you become its co-participant, open up new sides of your "I," submerge into state of We or state of Unity, and receive answers to questions that are important to you.

Since the opening of the school, many seminars have been organized, and we continue to organize more. In order to help you choose the right disc, and by freeing the conditioned mind from "helping" you in this action, we have developed the Index of materials: "Catalyst of Awareness." You can get acquainted with it and order audio and video recorded seminars on our site www.pint.ru in the section "Materials "Catalyst of Awareness."

Seminars—trainings

Seminars of The school of Holistic Psychology are as diverse as life itself and never repeat themselves. It is a combination of games, serious internal work, deep feelings and expressing yourself in action. Some students come with clear-cut formulated inquiries; some come simply due to the call of their hearts; some come to find and understand themselves—there are many motives. Seminar is a spectacle where everyone performs as a full-fledged actor, director, and screenwriter, while being aware of all his roles.

Of all types of work, seminar is the most efficient, as the degree of your involvement into understanding-feeling-action is the highest. By working with a book or a disc, one can put them aside for a time, occupy himself with something else, and return to it later at a more convenient time. On seminar, you experience yourself *here and now*, while the spectacle of your life, set up based on your own script, start to unfold right in front of your eyes. "What kind of script is it?" "What are its key parameters?" "How fully do I know my show?" "Are there any alternative scripts?" These are the questions any one of our seminars can holistically answer for you.

Seminar is an opportunity to get out of your habitual environment for a certain period of time and to look at your life from another point of view. It is an opportunity for the deepest immersion into an atmosphere of investigation of your inner space, a connection with your creative potential, and communication with those who have the same aim as you. It is a combination of internal work and pleasant vacation, useful for the body, happiness for the soul and spirit.

You can organize a seminar in your city.

The phone number of our school in Moscow (495) 506-74-18, (925) 506-74-18

You can also attend our seminars in Moscow and other cities. In order to do so, you need to contact its organizer. A schedule of seminars is available on our site www.pint.ru. If you want to get in touch with us, use our email contact@pint.ru.

ABOUT THE AUTHOR

•◆•◆• •◆•◆• •◆•◆• •◆•◆• •◆•◆• •◆•◆• •◆•◆• •◆•◆• •◆•◆• •◆•◆• •◆•◆• •◆•◆•

Alexander Pint is a self-investigator, founder of Holistic Psychology, writer, and conductor of seminars.

The author, inspired by examples from his own life, conducted self-investigation as a result of which basic laws of the dual world, which we currently occupy, were elucidated and formulated. In other words, the rules of the game we play in this reality were defined. Those are the rules that represent the system of coordinates, the axiom of this world; not the laws, norms, or morals created by people themselves in order to regulate interpersonal relationships in society. The personality of any given human being reflects dual principals of the organization of any given world. The author's discovery of duality allows receiving the answers to all questions related to the meaning of our presence in this world. In particular, it was determined how duality is installed into a human being and how it determines the screenplay of his life, how it operates and where its action leads, what kind of experience or lessons one lives through in connection to the presence of duality, how and precisely on what typical scenarios one's life are based, how can one change those scenarios, and how to exit the limits of duality that generate pain and suffering.

Read more at: www.pint.ru

"The essence of the game of our world is that when we are born we accept a certain condition, which we can express with the word "separation." This is the act of forgetting oneself. That is where all the difficult states and multiple problems we constantly talk about come from. We forgot the Source. The majority of people forget who they are, where their real House is, what they came here for. They feel lonely, they pity themselves, and they don't understand what's going on. But, in reality those are the rules of the game played here. This is not an accident but is the specifics of the game chosen by your Soul. The rules and mechanisms of the game and its meaning for you is the topic of this book."

– Alexander Pint, from *Caterpillar to Butterfly: A Way to Yourself*

www.ingramcontent.com/pod-product-compliance
Lightning Source LLC
Chambersburg PA
CBHW062047270326
41931CB00013B/2968